PENGUIN BOOKS

THE ULTIMATE OPERA QUIZ BOOK

Kenn Harris is the author of *Opera Recordings: A Critical Guide* and a biography of Renata Tebaldi. He has covered the opera scene in New York City since 1963 and currently appears as a weekly reviewer and guest host for the cable television program *What's On.*

THE ULTIMATE OPERA QUIZ BOOK

KENN HARRIS

PENGUIN BOOKS

Penguin Books Ltd, Harmondsworth,
Middlesex, England
Penguin Books, 625 Madison Avenue,
New York, New York 10022, U.S.A.
Penguin Books Australia Ltd, Ringwood,
Victoria, Australia
Penguin Books Canada Limited, 2801 John Street,
Markham, Ontario, Canada L3R 1B4
Penguin Books (N.Z.) Ltd, 182–190 Wairau Road,
Auckland 10, New Zealand

First published 1982

LIBRARY OF CONGRESS CATALOGING IN PUBLICATION DATA
Harris, Kenn, 1947–
The ultimate opera quiz book.
1. Opera–Miscellanea. I. Title.
ML63.H26 1982 782.1 82-11246
ISBN 0 14 00.5884 2

Printed in the United States of America by
R. R. Donnelley & Sons Company, Harrisonburg, Virginia
Set in Fototronic Garamond

Grateful acknowledgment is made to the following institutions and individuals for permission to reproduce the photographs in Quiz 107: Lucine Amara for photograph 5; Beth Bergman for photograph 25 (copyright © Beth Bergman, 1977); The Connecticut Opera for photograph 15 (photographed by Sylvian Ofiara on February 15, 1968, at Bushnell Hall, Hartford, Connecticut); Erika Davidson for photograph 4 (copyright © Erika Davidson); Deutsche Oper, Berlin, for photograph 23; The Granger Collection, New York City, for photographs 7, 21, 22, 24, 26, 27, 28, 29, and 31; J. Heffernan, Metropolitan Opera Association, for photographs 1, 2, 3, 6, 10, 11, and 14; Lyric Opera of Chicago for photograph 19; Metropolitan Opera Association for photographs 12, 13, 17, 30, 33, 34, 35, 36, 37, and 38; Margaret Norton, San Francisco Opera, for photographs 9, 16, and 20; La Scala Opera for photograph 32; Nancy Sorenson for photograph 8; The Vancouver Opera Association for photograph 18.

TO MY GREAT AND GOOD FRIEND

CHARLES D. LIEBER

CONTENTS

ACKNOWLEDGMENTS 11

PREFACE 13

THE ANECDOTES AND QUIZZES

COMPOSERS AND THEIR OPERAS

1. American Opera 17
2. English Opera 19
3. French Opera 20
4. German Opera 21
5. Italian Opera 22
6. Russian Opera 24
7. *Aida* 25
8. *Carmen* 26
9. *Cavalleria Rusticana* 27

10. *Madama Butterfly* 27
11. *I Pagliacci* 29
12. *Der Ring des Nibelungen* 29
13. *Der Rosenkavalier* 32
14. *Tosca* 32
15. *La Traviata* 34
16. I've Heard That Before 34
17. Wagner I 35
18. Wagner II 36
19. Mozart 37
20. Puccini Rarities 39
21. Verdi 40
22. Verdi Rarities 40

OPERA STARS AND SUPERNOVAS

23. Baritones 42
24. Mezzos 44
25. Sopranos 45
26. Tenors 47
27. Lucine Amara 49
28. Montserrat Caballé 50
29. Maria Callas 51
30. Enrico Caruso 53
31. Franco Corelli 53
32. Giuseppe di Stefano 55
33. Placido Domingo 56
34. Tito Gobbi 56
35. Luciano Pavarotti 57
36. Leontyne Price 58
37. Renata Scotto 59
38. Beverly Sills 60
39. Joan Sutherland 61
40. Renata Tebaldi 62
41. Debuts at the Met 63
42. Famous Firsts 64
43. The Younger Generation 65
44. Opera Stars on Broadway 66
45. Tiny Facts About Great Singers 67
46. Farewells at the Met 68

UNFORGETTABLE CHARACTERS

47. Title Roles 70
48. Noblesse Oblige 70
49. Their Masters' Voices 71
50. Servants, Slaves, and Companions 71
51. Holy Men and Women 72
52. Hi, Mom! Hi, Dad! 72
53. What's My Line? 73
54. Disguises 73
55. Aliases 74
56. Who Wears the Pants? 75
57. Home Wreckers 76
58. Good Dreams . . . Bad Dreams 76
59. Loco en el Coco 77
60. *Suicidio* 77
61. Murders Most Foul 78
62. Prisoners of Fate 79
63. Capital Punishment 80
64. Final Requests 80
65. Opening Lines 81
66. Famous First Words 82
67. Dramatic Entrances 83
68. Love Duets 83
69. *Cabalette* 84
70. Self-Awareness 85
71. Famous Last Words 86

AND THEN WHAT HAPPENS?
OPERA PLOTS AND PLOTTINGS

72. Extra! Extra! Read All About It! 88
73. The Rain in Spain 89
74. Little Things Mean a Lot 90
75. Hot Times 91
76. Holidays 92
77. Wine, Persons, and Song 92
78. Crimes Major and Minor 93
79. Hiding Places 94
80. Gifts 94
81. Members of the Wedding 95
82. Stop All That Singing and Let Us Dance! 96

83. Getting There Is Half the Fun 97
84. Faraway Places 97
85. Cruel and Unusual 98

A POTPOURRI

86. Opening Nights 99
87. Opera Houses Around the World 100
88. From Page to Stage 102
89. Play Versus Opera 102
90. Librettists 103
91. Record Collectors I 104
92. Rudolf Bing 106
93. Famous Operatic Conductors 108
94. Saturday Afternoons at the Met 110
95. Opera on the Silver Screen 111
96. Record Collectors II 112
97. Old Vienna 113
98. They Had Some Songs to Sing, O 115
99. Women's World 116
100. Off the Beaten Path 118
101. Don't Believe Everything You Read I 120
102. Operatic Scavenger Hunt 122
103. Don't Believe Everything You Read II 123
104. Out in the Cold 124
105. Record Collectors III 125
106. Ultimate Wagner 126
107. Opera Pix 127

THE ANSWERS

COMPOSERS AND THEIR OPERAS 155

OPERA STARS AND SUPERNOVAS 185

UNFORGETTABLE CHARACTERS 207

AND THEN WHAT HAPPENS?
OPERA PLOTS AND PLOTTINGS 240

A POTPOURRI 259

ACKNOWLEDGMENTS

The writing and preparation for *The Ultimate Operatic Quiz Book* occupied three years of my time. The time spent working on this book was the happiest episode in my life during those three years. The support and encouragement I received from my agent, my publisher, and my friends contributed largely to the pleasure I took in working on the manuscript.

I am deeply grateful to Ms. Linda Sirkus, and Messrs. Harvey Silbert, Robert E. Weiss, Paul Brynan, and Roy Herschaft for the interest they took in my labors, contributing hours of their weekends, as I tested questions on them. In particular, Messrs. Weiss, Brynan, and Howard Weiner were extraordinarily helpful, supplying answers to questions for which I myself had no proper response.

Merle Hubbard and Hans Boone, of the Herbert Breslin organization, generously supplied me with photographs of artists, a number of which are included in the finished book, and I am very much in their debt for this help.

Unquestionably, the lion's share of my gratitude is reserved for Penguin Books, which did me the honor of accepting my work for publication, and my eternal thanks must go to Martha Kinney, my editor, for her immensely supportive work in my behalf, and for her skillful and perceptive editing and shaping of my manuscript, without which this book would certainly be much the poorer. Martha, and the Penguin staff, most notably Mary Wachs and Anne Marie Demetz, became friends of mine, and did much to calm the nerves and soothe the psyche of this "newly hatched" Penguin author. To these individuals as well as to supportive friends and colleagues too numerous to list, I offer my heartfelt thanks.

K. H.

PREFACE

My agent, my editor, and my friends all agree that this book is one that I was born to write. People who have known me well over the years have suggested that with my passion for trivia, I might as well put the information to some use. Who knows, maybe there are other people out there who would enjoy it. This book is intended for people who share my lifelong passion for opera. Many a Saturday in my childhood and adolescence my mother would say, "It's gorgeous outside. Why don't you go out and play ball or do something instead of listening to the opera?" Our family doctor used to regale friends with the story of his ten-year-old patient who switched an appointment in order not to interrupt his enjoyment of the weekly Metropolitan Opera broadcast. This incident took place in February 1958, and the broadcast in question was the rather astonishing double bill of *Gianni Schicchi* and *Salome.* The principals were Fernando Corena and Laurel Hurley in *Schicchi,* and Inge Borkh and the late Mack Harrell in *Salome.* Would you believe that I recall these facts after all these years? It has always been this way for me with opera. I remember practically everything I have ever learned about the subject.

I remember my very first exposure to opera. My parents took me to see the film of *Carmen Jones* one Saturday night in the summer of 1955. I fell in love with Bizet's music as performed by Marilyn Horne (filling in on the soundtrack for Dorothy Dandridge's luscious on-screen Carmen), Harry Belafonte, Pearl Bailey, and Diahann Carroll. Shortly thereafter I borrowed *Carmen* recordings from the public library, and several months later I watched (on TV) my first real opera–*Madama Butterfly*–performed by the NBC Opera Company with Elaine Malbin as Cio-Cio-San. I was hooked.

My parents must take credit for my introduction to the lyric theater, even though there were countless times that they regretted ever taking me to that damned film in the first place. Now I find myself, at age thirty-five, having attended well over one thousand opera performances and amassed a record and tape collection that has practically pushed me and my cats out of our Manhattan home. I should mention that I have even burdened my feline companions with operatic names: Fedora and Adriana Lecouvreur. Imagine my surprise when once Adriana poisoned herself by chewing on a bouquet of violets, almost expiring in the manner of Cilea's less lucky heroine, for whom she is named.

People have called me a sort of operatic walking encyclopedia, and I have prepared this collection of quizzes and anecdotes to share some of the information I have amassed in the past quarter century. The book is intended to entertain, and I hope that purists will not object to my occasionally irreverent or whimsical ideas. Opera is an art form intended to amuse as well as instruct, and nothing about the lyric stage, including *Parsifal,* should be immune to a little gentle fun. I intend for my readers to have many a merry time and along the way gain knowledge that will stand them in good stead.

I want to make brief mention of the anecdotes that are sprinkled throughout the text. While I was an eyewitness to quite a few of them, they include a number of stories that have been told before. By now some have been handed down for a few generations. You doubtless have read some before; I know I have. Wherever possible, I have credited the original sources of these stories, a few of which are practically legends by this time. This is part of the glorious sharing experience that is operamania.

Thus having unburdened myself, I withdraw to the wings to let the questions "answer for themselves." Best of luck to all.

K. H.

THE ANECDOTES AND QUIZZES

COMPOSERS AND THEIR OPERAS

1. AMERICAN OPERA

1. Although born in Italy, this composer has spent most of his adult life in America. Among his many credits is the first opera to have been given its world premiere on television. Name the composer and the opera.
2. First performed in 1958, this opera was composed with Maria Callas in mind for the title role. Callas rejected the score. Who created the title role in this opera?
3. Beverly Sills had one of her first successes in an opera based on an incident in American history. Name the opera and its composer.
4. At the time of his murder, Marc Blitzstein was at work on an opera dealing with a controversial American court case. What was the subject matter?
5. Jack Beeson's most popular opera is based on the life of a notorious New Englander. Identify the opera. (The score does *not* include a well-known folk song about its title character.)
6. One of Arthur Miller's best-known plays was adapted into a splendid opera some years ago. Name Miller's play and the composer of the opera.

7. Although first produced on Broadway and later made into a Hollywood film, this wonderful work has begun slowly to make its way into the repertories of opera houses in America and around the world despite its special casting problems. Name the opera, composer, librettist, and its three original stars. What important American singer received her first "break" in a revival of this work?
8. Can you remember the title of Howard Hanson's opera, which was performed at the Metropolitan and elsewhere during the 1930s?
9. The great American soprano Helen Traubel made her Met debut in a now forgotten American opera. Name it.
10. A famous American playwright's book was used as the basis for this American opera which transplanted a Greek legend to American shores. Name the playwright, play, opera, composer, and the American soprano its world premiere introduced to Metropolitan Opera audiences.
11. The late Marie Powers had a great personal success as the tormented title character of this opera. The production premiered on Broadway and was later seen on television and around the world. Name the opera and composer.
12. What is the only opera that has a crucial scene set in a New York City subway station?
13. Gertrude Stein wrote the whimsical libretto for this opera dealing with a famous fighter for women's rights. Name the opera, the composer, and the protagonist.
14. This opera transplanted a Biblical story to the New World. Identify the opera, the composer, the Biblical story in question, and tell where the work was set. Where and when was the work premiered? Who starred in the New York premiere?
15. Name two American operas based on works by Charles Dickens and composed by American citizens.
16. Gian Carlo Menotti wrote the libretto but *not* the music for this Pulitzer Prize-winning opera. Name the composer and the young American artist whose career blossomed after she created a major role in this work.
17. This weighty opera, based on one of Eugene O'Neill's most ambitious tragedies, was first performed in 1967. Name the opera, its composer, and the four principal cast members. Unfortunately, the production was more highly praised for its staging than for its music. Who was the stage director?
18. What is the name of Aaron Copland's one opera?
19. Name two operas by Thomas Pasatieri.

20. Lawrence Tibbett sang two indigenous American roles during his years of Met stardom. What were they?
Answers on page 155.

2. ENGLISH OPERA

1. Name the first English opera composer and two of his operas.
2. One of Benjamin Britten's operas is based on a novel written by an American. Identify the opera and the novelist.
3. Another opera of Britten's is based on the exploits of which American folk hero?
4. Joan Sutherland, in her pre-star days, sang in an opera by Michael Tippett at the Royal Opera. Name the opera.
5. Name a contemporary British woman composer and two of her operas.
6. What has become of the former Sadler's Wells Opera Company?
7. Where did the D'Oyly Carte Opera Company, for which the Savoy Theatre was built, give its London performances?
8. Name the singer most often associated with the operas of Benjamin Britten.
9. In *Peter Grimes,* how did Grimes's first apprentice die?
10. Who created the title role at the world premiere of Britten's *Billy Budd*?
11. With what company does the Royal Opera share Covent Garden?
12. Who is the current (1982) musical director of the Royal Opera?
13. Name five British opera companies.
14. Who composed the opera written for the coronation of Queen Elizabeth II? Name the opera and identify its subject.
15. When Maria Callas canceled a series of performances of *Tosca* at Covent Garden in 1965, she was replaced by a young British soprano. Who was she?
16. British soprano Amy Shuard was acclaimed throughout Europe for which Puccini role?
17. Name four British singers, active in the last fifty years, who have been knighted.
18. What is the name of the mute character so crucial to the plot of Britten's *Death in Venice*?
19. List six members of the English National Opera who have enjoyed busy international careers.

20. Name two Italian composers who settled in London at the turn of the century, giving lessons and writing songs (and, in one case, an opera).
21. Who is the British artist well known for singing Wagnerian heroes in English?
22. Name two currently active singers, both born in Wales, who have achieved success throughout the operatic world.
23. Name four operatic roles that Benjamin Britten wrote for Sir Peter Pears.
24. Name the British music festival celebrated for its superlative Mozart and fancy dress rules.
25. Name two operas by Ralph Vaughan Williams.
26. What is Frederick Delius's best-known opera?

Answers on page 157.

3. FRENCH OPERA

1. Name two operas by Ambroise Thomas.
2. List three operas composed by Verdi for the Paris Opéra.
3. Who wrote the libretto for *Carmen*? On whose novel is it based?
4. Name the opera house in Paris where Verdi and Donizetti experienced early successes.
5. Name four operas (not necessarily by French composers) dealing with the French Revolution.
6. Who created the role of Mélisande in Debussy's opera?
7. Identify the following characters from French operas. Name the opera, composer, and briefly describe the character.

   a. Zuniga
   b. Spalanzani
   c. Philine
   d. Siebel
   e. Blanche
   f. Charlotte
   g. de Brétigny
   h. Schlémil
   i. Mercedes
   j. Rachel
   k. Leila
   l. Cassandre
   m. Athanaël
   n. Abimelech
   o. Nicklausse

8. Name two operas by Gustave Charpentier.
9. Which French composer wrote an opera dealing with King Henry VIII?
10. Where did the world premiere of Poulenc's *Dialogues des Carmélites* take place?

11. Who was the American soprano for whom Jules Massenet composed *Esclarmonde?*
12. Name two French cities where opera festivals are held in the summer.
13. What was the title of the opera left unfinished by Debussy at his death?
14. Which three Offenbach operettas have been recorded by Régine Crespin?
15. Which of the following is *not* a French opera: *Le Roi d'Ys; Robert le Diable; Le Coq d'Or; Le Roi de Lahor?*
16. Which of the following is *not* a French operatic conductor: Pierre Boulez; Jean Morel; Wilfred Pelletier; Georges Prêtre?
17. What is the current name of the Paris theater formerly known as the Opéra-Comique?
18. List Hoffmann's four great loves in Offenbach's opera.
19. From which operas do the following arias come from? Give the title, the composer's name, and the character who sings each:
    - a. "Pourquoi me réveiller, ô souffle du printemps?"
    - b. "Les oiseaux dans la charmille"
    - c. "Vois ma misère, hélas! Vois ma détresse."
    - d. "Je dis, que rien ne m'épouvante."
    - e. "Connais-tu le pays où fleurit l'oranger?"
    - f. "Ah! je ris de me voir si belle en ce miroir!"
    - g. "Avant de quitter ces lieux"
    - h. "Pleurez mes yeux!"
    - i. "Ô souverain, ô juge, ô père"
    - j. "Enfin, je suis ici."
    - k. "Il m'en souvient."
    - l. "Sois immobile."
    - m. "Ah! fuyez, douce image"
    - n. "Ah quel dîner je viens de faire."
    - o. "Où va la jeune indoue?"
20. Who is the composer of *Les Martyrs*? What is the title of the better-known Italian version?

Answers on page 158.

4. GERMAN OPERA

These concern German operas not *composed by Wagner or Richard Strauss.*

1. Name two operas by Albert Lortzing.

2. Who composed *The Merry Wives of Windsor?*
3. Who is the composer of *Margarete?*
4. Where and when was *Fidelio* first performed?
5. When this beloved artist took one of her children to a performance of *Hansel and Gretel* in which she sang the role of the witch, the child caused pandemonium when, seeing his mother being thrown into the oven, he began to scream, "They're killing my Mama!" Who was this artist? Where did this take place?
6. Who wrote the play on which Alban Berg based the opera *Wozzeck?*
7. Who are the trio who torment Wozzeck throughout Berg's opera?
8. Name Friedrich von Flotow's most enduring work?
9. What are the names of the tenor and soprano lovers in *Der Freischütz?*
10. "Ozean! Du Ungeheuer" comes from what opera? Who is the composer?
11. Who completed the orchestration of the third act of Berg's *Lulu,* left unfinished at the composer's death?
12. What held up the completion of *Lulu* for more than forty years?
13. Where and when did the premiere of the completed *Lulu* take place? Name the conductor and the soprano who performed the title role.
14. When Hans Werner Henze's opera *The Young Lord* was first produced by the New York City Opera, what famous operatic personality played an important, if mute, role?
15. The Bavarian State Opera in Munich recently gave the first performance of a new opera based on a Shakespearean tragedy. Name the opera, its composer, and the artist who sang the title role.

Answers on page 160.

5. ITALIAN OPERA

1. Name the two operas by Gioacchino Rossini that feature a leading tenor named Lindoro.
2. What is the title of the opera that Gaetano Donizetti left unfinished at the time of his death?
3. Johann Simon Mayr was the principal teacher of which famous Italian composer?
4. Who was Amilcare Ponchielli's most successful student of composition?

5. What was the occupation of Giuseppe Verdi's father?
6. Alfred Catalani composed two operas that were very highly regarded by Arturo Toscanini, who named one of his children after the title character of one. Name the two operas.
7. Saverio Mercadante's mid-nineteenth-century opera *Il Giuramento* is based on the same source as a much more famous Italian opera. Name the source, its author, the better-known opera, and its composer.
8. Which opera is sometimes referred to as "the Italian *Tristan*"?
9. A Jesuit priest composed an opera for a beautiful and famous soprano. Name the composer, the opera, and the lady for whom it was composed.
10. For each aria title listed below, provide the opera it is from, the composer, and the character who sings it.
    a. "Dai campi, dai prati"
    b. "Quando le sere al placido"
    c. "Son pochi fiori"
    d. "Voce di donna o d'angelo"
    e. "Il cavallo scalpita"
    f. "Quanto è bella, quanto è cara!"
    g. "Ah! non credea mirarti"
    h. "Nemico della patria"
    i. "A lui che adoro"
    j. "Paolo, datemi pace"
11. Why did the Austrian censors (servants of the government that occupied northern Italy in pre-Risorgimento days) object to the libretto for Verdi's *Un Ballo in Maschera*?
12. The following are titles of choruses from Italian opera. For each, give the title and composer of the opera the chorus is from.
    a. "O, Pastorelle addio!"
    b. "Trema, Banco!"
    c. "Regina Coeli"
    d. "Guerra guerra!"
    e. "Va pensiero, sull'ali dorate"
13. Name the famous composers of the following relatively obscure Italian operas:
    a. *Emilia di Liverpool*
    b. *La Cena delle Beffe*
    c. *Alzira*
    d. *Gemma di Vergy*
    e. *Chatterton*
    f. *Giulietta e Romeo*
    g. *Adelson e Salvini*
    h. *I Promessi Sposi*
    i. *Nerone* (name two)
    j. *La Finta Giardiniera*
    k. *Edgar*
    l. *Tancredi*

14. Giuseppe Verdi started and abandoned several times a work based on what celebrated tragedy?

Answers on page 161.

6. RUSSIAN OPERA

1. Who was the librettist for Modest Mussorgsky's *Boris Godunov?*
2. Name two composers who tampered with the orchestration of *Boris Godunov* after Mussorgsky's death. Which of the three versions of the opera is most often performed?
3. What are the sources of Pyotr Ilich Tchaikovsky's *Pique Dame* and *Eugene Onegin?*
4. Music from Alexander Borodin's opera *Prince Igor* was adapted for a Broadway musical. One piece, with a new, "American" lyric, has become a popular standard.
   a. Name the Broadway show in question.
   b. Identify the section of the opera from which most of the music was adapted.
   c. Who did the adaptation?
   d. Name the song that became a popular hit.
   e. Who sang it on Broadway and who recorded the hit record?
5. In *Eugene Onegin* there is an aria known as the Letter Scene. In this opera, who mails the letter, who receives it, what are the letter's contents, and what ultimately happens between the sender and recipient?
6. Under what circumstances did the United States premiere of Serge Prokofiev's *War and Peace* take place?
7. When the Bolshoi Opera visited the United States in 1975, three of its leading artists became favorites of American audiences. Two artists have been enjoying success at several American opera houses, but Soviet authorities have not allowed the third to sing in America since 1975. Name the three singers.
8. Who was the first Bolshoi soprano to sing at the Met? Which roles has she sung there, and in what languages?
9. After the first production of *Boris Godunov,* Mussorgsky was urged to make a certain addition to his opera that would tend to make the work more enjoyable to the audience. The composer took the advice. What did he do?

10. Prokofiev created an opera based on Leo Tolstoy's *War and Peace.* He also composed an opera based on a novel by Feodor Dostoevsky. Name that novel.
11. Which of the following works is *not* a Russian opera: *The Czar's Bride; The Czarevitch; A Life for the Czar*? Name its composer and the composers of the other two operas.
12. In Tchaikovsky's *Pique Dame,* who is Herman's rival for the hand of Lisa?

Answers on page 162.

The great conductor Sir Thomas Beecham was presiding over a performance of *Aida* beset by many stylistic problems, not the least of which was a camel that relieved itself on the stage during the Triumphal Scene. Sir Thomas watched the havoc on the stage and then was heard to mutter to himself, "Terribly vulgar, but, Lord, what a critic!"

7. *AIDA*

1. What is the name of the god worshiped by the Egyptians in *Aida*?
2. How does Amneris trick Aida into revealing her true feelings about Radames?
3. Who created the role of Aida, and in what other way was this artist important to Verdi?
4. What change did Verdi make in the score of *Aida* after the first performance in Egypt and before the Italian premiere at La Scala?
5. Describe the two alternate endings Verdi composed for Radames's aria, "Celeste Aida."
6. In a well-known Italian film of *Aida* a popular screen beauty was cast

in the title role; the singing was dubbed by an equally beloved artist. Who is seen and who is heard in this 1953 film?

7. Aida, with her father offstage eavesdropping, tricks Radames into revealing the route the Egyptian soldiers are planning to take. Name the route in question.
8. *Aida* was the only opera conducted by Arturo Toscanini to be telecast, albeit in concert form, in the United States. A recording of this performance survives today on a major label. Name the singers heard as Aida, Radames, Amneris, and Amonasro.
9. A performance of *Aida* in Mexico City became one of the legendary evenings in Maria Callas's career. What was the reason for all the excitement?
10. Who wrote the libretto for *Aida*?

Answers on page 164.

8. *CARMEN*

1. In Act I, Micaela brings Don José three gifts from his mother. What are they?
2. What is the fight about between Carmen and her coworker in the cigarette factory?
3. What is the name of Carmen's adversary in that fight?
4. Which of Bizet's operas was composed first, *Carmen* or *Les Pêcheurs de Perles*?
5. What were the objections voiced by the management of the Opéra-Comique to Carmen's onstage activities?
6. Which of Carmen's two smuggler friends is the chief of the outlaws, El Remendado or El Dancaïro?
7. Who composed the music to the recitatives in the revised, "operatic" version of *Carmen*?
8. When Escamillo duels with José, he spares the corporal's life, giving a specific reason for doing so. What is this reason, and how does José repay the toreador?
9. Early unfavorable reviews of the first production of *Carmen* accused its composer of being in the thrall of what other well-known nineteenth-century opera composer?

10. Who was the famous American Carmen who graduated to that role after many performances of the role of Micaela?
Answers on page 165.

9. *CAVALLERIA RUSTICANA*

1. Why has Santuzza been excommunicated?
2. Who was the first Santuzza?
3. What is the name of Turiddu's other girl friend?
4. When Alfio refuses the glass of wine that Turiddu offers him, what reason does he give for not taking the drink?
5. During his "Addio" aria, Turiddu asks his mother, Mamma Lucia, to do three things for him. What are they?
6. What is the curse that Santuzza hurls at Turiddu at the climax of their quarrel? In what way might it be said to have been fulfilled?
Answers on page 166.

10. *MADAMA BUTTERFLY*

1. Puccini based his opera *Madama Butterfly* upon a play by David Belasco. Belasco, in turn, based his drama upon a short story by a then noted American author. Who wrote that original story?
2. Early in *Madama Butterfly*'s first act, Pinkerton describes the lease on the house he has rented. What were the lease's two clauses, and what relationship does one of them have to the marriage contract between Butterfly and Pinkerton?
3. When Butterfly shows Pinkerton a few of her possessions, he shows displeasure at one of them, which Butterfly promptly discards. What arouses Pinkerton's displeasure?
4. At *Madama Butterfly*'s world premiere at La Scala, one of the many things that the hostile audience carped at was a seemingly inadvertent

quotation from another Puccini opera. What tune was quoted (give the opera, too, of course) and where does the intrusion occur?

5. One of the most famous recordings of *Madama Butterfly* was made in Rome shortly before the outbreak of World War II. This recording is still available. Who sings Butterfly and Pinkerton on this album?
6. When does Pinkerton promise that he will return to Butterfly? What happens when Butterfly asks Consul Sharpless about this?
7. Where in Japan does *Madama Butterfly* take place?
8. After *Madama Butterfly*'s disastrous first performance, Puccini withdrew the opera from La Scala and made a series of revisions before he would allow the opera to be produced again, several months later, in Brescia. Four of these changes are important enough to be noted here. Name them.
9. Name the three sopranos who have twice recorded the title role of *Madama Butterfly.* Name the tenors on each of the six recordings.
10. What is the name of the wealthy suitor to whom the marriage broker Goro introduces Butterfly while she is still waiting for Pinkerton to return to Japan?
11. A famous visual element in many performances of this opera represents faulty knowledge of insect lore on the part of most designers. What is this? (*Hint:* This answer has nothing whatsoever to do with butterflies!)
12. In Act II the heroine orders the American consul to leave her home at once, although she immediately reconsiders. What has Sharpless done to incur Butterfly's wrath?

Answers on page 166.

One of the most catastrophic yet hilarious gaffes I have ever seen in an opera house occurred during a performance of *Die Walküre.* The first act was spectacularly cast—Birgit Nilsson was Sieglinde and Jon Vickers sang Siegmund. The performance grew from strength to strength musically, and then came that powerful moment when Siegmund pulls his father's sword from the tree into which it had been thrust by Wotan. Vickers pulled, Nilsson gasped in awe—and the sword fell apart into little pieces across the floor of the stage!

How the two singers managed to finish the act without dissolving into hysterics, I'll never know. (Vickers, of course, has been known to erupt with fury on lesser provocation.) However, Siegmund led his sister off to conceive Siegfried, and it can only be hoped that the Wälsungs' night of love went off more smoothly than did their escape from Hunding.

11. *I PAGLIACCI*

1. In the original score of *I Pagliacci,* which character is given the opera's final line?
2. What *is* that final line?
3. On what source did Ruggiero Leoncavallo base *I Pagliacci*?
4. What is the name of Nedda's lover?
5. What advice does Tonio give Canio after the latter's unsuccessful pursuit of Nedda's lover?
6. Who is the only major tenor in recent years who has made a practice of singing Turiddu and Canio on the same evening?

Answers on page 168.

12. *DER RING DES NIBELUNGEN*

1. In *Das Rheingold,* in order to steal the gold from the Rhinemaidens, what does Alberich have to do?
2. What are gods Wotan and Fricka worried about when we first meet them in scene 2 of *Das Rheingold*?
3. What is Freia's special contribution to the gods' lifestyle?
4. How does Alberich make himself invisible?
5. What is the name of the gods' new home?

6. Kirsten Flagstad, arguably the greatest Brünnhilde of all time, appears on the first complete recording of the *Ring* (led by Solti on Decca/London) singing what role?
7. What is the name of Sieglinde's caveman husband?
8. Why does the gentleman named in the answer to Question 7 not stop Sieglinde and Siegmund when they run off together?
9. What mode of transportation does Fricka employ in Valhalla?
10. How does Siegmund react when Brünnhilde tells him about the fate that awaits him?
11. How does Wotan initially plan to punish Brünnhilde for having defied him by trying to aid Siegmund in his battle with Sieglinde's husband? What mercy does she ultimately receive from him?
12. What does Brünnhilde tell Sieglinde, and what does she give her?
13. Why is *Siegfried* often referred to as the "scherzo" of the *Ring*?
14. What happens to Siegfried after he tastes the blood of the dragon that he has slain?
15. Why does Siegfried kill Mime?
16. How does Siegfried learn of Brünnhilde's existence?
17. Who is the Wanderer?
18. Early in Act III of *Siegfried,* the Wanderer encounters earth goddess Erda, who thus makes her first appearance on stage since *Das Rheingold.* What, however, has happened between these two characters since then?
19. In the first scene of the prologue to *Die Götterdämmerung*, what are the three Norns doing? When this activity is interrupted, what is foreshadowed?
20. Name the musical interlude played between the second scene of *Die Götterdämmerung*'s prologue and scene 1 of Act I.
21. Why does Waltraute visit Brünnhilde?
22. In what order were the libretti for the *Ring* operas written?
23. Who wrote the libretti for the *Ring*?
24. What reason does Hagen give for killing Siegfried?
25. What is the name of Brünnhilde's horse?
26. Name five orchestral highlights of the *Ring.*
27. Who wrote the English translation of the *Ring* used by the English National Opera and the Seattle Opera, and heard in the ENO's recording of the *Ring*?
28. Returning to *Die Walküre*, why does Fricka insist that Wotan protect Hunding in his fight with Siegmund?
29. What is Wotan's relationship to Siegmund?
30. What is Brünnhilde's relationship to Siegmund?
31. Therefore, what is Brünnhilde's relationship to Siegfried?

32. What are Brünnhilde's first words upon waking up at Siegfried's kiss?
33. What does Siegfried say upon seeing Brünnhilde for the first time?
34. Which *Ring* opera requires the services of a chorus? What is the scene in which the chorus performs?
35. Who devised the so-called "neo-Bayreuth" style of staging the *Ring* (and other Wagnerian works) that, after World War II, helped remove the Nazi stigma from these operas?
36. Name five famous Brünnhildes who also were celebrated for singing Sieglinde.
37. Who was the principal American Brünnhilde during World War II, when Flagstad was trapped in her native Norway?
38. Who conducted the notorious 1978 Bayreuth *Ring* cycle, in which the unorthodox production incited much booing from the audience?
39. Where did Herbert von Karajan first stage his own, controversial *Ring* production? What opera house subsequently produced a *Ring* based upon the von Karajan one?
40. Who is the English soprano who sings Brünnhilde in English as well as German, and who had the unenviable task of replacing Birgit Nilsson in that role when Nilsson injured herself in a backstage accident at the Metropolitan?
41. At what opera house was there a performance of *Die Walküre* that had Nilsson as Brünnhilde and Montserrat Caballé as Sieglinde? Who sang Siegmund?
42. Maria Callas sang the *Walküre* Brünnhilde in Italy, in Italian. At what theater did the performance take place, and who was the conductor?
43. Arturo Toscanini recorded a few vocal excerpts from *Die Walküre* and *Die Götterdämmerung* for RCA during the 1940s. What were the scenes that were performed, and who were the soprano and tenor?
44. The role of Wotan was shared by which two artists on the von Karajan recording of the *Ring*?
45. Who are the two Brünnhildes on the von Karajan recording of the *Ring?*
46. A world-famous soprano performed a tiny part on the Solti recording of *Siegfried.* Name the lady and the role she sang.
47. In the years between the *Ring* performances of Helen Traubel and Birgit Nilsson, who was the principal Brünnhilde at the Metropolitan Opera?
48. Name the American soprano who achieved great success as Brünnhilde at Bayreuth during the 1950s.
49. What is the curse that Alberich places on the ring, and why does he do so in the first place?

Answers on page 168.

13. *DER ROSENKAVALIER*

1. What are the nicknames that the Marschallin and Octavian have for one another?
2. What is Baron Ochs's full name?
3. Who is Leopold?
4. Octavian feels quite badly when the suddenly melancholy Marschallin dismisses him. What does his lover offer to allow him to do as a way of cheering him up?
5. Why does the Marschallin summon little Mahomet at the end of the first act?
6. Describe Ochs's reaction when he discovers Sophie and Octavian in each other's arms in Act II?
7. In Act II what choice concerning her future does Faninal give his daughter Sophie?
8. In the well-known film of the opera made at the Salzburg Festival, who are the artists who portray the Marschallin, Octavian, Sophie, and Ochs? Who conducts?
9. In the famous 1930 abridged recording of *Der Rosenkavalier* (currently available on Seraphim Records), who are the artists in the same roles listed in Question 8? Who conducts?
10. Why is Annina furious with Ochs as Act II draws to a close?
11. In Act III, the Marschallin gives advice first to Ochs and then to Sophie. What does she say to each?
12. Why does Mahomet come back onstage at the very end of the opera?

Answers on page 172.

14. *TOSCA*

1. Name the playwright who wrote *La Tosca* and the actress who made the play a success.
2. Puccini, with the help of his publisher, Giulio Ricordi, convinced what composer to relinquish the rights to the play on which the opera

is based, and what reason did they give to lure the gullible chap away from *La Tosca*?

3. Who is the model for the painting of Mary Magdalene on which Mario Cavaradossi, the hero of the opera, is working? What is this woman's bearing on the plot?
4. From where does the prisoner Angelotti escape?
5. Why does Tosca return to the church of Sant'Andrea della Valle after leaving Mario to return to his painting?
6. Which aria in *Tosca* did Puccini grow to dislike, and why?
7. When Scarpia prepares a safe conduct for Tosca, which route does she request him to specify?
8. How did the tradition of singing the aria "Vissi d'arte" from a prone position on the floor originate?
9. Why was the world premiere performance of *Tosca* interrupted moments after the opera began?
10. Who composed the music for the Te Deum that Tosca is heard singing offstage during the second act of the opera?

Answers on page 173.

Galina Vishnevskaya had a scary experience while singing *Tosca* in Vienna. Having stabbed Scarpia, the Russian soprano searched the dead man's desk, looking for the safe conduct that would allow her and Mario to leave Rome. Vishnevskaya inadvertently backed into a candle, and her wig caught fire. Fortunately her Scarpia was lying "dead" with his eyes open and saw his colleague was in danger of performing a non-Wagnerian immolation scene. He leapt up, ran to the still oblivious soprano, and began whacking the flames in her hair with his bare hands. Vishnevskaya screamed, unsure whether her Scarpia had suddenly gone mad or was indulging in a bizarre new piece of stage business. Only after the act ended did Vishnevskaya realize that her resurrected Scarpia had saved her life.

15. *LA TRAVIATA*

1. Where and when did *La Traviata* have its world premiere?
2. The opera's first performance was not a success. What were the two main reasons that the opera failed to please the audience?
3. What is the name of Violetta's protector at the beginning of the opera?
4. Name the six "solo" guests at Violetta's party.
5. Which character sings "De' miei bollenti spiriti"?
6. Why is Alfredo's father so insistent that Violetta give up Alfredo?
7. How does the elder Germont know that Alfredo will be at Flora's party?
8. What are Papa Germont's words after he witnesses Alfredo insulting Violetta, and why might they seem hypocritical?
9. Who sang the principal roles in the famous 1955 *La Traviata* at La Scala, immortalized by a pirated recording? Who designed and staged the opera? Who was the conductor?
10. Toscanini led a famous broadcast of *La Traviata* long available as a commercial recording. The broadcast was done in New York in 1946. Who were the artists singing Violetta, Alfredo, and Germont?
11. Violetta's poignant outburst "Ah, gran Dio, morir sì giovine" comes after what sign that she is dying?
12. What are Violetta's final, inappropriately joyous words?

Answers on page 174.

16. I'VE HEARD THAT BEFORE

Operatic composers occasionally pay other composers the compliment of quoting someone else's aria in their own score. Below are listed a number of operas where such quotations occur. Give the name of the opera quoted, its composer, and the reason that the quotation is made.

1. *Don Giovanni*
2. *Il Tabarro*
3. *Les Contes d'Hoffmann*

4. *Die Meistersinger von Nürnberg*
5. *Madama Butterfly*

Answers on page 175.

17. WAGNER I

1. What was Wagner's first opera?
2. Name Wagner's first wife.
3. Who was the influential music critic whom Wagner hated and used as the basis for a nasty character in one of his operas? Name the character and the opera.
4. The original version of *Tannhäuser* is known by the city in which it was produced. The revised version of that opera, first produced elsewhere, is also known by the city of its "birth." Name both cities and describe the principal difference between the two versions.
5. Name the monarch who, for many years, was Wagner's principal patron.
6. Name Wagner's second wife. Who was her father?
7. What was Mathilde Wesendonck's relationship to Wagner?
8. Which of Wagner's works is foreshadowed in themes found in the Wesendonck Lieder?
9. A brilliant and celebrated Briton adored Wagner's music and wrote a famous book on that subject. Name the writer and his book.
10. Which of Wagner's operas involve relationships between fathers and sons?
11. In what circumstance did Wagner hit upon the idea of composing *The Flying Dutchman*?
12. The Viennese soprano Leonie Rysanek is especially admired for her Wagnerian roles. What are they?
13. A young composer, who eventually achieved fame with a very popular opera of his own, once served as an assistant at Bayreuth during the preparation for the world premiere of *Parsifal.* In fact, this chap synthesized a few bars to be added to an orchestral interlude to facilitate a scene change. Identify the composer and his most famous opera.
14. For what occasion was the *Siegfried Idyll* composed?

15. In which of Wagner's operas do the following characters appear? Briefly discuss each one in terms of his or her importance to the opera in which he appears.

a. Melot	f. Mary
b. Henry the Fowler	g. Pogner
c. Wolfram	h. Waltraute
d. Erik	i. Woglinde
e. Fafner	j. Brangäne

16. Which Wagnerian characters sing the following well-known lines:
    a. "Amfortas–die Wunde!"
    b. "In fernem Land"
    c. "Du bist der Lenz."
    d. "Die Frist ist um."
    e. "Mild und leise"
    f. "Weia! Waga!"
    g. "Dich, teure Halle"
    h. "O sink hernieder"
    i. "Gerechter Gott, so ist's entschieden schon."
    j. "So ist denn aus mit der ewigen Göttern."
17. Klingsor, the villain in *Parsifal,* had once been a Knight of the Grail. Why is this knight different from all other knights?
18. In *Parsifal*, why has Kundry been condemned to her miserable existence?
19. What was Wagner's final opera?
20. Where and when did Wagner die?

Answers on page 176.

18. WAGNER II

1. Name the one-time operetta singer who, under the tutelage of Herbert von Karajan, became a noted exponent of Lohengrin, Rienzi, and Walther?
2. Who was the first American artist to sing at Bayreuth?
3. What is Cesare Siepi's one Wagnerian role?
4. What is the name of Tristan's loyal servant?
5. When the wounded Tristan was being cared for by Isolde (in Ireland, months before the action of the opera begins), what alias did he use?

6. Which of the following characters does *not* appear in a Wagnerian opera: Herzelaide; Ortrud; Brangäne; Magdalene?
7. Which of the following artists has never sung a complete Wagnerian role in the opera house: Renata Tebaldi; Leontyne Price; Maria Callas; Mario del Monaco?
8. Name the celebrated comedienne who for years has convulsed audiences with her satirical lectures on Wagner's music.
9. One of the greatest of Wagnerian conductors was Italian. Name him.
10. In which of Wagner's stage works is a musical theme from *Tristan* quoted? Describe the dramatic situation.
11. Name all of the Mastersingers.
12. Which of Wagner's mature operas are devoid of all supernatural elements?
13. Who is the British conductor who led the English-language performances and recordings of the *Ring* given at the English National Opera?
14. Which was the Wagnerian role that Nellie Melba foolishly insisted upon singing, nearly wrecking her voice in the process?
15. Who was the "Schwarze Venus" of Bayreuth?

Answers on page 179.

19. MOZART

1. What is the title of Mozart's first opera, and how old was he when he wrote it?
2. What is the familial relationship between Fiordiligi and Dorabella in *Così Fan Tutte*?
3. Listed below are several arias, duets, and ensembles from Mozart operas. For each, name the opera it is from, and the character or characters who sing them.

   a. "Dalla sua pace"
   b. "Ein Mädchen oder Weibchen"
   c. "Vedrò mentr'io sospiro"
   d. "Un'aura amorosa"
   e. "Pace, pace mio dolce tesoro!"
   f. "Bei Männern, welche Liebe fühlen"

4. In which of Mozart's operas do the characters listed below appear?
   a. Sesto
   b. Elettra
   c. Don Curzio
   d. Masetto
   e. Astrafiammante
   f. Guglielmo
5. For which single Mozart role was soprano Zinka Milanov celebrated?
6. Which two Mozart operas had their world premiere in Prague?
7. Which of Mozart's operas is a thorough debunking of the world of opera?
8. Two of the most famous arias in *Don Giovanni* were inserted after that work's first performance. Name them.
9. Which of the following operatic conductors is *not* renowned for his Mozart performances: Bruno Walter; Fritz Busch; Clemens Krauss; Josef Krips?
10. Richard Strauss was a great admirer of Mozart. Two of Strauss's operas are acknowledged homages to Mozart works. Name these operas and the Mozart operas that, in a sense, inspired them.
11. At the end of *Don Giovanni*, the six surviving characters announce their plans for the future. For each of these people–Donna Anna, Don Ottavio, Donna Elvira, Zerlina, Masetto, and Leporello–describe their projected activities.
12. In *The Magic Flute*, what is Monostatos's reward for telling Sarastro of Pamina's attempt to escape?
13. Which Mozartean character is a "valentine" to the composer's wife?
14. Which of the following celebrated basses was *not* a great exponent of *Le Nozze di Figaro* and *Don Giovanni:* Feodor Chaliapin; Cesare Siepi; Ezio Pinza; George London?
15. Which Mozart aria was often sung by Maria Callas in concerts? (Callas was rarely associated with Mozart's music.)
16. Who directed the 1979 film version of *Don Giovanni*? Who conducted this performance? Who sang the title role, and who were the three ladies heard and seen in the film?
17. Actor Alfred Lunt staged a Metropolitan Opera production of one of Mozart's most brilliant operas that established that work as a repertory opera in America. Name the opera.
18. When Ingmar Bergman filmed *The Magic Flute* in 1974, he made a major change in one aspect of the plot. What was this alteration?
19. Name the two European music festivals closely associated with Mozart operas.

20. What is the name of the love song that Cherubino has written in honor of the Countess Almaviva in *Le Nozze di Figaro*?
21. At the ripe old age of fourteen, Mozart was commissioned by an Italian theater to compose an *opera seria.* Name the work that resulted.
22. Name the three libretti written for Mozart by Lorenzo da Ponte.
23. Freemasonry is the ever present theme of which Mozart opera?
24. Janet Baker has won plaudits for her work in which relatively unknown Mozart opera?
25. Marc Chagall created the decor for a landmark production of a Mozart opera in a famous opera house. Name the opera and the opera house.

Answers on page 180.

20. PUCCINI RARITIES

1. Where and when was Puccini born?
2. All of Puccini's operas except one were published and managed by the famous publishing house Ricordi. Which opera was handled by another publisher, and who was that publisher?
3. Who sang the title role at the premiere of *Turandot*?
4. Name the country town where Puccini had his hunting lodge.
5. What was the title and who was the playwright and the star of the hit Broadway show that Puccini saw in London and which inspired him to compose *Madama Butterfly*?
6. From whom did Puccini steal the idea for his opera *La Bohème*?
7. Which four Puccini operas had world premieres at the Metropolitan Opera House?
8. Puccini once auditioned a young singer and said to him: "Who sent you to me? . . . God?" Whom was he addressing?
9. Can you name the first artists to sing the roles of Minnie, Johnson, and Rance in Puccini's *La Fanciulla del West*? Who conducted the premiere?
10. Who were the librettists for Puccini's "big three"–*La Bohème, Tosca,* and *Madama Butterfly*?
11. A famous recording was made of a performance that celebrated the fiftieth anniversary of the world premiere of *La Bohème.* Where was this performance given, and who were the conductor and the principal artists?

12. A famous playwright turned down Puccini's request for the operatic rights to one of the author's most successful plays. What reason was given for the refusal, and what was the eventual fate of the play in question?
Answers on page 181.

21. VERDI

1. Where was Verdi born?
2. Name Verdi's influential patron and father-in-law.
3. What did the slogan "Viva Verdi" actually mean?
4. Which of Verdi's twenty-six operas were composed to French texts?
5. Which of Verdi's operas was composed as a vehicle for Jenny Lind?
6. What was the name of Verdi's country estate?
7. Verdi revised *Simon Boccanegra* in 1881. Who worked on the revised libretto, and what was the principal addition to the opera?
8. To whom did Verdi dedicate his *Requiem*?
9. Who was the librettist for *Rigoletto*?
10. Name three nonoperatic songs by Verdi.
11. Who was the second cellist at the premiere of *Otello*?
12. Which Verdi chorus became a patriotic anthem of a newly unified Italy?
13. In which of Verdi's operas did the woman who was to become the composer's second wife create the leading female role?
14. Who created the role of Falstaff?
15. Which Verdi work was made into a propaganda film by the Allies in World War II?
16. Why did Verdi decide not to compose an opera based on Sardou's play *La Tosca*?
17. Where did Verdi die?
18. What was the charitable organization created by Verdi?
Answers on page 183.

22. VERDI RARITIES

1. In which operas do the following ladies appear: Griselda; Federica; Fenena; Odabella?

2. The aria "La mia letizia infondere" is from which of the following Verdi operas: *Alzira; Un Giorno di Regno; I Lombardi alla Prima Crociata; Simon Boccanegra*? Who sings it, and for what kind of voice is it written?
3. Ernani, in Verdi's opera, is offered a choice of two means of killing himself. What are they, and which does the poor tenor choose?
4. Who is the author of the libretto of *Nabucco*?
5. In Verdi's *Macbeth,* the aria for Lady M., heard early in the second act of the revised version of the opera, is completely different from that composed for the original 1847 production. Name the aria in the second version and also the one it replaced.
6. What Verdi opera is based on a poetic drama by Lord Byron?
7. In what country does Verdi's *Un Giorno di Regno* take place?
8. Verdi attempted to compose an opera based on Shakespeare's *King Lear* but never completed it. Although Verdi destroyed most of the music, one aria was later used in another famous work. Name the aria, the opera, and the character who sings it. Who was the character in *Lear* for whom it was intended?
9. Verdi borrowed the theme from one of his early songs and gave it to the heroine of one of his most popular operas. Name the song, the opera in which it appears, the aria, and the character who sings it.
10. Verdi often portrayed tender relations between fathers and daughters in his operas. Perhaps he was drawn by such themes due to his having lost his own two children when they were still very young. Here is a list of daughters. For each, provide the name of her father and the title of the opera in which they appear.
    a. Amelia Grimaldi
    b. Abigaille
    c. Nannetta
    d. Gilda
    e. Leonora di Vargas
11. Although there are many drinking songs in Verdi's operas, only one major Verdian character is shown to be drunk. Name the character, the opera, and the significance of the figure's inebriation.
12. Which of the following plays is *not* the source of a Verdi opera: *Die Räuber; Henry V; La Fuerza del Sino; Henry IV, Part 1*?

Answers on page 184.

OPERA STARS AND SUPERNOVAS

23. BARITONES

Try to identify the baritones from the clues given below.

1. Celebrated for his Verdi, this artist died on the stage of the Metropolitan Opera.
2. Skipping out on his Metropolitan contract to make a film called *Aaron Slick of Punkin Crick* almost cost this artist his career with that opera company.
3. Renowned as a frightening Baron Scarpia, this singer is also a noted stage director, painter, and teacher.
4. This heroic baritone continued to sing although suffering from cancer of the vocal cords; he died at a young age.
5. He created the roles of Iago, Falstaff, and Tonio.
6. Although alcoholism shortened his career, this baritone enjoyed great popularity at the Met, on radio, and through his recordings.
7. This American baritone was brave enough to talk back to the gallery patrons at the opera in Parma and was punched in the jaw by the stage manager of that opera house.
8. He excells in the operas of Strauss, Mozart, and Wagner, and once was

married to a famous artist with whom he frequently appeared in performance.

9. This baritone, who has performed in many contemporary operas, once costarred in a Broadway musical with Phil Silvers and Nancy Walker.
10. He sang at the Metropolitan for thirty-three consecutive years, setting a record for longevity in that theater by a leading artist. He often sang exotic villains.
11. Although he is a star all over the world, this baritone has sung exactly one performance at the Metropolitan Opera, replacing Leonard Warren after that artist's sudden death.
12. A farmboy from Illinois, this gentleman is the handsome villain in Verdi operas from Hamburg to San Francisco, and all points in between.
13. This baritone had a distinguished career throughout the United States and Latin America, and costarred with Maria Callas in many of her early triumphs. Most Americans know him as the star of a Frank Loesser musical
14. The most famous Baron Ochs of his day, he fled the Nazis and ended his career at the Metropolitan.
15. England's most noted contemporary baritone, this artist, knighted by Queen Elizabeth, is hailed for his acting as well as his voice.
16. One of the first Americans to make a career in postwar Europe, he was noted for his versatility and his powers as an actor.
17. He was the first black male to sing at the Metropolitan Opera.
18. A redoubtable Viennese baritone, this artist has aged gracefully from leading man to character singer. He is well known for his work in operetta.
19. This Swiss artist began his long career as a baritone, but in recent years he has displayed comic gifts as a *basso buffo.*
20. He has recorded each of Schubert's six hundred songs and has sung operas by Gluck, Berg, Busoni, and virtually everybody else.
21. Once married to a celebrated Octavian, this veteran baritone is a Rossini specialist and a pillar of the Glyndebourne Festival.
22. One of the few French artists to enjoy an international career, this baritone has gone from villains to character roles, always impressing as an actor and a linguist.
23. A product of the New York City Opera, this young baritone sings everything from *Il Barbiere di Siviglia* to *Billy Budd* in opera houses throughout the world.
24. Beloved as a character singer for forty years, this baritone was married to a great soprano.

25. A stage actor and director of great skill and charm, he called himself a baritone and sang the comic villain in a popular operetta.

Answers on page 185.

24. MEZZOS

Try to identify these mezzos from the clues given below.

1. The most famous Carmen of her time, this mezzo once made a movie with Bing Crosby.
2. This beautiful lady invaded New York with the Bolshoi and conquered the city with her Marina. She also sings at La Scala, Vienna, and Paris.
3. Although she started her career singing small roles at La Scala, this artist soon set the world standard for such roles as Azucena, Amneris, Adalgisa, and Rosina.
4. She was the first American Carmen.
5. This large lady from Germany helped the American war effort in World War I, although two of her sons fought in the Kaiser's army.
6. Samuel Barber's aunt, she sang Dalila and Suzuki in the company of Enrico Caruso.
7. This mezzo is married to a leading bass at La Scala and is a great favorite of American audiences.
8. Making her Metropolitan debut as a "boy" in *The Magic Flute,* this young artist has charmed audiences in the ensuing years as Cherubino, Rosina, Mélisande, and Cenerentola. She is also an admired recitalist.
9. This matronly artist, who eschewed high fashion onstage and off, was nonetheless one of the very finest singers of this century. Her performances opposite Maria Callas in *Norma* and *La Vestale* were greatly admired.
10. Before becoming a soprano, this mezzo stunned her audience by singing both Cassandra and Dido in the long-overdue Met premiere of Berlioz's *Les Troyens.*
11. Once a soprano, this New York-born artist lowered her vocal range and became a famous Dame Quickly and Carmen.
12. The artist in Question 10 replaced this lady at the last moment in the role of Dido at the first Met *Les Troyens.* This artist, a beloved Viennese, soon recovered from the illness that had sidelined her.
13. A famous Bolshoi Carmen, this lady sang that role in Russian oppo-

site Mario del Monaco, who performed that night in a mixture of French and Italian.

14. A favorite of Toscanini, this exciting mezzo's voice failed her quite early, ending a brilliantly promising career.

Answers on page 186.

A Spanish soprano celebrated for her glorious *pianissimi* found herself singing her first *Aida* in a major opera house with a Radames understudy who was singing the part for the first time. The lady acquitted herself notably, and the understudy, whose usual role in Verdi's opera was that of the messenger, performed well. However, as the end of the Tomb Scene drew near, Madame — decided to take no chances with the newcomer. In an aside clearly audible in the house (and preserved on numerous in-house tapes), she stopped singing a moment before her last opportunity of the evening to dazzle the audience and said to the tenor, *"Canta piano"* (Sing softly). The poor tenor obeyed his Aida, but many in the house were chuckling too loudly to hear the high note!

25. SOPRANOS

Try to identify these sopranos from the clues given below.

1. Forty years old when she achieved stardom, this lady provided a glorious voice that could accomplish miracles with the music of Wagner, Gluck, or Beethoven.
2. She was the first American Butterfly.
3. Her operatic debut was televised throughout the United States, and within a few years' time, her Verdi interpretations were acclaimed throughout the world.
4. Whether singing Mozart, Verdi, or Samuel Barber, this lady impressed

with her beautiful tone and handsome stage presence. She learned the score of a brand new opera within a few weeks, and after its world premiere the critics believed that the role had been composed for this soprano.

5. She recorded *Carmen,* in an interpretation that is considered a classic, twenty years *before* she sang that role on the stage.
6. This famous Marschallin had a celebrated career as a recitalist, then retired to California, where she taught for the last two decades of her life. Several of her former pupils (Grace Bumbry, Régine Crespin, and Frederica von Stade) are themselves famous singers.
7. Toscanini told her that she had the voice of an angel, and throughout her career, her fans swore that she had a similarly angelic personality.
8. This portly lady was no actress, but when her *pianissimo* floated upward in the opera house, few cared about her dramatic shortcomings.
9. This pretty lady is noted for her Violetta and her Lucia, but she has also starred in a horror film, an Italian movie, and had her own television show in Italy for many years.
10. She made her debut at the Royal Opera in a tiny role, then sang dramatic soprano parts for several seasons until one night when, apparently cast "against type," she stunned the world with her abilities as a coloratura at the premiere of a new production of a *bel canto* favorite.
11. This exciting artist started her career as a mezzo-soprano, then let her voice fly upward until her repertoire included Lady Macbeth, Norma, and Tosca.
12. A beautiful woman with a heavenly voice, this artist had a great career in Europe and America despite her alleged former association with Nazi politics.
13. The first American to sing at Bayreuth, she was known as the "Yankee Diva."
14. She sang 700 performances in 27 seasons at the Metropolitan Opera, and has been celebrated for her ability to step into a role at a moment's notice.
15. The modern world's most fabulous singer of Wagner, this artist elected to give up her American career rather than accept defeat in a tax case.
16. She made her New York debut as a last-minute replacement for Marilyn Horne. Within a year she was a star at the Metropolitan Opera. When she appears, she is often glorious, but her reputation as a "canceler" is all too well deserved.
17. This Viennese artist sings Verdi and Puccini roles as brilliantly as she performs the heroines of Strauss and Wagner.

18. Caruso insisted that she sing with him at the Met. Her voice has been called one of the greatest in history, but her chronic stage fright led to an early retirement.
19. A plane crash cut short the life of this beautiful soprano who combined Hollywood stardom with a career as an opera star.
20. Her every move seemed to guarantee her headlines, yet the constant publicity, much of which was unjustly negative, could not obscure the fact that she was one of the most brilliant operatic artists of all time.
21. Brooklyn-born, she achieved fame singing queens from Egypt, Scotland, and England.
22. This petite soprano boasted a voice that could soar an octave *above* high C.
23. After a long career in her native Italy, this soprano became a controversial leading lady at the Metropolitan Opera, appearing in many new productions and TV broadcasts.
24. In her day a fine coloratura, she is perhaps best remembered because a chicken recipe takes its name from her.
25. Although she has never sung with a major opera company, this charming lady's satirical treatments of Wagner, Verdi, and "The Art of the Lied" have endeared her to music lovers around the world.

Answers on page 186.

Luciano Pavarotti likes to tell this joke about a chap who suffered a head injury and had to be rushed to the local hospital for brain surgery. When the victim regained consciousness, the surgeon told him: "I'm afraid we had to remove half of your brain. I hope this doesn't affect your life too much." The patient smiled and reassured the doctor: "Oh, that's all right—you see, I'm a tenor!"

26. TENORS

Try to identify these tenors from the clues given below.

1. Italian journalists nicknamed this feisty divo "Golden Calves" be-

cause his handsome appearance thrilled people nearly as much as his charismatic tenorizing.

2. Not content with being a leading singer in theaters around the world, this tenor also conducts and has directed performances in many of the theaters in which he sings.
3. This tenor began his career as a baritone, achieved his greatest successes as Tristan and Otello, and ended his career singing *basso buffo* roles.
4. This artist once took part in a bizarrely comic fund-raising gala for the Met, in which he was photographed doing an Apache dance with a celebrated prima donna with whom he had rarely, if ever, shared the stage. Name the tenor and his dancing partner.
5. These two tenors, brothers-in-law, were stars for decades and would not speak to each other.
6. At the age of eighty, this famous artist sang a small role in an opera in which he often sang the tenor lead.
7. Equally at home in operetta and grand opera, he fled the Nazis only to die prematurely in England.
8. Although he only sang one fully staged opera performance in his entire life, this tenor was chosen to portray Enrico Caruso in a famous movie.
9. After singing a particularly thrilling high C, he stopped the performance to announce that the note had been dedicated to a newspaper critic who, a few days earlier, had written that the tenor could no longer hit high C.
10. After missing his entrance in *Lohengrin,* this tenor made the oft-repeated request to a chorister: "What time does the next swan leave?"
11. Many boy sopranos turn out to be basses, but this boy (who once turned down the opportunity to hear Caruso in order to go to a silent film instead) was often hailed in later life as Caruso's "successor."
12. Although he sang in many operas, this tenor made many fans through his appearances in Broadway musicals, including *Candide* and *Man of La Mancha.*
13. Although he was five feet eight inches tall, much shorter than the two ladies with whom he costarred most frequently, this brilliant tenor was considered one of opera's most potent sex symbols during the peak of his career.
14. Although he is as Italian as the tower at Pisa, this tenor received his first major engagements in Australia and England.
15. This gentleman recorded one of his best roles in an opera that has the

rare distinction of being conducted by its composer in this recording. Name the tenor, the opera, the role he sang, and the work's composer.

16. This Polish-born tenor made life miserable for Grace Moore (and was repaid in kind) whenever the two sang together.
17. During a performance of *Tristan und Isolde,* this glorious but temperamental tenor once got up from the dying hero's bed to demand that noisy members of the audience "stop their damned coughing."
18. This polyglot artist has recorded more complete operatic roles than any other singer.
19. He rarely sang in staged operas, but his way with songs made him one of the most popular concert stars of his age, as his recordings still testify.
20. In between engagements at the world's leading opera houses, this outstanding tenor (whose admittedly bland stage presence led one exasperated critic to compare him to a trained seal) runs an inn in Verdi's hometown.
21. Although he excels as Faust, Hoffmann, and Werther, this aristocratic tenor is not French at all and, in fact, made his operatic debut in Cairo.
22. Beginning his career singing such tiny roles as Parpignol and Roderigo, this hefty gentleman eventually earned a place for himself in many opera houses in such roles as Samson, Otello, Canio, and Tannhäuser.
23. This tenor made some of his first recordings while interned in a POW camp, later going on to thrill audiences at La Scala, Vienna, and the Met.
24. As a young man, this Neapolitan was so poor that he owned only one shirt. Once, at the beginning of his singing career, a photographer called on the singer at home. The tenor's shirt was soaking wet from having been washed, and the photography session was salvaged only when the rotund little man wrapped a bed sheet, toga-fashion, around his middle. In his peak years, this tenor had no trouble keeping himself in shirts.

Answers on page 187.

27. LUCINE AMARA

1. With which opera company did Amara score her first successes?
2. What was Amara's nickname during her first years as a singer?

3. Who was the conductor who guided Amara's career in its early years?
4. Lucine Amara has sung in five opening night performances at the Met. Give the dates, and name the operas and roles she sang on these occasions.
5. Name four complete opera recordings Amara made for commercial recording companies. For each, name her principal colleagues and the conductor.
6. Name seven roles Amara recorded for the now defunct Metropolitan Opera Record Club. (These discs are long out of print and are highly prized collector's items.)
7. Amara sang with Mario Lanza in what film?
8. Amara is renowned for her ability to assume a role at a moment's notice. She has occasionally rescued a performance by replacing an ailing soprano partway through a performance. One evening at the Met, Amara had to go on in mid-scene, without benefit of an announcement. Name the opera, the role, and the singer Amara replaced that evening.
9. Name five operas in which Amara has sung more than one role.
10. As of 1982, Lucine Amara had sung 505 performances at the Metropolitan Opera. (She has also sung more than 200 times with the Met on tour.) Who is the only other soprano, also an American, who sang at the Met more often?

Answers on page 187.

28. MONTSERRAT CABALLÉ

1. Describe the unusual circumstances under which Caballé made her entrance into American operatic life.
2. What was the soprano's childhood ambition?
3. Irving Kolodin, reviewing a Caballé performance of Desdemona that did not impress him, made a devastating comment about her abilities as an interpreter. Do you remember what he said?
4. Name the tenor to whom she is married.
5. Which opera did Caballé and her husband sing together on records?
6. Caballé "discovered" a young tenor during a 1970 performance of *Norma.* Who was he?
7. In which two operas has Caballé appeared with Birgit Nilsson?

8. Which three Richard Strauss heroines has Caballé sung?
9. Where did Caballé sing her first Turandot?
10. For what foible is Caballé notorious?
11. List two productions from which Caballé has withdrawn at almost the last possible moment.
12. Which two operas by Rossini has Caballé recorded?

Answers on page 188.

Several years ago, I attended a performance of Puccini's *Tosca* in which the title role was sung by a glamorous and justly renowned dramatic soprano from France. This lady, long highly regarded in many Wagnerian roles, not to mention her incandescent Marschallin in *Der Rosenkavalier,* sang an overwhelmingly fine Tosca, certainly one of the two or three best interpretations of that Puccini heroine that I've ever heard. I went backstage that night to see the tenor, a friend of mine. However, when the diva swept by me in the corridor, I took her hand and gushed words to the effect that she had sung a truly great Tosca that night. The lady, proving to be as self-confident as she was talented, looked at me and, matter-of-factly, in a speaking voice that sounded something like a contrabass Maurice Chevalier, replied: "Well, when you have a great voice like I do, how can you help but be great?" *Zut alors!*

29. MARIA CALLAS

1. In what role did Callas have her first major success? Name the opera and its composer, and give the place and year of performance.
2. Callas made her La Scala debut in 1950 as Aida, replacing which well-known artist?

3. What was Callas's American debut role? Where and when was this performance?
4. What was the name of Callas's little poodle?
5. Maria Callas's American debut was preceded by the issuing of three complete opera recordings on EMI/Angel that received much critical acclaim. Name the operas, her costars, and the conductors.
6. Which roles did Callas sing at the Metropolitan?
7. Maria Callas and Jussi Bjoerling sang together only once. In what opera did they appear, and where did they sing it?
8. What was Callas's final new role at La Scala? Who were her tenor and baritone colleagues that night?
9. Name at least five operas revived at La Scala especially for Callas.
10. What opera was to have been staged for Callas at the Met when Rudolf Bing discharged her? Who replaced her?
11. Several of Callas's most famous operatic recordings were of roles that she never actually performed in the theater. Name three of these roles.
12. When Callas canceled a performance scheduled for the Edinburgh Festival, a little-known soprano replaced her and went on to become a major star. Who was she and what was the opera?
13. What incident allegedly began the Callas-Tebaldi feud?
14. How did Callas (allegedly) compare her voice to that of Tebaldi?
15. What was the name of Callas's husband?
16. Callas sang only two comic roles. Name them and their composers.
17. In 1946 Edward Johnson, the general manager of the Metropolitan Opera, invited Callas to sing two roles at the Met. Callas refused the offer. What were the roles, and why did she decline them?
18. Who was Callas's costar on her final concert tour in 1973–74?
19. Where and when did Callas's final public appearance take place?
20. What was the last staged opera in which Callas appeared? Where and when?
21. Who was the conductor under whose guidance Callas shaped the early years of her career? Who was her principal voice teacher?
22. What was Callas's only film? Who directed it?
23. What were Callas's three Wagnerian roles? In what language did she sing them?
24. A great figure in musical life and in Callas's own career died a few hours before Callas's first New York concert in eight and a half years. Who was he?
25. Name the only role Maria Callas ever broadcast live from the Met. Who was the baritone that afternoon, and why was Callas significant in his career?

Answers on page 189.

30. ENRICO CARUSO

1. Caruso was accorded the honor of being the first singer for whom a song was written especially for the purpose of making a recording. Name the composer and the title of the song.
2. Eleazar in Jacques Halévy's *La Juive* was Caruso's final role at the Metropolitan Opera. What was his debut role and the year?
3. Caruso recorded a patriotic song for the American effort in World War I. What was it?
4. One night, a basso colleague of Caruso's found himself voiceless seconds before the cue for his aria. Whispering his problem to Caruso, the unfortunate artist was assured by the tenor that Caruso would cover for him. What aria did Caruso perform?
5. Caruso, at the height of his fame, was arrested in New York. Of what crime was he accused, and what was the outcome of the case?
6. Puccini composed a famous role with Caruso in mind for the world premiere. As it turned out, Caruso did not appear in that opera's first performance but went on to sing the role with great success for the next two decades. Name the opera and the role.
7. There was only one singer with whom Caruso had a long-standing disagreement that prevented the two from appearing together. Who was that singer, and what was the one duet the two artists recorded together?
8. Caruso was a poor man's son, born in a poverty-stricken neighborhood in Naples, yet he often portrayed royal or noble characters. Name six blue-blooded characters from Caruso's repertoire.
9. What soprano, who often sang with the great tenor, was called by critics "Caruso in skirts"?
10. Caruso arrived at a recording session after having had a few drinks. His colleague Geraldine Farrar immortalized this fact during the duet the two sang that day. How?

Answers on page 191.

31. FRANCO CORELLI

1. Where was Corelli born?
2. With which celebrated tenor did Corelli study?

3. Corelli sang in the La Scala premiere of which contemporary Russian opera?
4. When Corelli canceled a performance of Maurizio in *Adriana Lecouvreur* at the Metropolitan Opera in 1968, who made a very successful surprise debut, replacing him on an hour's notice?
5. Which of Corelli's roles has been preserved on film? Who sings opposite him in that film?
6. Which three operas has Corelli recorded with Birgit Nilsson?
7. Corelli and Renata Tebaldi were a powerful team when they sang together at the Metropolitan. Name the five operas they sang together there.
8. Corelli sang the tenor lead in this *verismo* opera at La Scala opposite Maria Callas in the title role. This is one of the few Callas performances at La Scala that has not survived on tape. Name the opera.
9. Corelli's wife is a former opera singer. What was her stage name, and what are the three opera recordings in which she is heard?
10. Corelli once leapt from the stage of the Rome opera into a box. Why?
11. Who is the music critic whom Corelli once threatened to punch in the nose?
12. Corelli has performed two operas by Handel. What are they?

Answers on page 192.

The following story about Birgit Nilsson and Franco Corelli has been told so many times that it has entered the realm of folklore, but it is so endearing that it bears telling again. During the Met's spring tour, Nilsson and Corelli were singing in *Turandot.* After the second act, the tenor began to sulk, ostensibly because Nilsson had outshouted him on a jointly held high note. Rudolf Bing, faced with having to inform the capacity audience that Corelli had left the theater, advised the irritated tenor to bite Nilsson's lip when the two embraced in the final scene. Corelli thought this to be a wonderful idea and, one is told, nipped the soprano when the magic moment arrived. Nilsson finished the opera but the next day cabled Bing to say: "Cannot continue tour. Have rabies."

32. GIUSEPPE DI STEFANO

1. Name five operas that di Stefano sang in performance with Maria Callas.
2. Name two operas that he recorded with Callas but never sang on the stage with her.
3. Name the operetta that di Stefano sang first in Vienna, then on an international tour. What role did he sing?
4. Di Stefano made only one commercial recording with soprano Renata Tebaldi. What was it, and what unfortunate event occurred during the recording sessions?
5. What is the nickname by which di Stefano is known to his friends?
6. In a well-remembered incident, di Stefano, having completed dressing for a performance of Verdi's *Un Ballo in Maschera* in Philadelphia, was leafing through the opera house's program shortly before the performance was to begin. An advertisement caught his eye, and the tenor became angry. He summoned the theater manager to his dressing room and announced that he would not walk onto the stage until the offending page was excised from all the playbills. The poor manager had no choice but to accede to di Stefano's demand, delaying the start of the opera by more than an hour. What terrible thing did the playbill contain?
7. Once, while singing the third act of *Carmen* at the Met, di Stefano threw his Carmen to the ground with such force that the lady broke her arm. Who was the unfortunate Carmen?
8. Di Stefano took part in celebrated productions of *Fedora* and *Adriana Lecouvreur* at the Chicago Lyric Opera. Who were his principal colleagues in those productions?
9. Name five French operas in di Stefano's repertoire.
10. Arturo Toscanini chose di Stefano for one of the conductor's celebrated radio concerts with the NBC Symphony. This performance is available on records. What is the work in question, and who are di Stefano's colleagues?
11. In what role (and when) did di Stefano make his final Met appearance?
12. Di Stefano sang Otello once, in a performance that has survived as a "private" recording. Where and when did this *Otello* take place, and who were the soprano and baritone?

Answers on page 192.

33. PLACIDO DOMINGO

1. Domingo spent the early part of his career as lead tenor of an opera company in a rather small country, not famous for its opera. He sang his roles in the language of this nation. Name the country and the language.
2. Domingo recorded the prison scene from Verdi's *Don Carlo,* singing the title role, on a special disc made by Deutsche Grammophon as a benefit for an anti-cancer crusade. Who sang the role of Rodrigo on that recording?
3. Domingo's first operatic appearance in the U.S.A. coincided with the final appearance of a famous and beloved soprano. Name the opera and the soprano, and give the year and the place.
4. In what role did Domingo first attract major critical attention in America?
5. Domingo was invited to make his debut at La Scala at the suggestion of an American artist who turned down the role in question. Who recommended Domingo, and what was the role?
6. Domingo has another musical ambition besides being a star tenor. He has worked in this capacity at the Vienna State Opera and the New York City Opera. What is this second field of endeavor?
7. Name the two Wagnerian roles currently in Domingo's repertoire.
8. One of Placido Domingo's first professional engagements was a small role in the Mexico City production of an American musical comedy. Name the show.
9. In what theater did Domingo sing his first performance of Verdi's *Otello*? Name his conductor, soprano, baritone, and the year when the performance took place.
10. Which celebrated soprano once slapped Domingo across the face so hard that he required the services of a dentist? What opera were they performing and where?

Answers on page 193.

34. TITO GOBBI

1. Which Italian theater has been Gobbi's primary artistic home?
2. Name three Wagnerian roles that Gobbi has sung in Italian.

3. Gobbi's brother-in-law is also a famous singer. The two men frequently appeared with one another in a pair of Verdi operas that threw them into adversary positions. Name Gobbi's brother-in-law, the operas in question, and the roles each man sang in them.
4. According to the baritone's memoirs, a guest appearance he made at La Scala in a very difficult contemporary role was a great success, but one that so inflamed the jealousy of certain members of La Scala that Gobbi never felt really welcome at that Milanese theater again.
5. During the 1964–65 season Gobbi was asked to sing Baron Scarpia opposite two very famous Toscas who were returning to the operatic stage after prolonged absences. Name the sopranos and the opera companies.
6. Gobbi, as were a number of the best singers of his generation, was nurtured in his early days by proximity to which great Italian maestro?
7. In later years, Gobbi became well known as a stage director. For which company did he stage his first opera? What was the opera?
8. Gobbi appeared in Italian-made films of which three famous operas?
9. Gobbi's principal voice teacher was which well-known tenor?
10. Gobbi and Maria Callas were closely identified with roles in an opera they sang together only twelve times. Since their performances were considered by many observers to have been all but perfect, it is generally assumed that they performed this opera with one another on a great many occasions. Name the opera.
11. In addition to his work as a singer and stage director, Gobbi excels in which other artistic pursuit?
12. With which sopranos has Gobbi recorded the Puccini roles of Marcello, Sharpless, and Michele?

Answers on page 194.

35. LUCIANO PAVAROTTI

1. Where and when was Pavarotti born?
2. A childhood friend of the tenor's grew up to become an internationally famous artist and sings with Pavarotti frequently. Who is she?
3. What is Pavarotti's "good luck role" and, thus, the role that he prefers to sing when making a debut at an opera house?

4. Who was the soprano who was instrumental in establishing Pavarotti's reputation?
5. What did Pavarotti do for a living before he became a professional tenor?
6. What was Pavarotti's first complete operatic recording?
7. What was the role that can be said to have made Pavarotti into a superstar in America?
8. When Pavarotti sang *La Bohème* on a live telecast from the Metropolitan Opera House, who was the soprano who sang Mimi?
9. Pavarotti sang his very first performances of two of his most important roles in America. What were they, and where did he sing them?
10. What has Pavarotti advertised on American television?

Answers on page 195.

According to an article in *Time* magazine, Leontyne Price was readying herself backstage for her first *Aida* at La Scala. Shortly before the curtain rose, a representative of the company's makeup department stopped at Price's dressing room to wish the soprano good luck. Momentarily forgetting herself, the visitor reminded the star to be careful lest her "Ethiopian" makeup start to run and soil her costume. Laughing it off, the soprano shook her head and said, "Oh, sweetie, you'd be surprised how well it stays on me!"

36. LEONTYNE PRICE

1. Where is Miss Price's birthplace?
2. What is her birth date?
3. Before singing at the Metropolitan, Price sang three major operatic roles on NBC television. Name them.
4. Where and in what role did Price make her operatic stage debut?

5. Name three roles Price sang during her first Metropolitan season.
6. In what role did Leontyne Price appear on Broadway?
7. She sang at the inauguration of which United States president?
8. What was the name of Price's late, beloved housekeeper?
9. Who was Price's husband?
10. Leontyne Price has sung three opening night performances at the Metropolitan. Name the operas, the roles, and her costars.
11. Which complete operatic role has Price recorded three times?
12. What was Price's first role in German, and where did she first sing it?
13. Price has recorded a beautiful album of Christmas songs. Who is the world-famous conductor of that album?
14. What was the first role Price sang at the new Metropolitan Opera *after* her opening night Cleopatra?
15. In what opera did Price appear in the Soviet Union as a member of the visiting La Scala company?

Answers on page 196.

37. RENATA SCOTTO

1. In what opera did Scotto make her debut at La Scala? What role did she sing, and what other famous soprano was in the cast that night?
2. Renata Scotto once sang in an opera with Maria Callas at La Scala. What was the opera and what roles were sung by the two sopranos?
3. Although Scotto made her reputation in the *bel canto* repertoire, in recent years she has sung a number of the heavier, *verismo* roles. Name five of these roles that Scotto has sung.
4. To whom is Scotto married, and what was her husband's former profession?
5. Early in her career Scotto recorded *Lucia di Lammermoor.* Who are the tenor and baritone who sing with her on this recording?
6. In 1972 Scotto sang the role of Griselda in a New York concert version of Verdi's *I Lombardi,* which marked that work's first New York hearing in half a century. Who were the leading tenor and bass that evening, and who conducted? (The performance has been preserved on pirate records.)
7. List four operas that Scotto has recorded with tenor Placido Domingo.
8. Scotto once complained to a journalist that she had never been invited

to sing an opening night at the Met. In 1976 that injustice was corrected. Name the opera in which Scotto opened the Met's 1976–77 season, and list her tenor, mezzo, and baritone costars, as well as the conductor.

9. In what city did Scotto sing her first Norma?
10. Name two French operas in Scotto's repertoire.

Answers on page 196.

Leontyne Price once related that, while browsing through Saks Fifth Avenue one wintry afternoon, a shopper walked up to her, stared, and finally said, "You're Joan Sutherland."

"Oh, no, I'm not," purred Miss Price. "I'm Beverly Sills!"

38. BEVERLY SILLS

1. What was the name of the radio serial in which Sills had a featured role?
2. What role did Sills sing at her New York City Opera debut? When was it?
3. To whom is she married?
4. In what opera did Sills achieve her first major triumph?
5. Beverly Sills made her debut at La Scala in 1969, replacing another artist in a rarely performed opera. Name the opera, the soprano whom she replaced, and the reason that artist withdrew from the production.
6. What are the three operas that make up Donizetti's trilogy of operas dealing with queens of England? Which role has Sills sung in each opera?
7. Name the late bass who often costarred with Sills at the New York City Opera.

8. How many roles did Sills perform during her five seasons with the Metropolitan Opera? Name them.
9. Name the opera in which Sills and Joan Sutherland costarred. Where and when did this take place? Which roles did each soprano sing?
10. What was the first role Sills sang with the Metropolitan Opera Company?
11. Although Sills has been acclaimed in such diverse operatic capitals as Milan, Naples, Paris, and Vienna, which is the one European city whose critics have consistently rejected her?
12. When Sills was named director of the New York City Opera in 1978, whom did she replace?

Answers on page 197.

39. JOAN SUTHERLAND

1. In what role did Sutherland make her Covent Garden debut?
2. Who was the designer/director of the production that catapulted Sutherland into the realm of international opera? By the way, name the opera as well!
3. The first time Sutherland auditioned for this famous impresario, he rejected her attempt to join his very famous company. Who was he?
4. Name the two major singers whom Sutherland can justly be credited with discovering.
5. After Sutherland's Italian debut, the local journalists coined a nickname for her. What is it?
6. Sutherland's coach first became her husband and then her preferred conductor. What is his name?
7. What are three of the non-*bel canto* roles that Sutherland sang at the Royal Opera in the years between her debut and her eventual superstardom?
8. After years of singing tragic or, at least, long-suffering heroines, Sutherland finally achieved a success with a charming heroine in an *opera buffa.* Name the role, the composer, and the tenor who costarred with her in both the London and Metropolitan Opera performances of this work.
9. American opera fans often request the Metropolitan to rebroadcast an intermission feature in which Sutherland exchanged shop talk and

demonstrated different technical terms in singing with another great soprano. Who is the other soprano?

10. Before her husband took over the training of Sutherland's voice, a highly distinguished maestro helped the soprano prepare for several of her *bel canto* roles. Name him.

Answers on page 198.

40. RENATA TEBALDI

1. A noted Italian composer and a celebrated Italian soprano were among the first to recognize Tebaldi's talent. Who were they?
2. Tebaldi absented herself from La Scala for five years during the 1950s. During this time the soprano reigned as the public's favorite *prima donna* at the Met while Maria Callas, who sang only sporadically in New York, was the *diva suprema* at La Scala. Tebaldi, however, returned to Milan in a tumultuously successful performance in 1959. Name the opera in which she appeared. Who were her tenor and baritone costars?
3. Where did Tebaldi's 1950 American debut take place?
4. Who was the tenor who sang opposite Tebaldi at both her American and Metropolitan debuts? What were his and Tebaldi's roles on those occasions?
5. In 1958 Tebaldi sang the role of Mistress Alice Ford in a Chicago Lyric Opera production of Verdi's *Falstaff.* This was a truly "star-studded" event, and one that has been preserved as a pirated recording. Who sang the following roles with Tebaldi that night of Falstaff, Mistress Quickly, Meg Page, Nanetta, Ford? Who was the conductor?
6. Tebaldi had a favorite role in an opera that has never been fully admired by critics. Name the opera, the role, and its composer.
7. Once, on American television, Tebaldi took part in an hour-long broadcast devoted to four reigning prima donnas. Who were the other three ladies on this historic telecast?
8. Although she never sang German operas outside of Italy or in their original language, Renata Tebaldi, in the first decade of her career, was greatly admired in three Wagnerian roles. Name them.
9. In the last decade of her singing career, Tebaldi often shared the operatic and concert stage with this famous tenor, with whom she made only one commercial recording. Name him.

10. Tebaldi returned to sing in Italy in the autumn of 1967. She had not sung in her native land since 1962. What role in which opera did Tebaldi choose for her return, and at what opera house did the performance take place?
Answers on page 199.

Lucky opera groupies who got backstage after the Metropolitan Opera's 1968 opening night *Adriana Lecouvreur* witnessed the public ending of the "feud" that allegedly existed between Renata Tebaldi (Adriana) and Maria Callas, who had attended the opening and had been brought backstage by Rudolf Bing. As the two prima donnas tearfully embraced, one of Tebaldi's fans was overheard to say, "Thank God! Now we can play our Callas records in the open!"

41. DEBUTS AT THE MET

Can you give the debut role for each famous Metropolitan Opera star listed here? For "extra credit," give both the year of the debut and the year he or she joined the company.

1. Renata Tebaldi
2. Leontyne Price
3. Mario del Monaco
4. Grace Bumbry
5. Tito Gobbi
6. Marian Anderson
7. Robert Merrill
8. Montserrat Caballé
9. Cesare Siepi
10. Giulietta Simionato
11. Kirsten Flagstad
12. Rosa Ponselle
13. Birgit Nilsson
14. Cornell MacNeil
15. Joan Sutherland
16. Maria Callas
17. Franco Corelli
18. Marcella Sembrich
19. Beverly Sills
20. Shirley Verrett

21. Placido Domingo
22. Sherrill Milnes
23. Renata Scotto
24. Mirella Freni
25. Luciano Pavarotti

Answers on page 199.

42. FAMOUS FIRSTS

Can you name the singers who created the following roles at the world premieres of these operas? If you can, give the part he or she sang, and the place and year of performance.

1. Abigaille in Verdi's *Nabucco.*
2. Tosca in Puccini's opera.
3. Otello in Verdi's opera.
4. Ariadne in Richard Strauss's *Ariadne auf Naxos.*
5. Anne Trulove in Stravinsky's *The Rake's Progress.*
6. Sophie in Richard Strauss's *Der Rosenkavalier.*
7. Dick Johnson in Puccini's *La Fanciulla del West.*
8. Cleopatra in Barber's *Antony and Cleopatra.*
9. Canio in Leoncavallo's *I Pagliacci.*
10. Falstaff in Verdi's opera.
11. Mélisande in Debussy's *Pelléas et Mélisande.*
12. Santuzza in Mascagni's *Cavalleria Rusticana.*
13. Peter Grimes in Britten's opera.
14. The Old Prioress in Poulenc's *Les Dialogues des Carmélites.*
15. Cecilia in Licino Refice's opera.
16. Cio-Cio-San in Puccini's *Madama Butterfly.*
17. Turandot in Puccini's opera.
18. Norma in Bellini's opera.
19. Juana in Menotti's *La Loca.*
20. Lulu at the world premiere of the complete, three-act version of Berg's opera.

Answers on page 203.

Even the nicest of opera stars tend to be egocentric. Self-preservation is vital in the world of international opera, and it is useful for a

singer to feel that he or she is indispensable. On the closing night of the old Met, a hasty decision was made: after the final scheduled number, the curtain was to rise and the entire company of soloists, chorus, and honored guests would lead the audience in "Auld Lang Syne." Informed of this, superdiva Birgit Nilsson frowned and shook her head. "Oh, no, we can't," she wailed. "*I* don't know the words!"

43. THE YOUNGER GENERATION

Can you identify a number of today's most promising singers from the clues below?

1. This young soprano won an Italian singing contest when just twenty-one and is now celebrated for her roles in Verdi operas. She will soon add Bellini's *Norma* to her repertoire, in a recording conducted by Herbert von Karajan.
2. This mezzo-soprano from Greece made her American debut when the Deutsche Oper of Berlin visited the Kennedy Center in 1975. Since then she has sung in Vienna and New York, making her Metropolitan debut as Octavian in 1979.
3. This beautiful and unconventional soprano, highly regarded in such diverse roles as Salome and Leonora in *Fidelio,* sang in the first digital operatic recording.
4. This young tenor from New York City was a protégé of the late Richard Tucker. He has sung in Europe and the United States, and has become well known for his Werther and Duke of Mantua.
5. This handsome Spanish tenor scored his first major successes at the New York City Opera and now sings at the Met, San Francisco, Chicago, La Scala, and Royal Opera.
6. This young bass, who studied with Rosa Ponselle, made his Metropolitan debut at the age of twenty-three and soon rose from *comprimario* roles to such leading roles as Don Giovanni.
7. This Junoesque soprano, who won both the Japanese *Madama Butterfly* contest and the Met national auditions, is now celebrated for her Puccini and Verdi heroines in many of the world's leading opera houses and recently added Norma to her repertoire.
8. This young soprano followed her recording of Bess in Gershwin's

opera with appearances at the San Francisco and Metropolitan Opera companies, singing with such tenors as Domingo and Pavarotti.

9. A native of Puerto Rico, this baritone began his career as a jazz musician.
10. A New Yorker, this exotically named mezzo has an extensive repertoire that includes Octavian, Carmen, Kundry, and Amneris.
11. Hailed as Cherubino and Rosina, this beautiful young woman made her Metropolitan debut as one of the three genii in *The Magic Flute.*
12. This young baritone came to opera by way of musical comedy. His operatic roles include characters inspired by such writers as Shakespeare and Melville.

Answers on page 204.

44. OPERA STARS ON BROADWAY

Since Ezio Pinza conquered Broadway, singing in South Pacific, *many opera singers have combined the musical theater with operatic engagements. Listed below are some prominent singers who have also starred on Broadway. In which shows did they appear?*

1. Robert Weede
2. Cesare Siepi
3. Robert Rounseville
4. Risë Stevens
5. Giorgio Tozzi
6. Eleanor Steber
7. William Warfield
8. Irra Petina
9. William Chapman
10. Mimi Benzell
11. Helen Traubel
12. Ezio Pinza (besides *South Pacific*)
13. Leontyne Price
14. Jan Peerce
15. Dolores Wilson

a. *Where's Charley?*
b. *Man of La Mancha*
c. *Shenandoah*
d. *Carmelina*
e. *Porgy and Bess*
f. *Milk and Honey*
g. *Candide*
h. *The Yearling*
i. *I Remember Mama*
j. *Bravo, Giovanni*
k. *Show Boat*
l. *The Most Happy Fella*
m. *Fiddler on the Roof*
n. *The Sound of Music*
o. *Annie*
p. *Cry for Us All*
q. *The King and I*
r. *Fanny*
s. *Pipe Dream*
t. *South Pacific*
u. *Greenwillow*

Answers on page 204.

Theatergoers were amused when Lily Tomlin, the comedienne, playing an engagement at a Broadway theater, listed Zinka Milanov as her understudy in the playbill.

Someone reported this to Madame Milanov, who immediately slapped a multimillion-dollar libel suit on Ms. Tomlin, claiming great anguish and damage to her image (note that this was twelve years after her retirement from singing), since Milanov never served as anyone's understudy. The suit was settled out of court.

Fortunately for playwright and opera buff Terrence McNally, Madame Milanov never attended his play *The Ritz.* This work, a farce set in a gay Turkish bath, ended with the show's villain being thrown into a baggy green dress and named winner of the "Zinka Milanov Look-Alike Contest." One imagines the diva sniffing: "Ve are not amused!"

45. TINY FACTS ABOUT GREAT SINGERS

1. Name the American radio program on which both Callas and Sills appeared as children.
2. How did Richard Tucker support himself before he scored as a tenor?
3. To whom is mezzo Fiorenza Cossotto married?
4. What is the title of Risë Stevens's biography?
5. Piero Cappuccilli, the great Italian baritone, has sung only one performance at the Metropolitan. When did it take place, whom did Cappuccilli replace, and what year did this all happen?
6. For what reason did Kirsten Flagstad receive bad publicity after the end of World War II?
7. In what role and with which company did tenor José Carreras make his American debut?
8. Why was bass Boris Christoff prevented from making his American debut at the Met in 1950?
9. Sherrill Milnes, prior to his recognition as a major baritone, sang the television jingle for which popular brand of cigarette?
10. How is Sara (Mrs. Richard) Tucker related to Jan Peerce?

11. Where did Placido Domingo sing his first *Otello*? When did it take place, who was the conductor, and who were his soprano and baritone colleagues?
12. Turn-of-the-century mezzo star Louise Homer was the aunt of which famous American composer?
13. Birgit Nilsson has had a bitter feud with which celebrated conductor?
14. Lily Pons once was married to which famous conductor?
15. Grace Moore was the mentor of which other successful American soprano?

Answers on page 205.

Few singers were more beloved in their time than was contralto Ernestine Schumann-Heink, whose career lasted from the turn of the century through the 1930s, when she ended her public life as a network radio star in the United States. She was a large woman, and one night during an orchestral concert, the dear lady had great difficulty threading her way past the musicians and their music stands. One player, attempting to be helpful, whispered, "Madame, move sideways."

Schumann-Heink snapped back, "With me, there *is* no sideways!"

46. FAREWELLS AT THE MET

For each artist listed, give the last role sung at the Metropolitan Opera House. Can you also give the year?

1. Kirsten Flagstad
2. Zinka Milanov
3. Enrico Caruso
4. Leonard Warren
5. Maria Callas
6. Dorothy Kirsten
7. Richard Tucker
8. Lily Pons

9. Renata Tebaldi
10. Risë Stevens
11. Maria Jeritza
12. Giuseppe di Stefano
13. Birgit Nilsson
14. Elisabeth Schwarzkopf
15. Jussi Bjoerling
16. Beverly Sills
17. Robert Merrill
18. Geraldine Farrar
19. Jan Peerce
20. Eleanor Steber

Answers on page 206.

A beloved soprano and an equally admired tenor exchanged some harsh words during the curtain calls after the second act of Ponchielli's *La Gioconda.* Each accused the other of upstaging during the act's finale. "Callas is a better Gioconda than you," shouted the tenor, certain that that remark would draw blood. Hardly batting an eyelash, the diva retorted, "Tucker is a better *tenor* than you." They finished the opera amid an atmosphere reminiscent of the third act of *Who's Afraid of Virginia Woolf?* and didn't speak for weeks.

UNFORGETTABLE CHARACTERS

47. TITLE ROLES

Give the names of the characters referred to by the titles of the following operas:

1. *Der Rosenkavalier*
2. *Il Trovatore*
3. *L'Amore dei Tre Re*
4. *Die Walküre*
5. *La Fanciulla del West*
6. *The Flying Dutchman*
7. *The Gypsy Baron*
8. *The Merry Widow*
9. *The Bartered Bride*
10. *La Sonnambula*
11. *La Rondine*
12. *Il Barbiere di Siviglia*
13. *La Favorita*
14. *I Pagliacci*
15. *Die Fledermaus*

Answers on page 207.

48. NOBLESSE OBLIGE

In many operas, the affairs of men are influenced by the wishes of royalty. Below is a list of kings, queens, and other noble men and women who appear in operas.

Name the opera and composer, and describe the influence each character has on the action. Note that these people are not "title characters."

1. King Philip II
2. Cleopatra
3. Queen Elizabeth I (name two)
4. Charles V (name two)
5. Henry the Fowler
6. Gustavus III
7. Dmitri Ivanovich
8. Jane Seymour
9. Emperor Altoum

Answers on page 207.

49. THEIR MASTERS' VOICES

Each character listed below either owns slaves or employs servants. Identify the servants and the operas in which these characters appear.

1. Violetta Valery
2. Sir John Falstaff
3. Leonora di Vargas
4. Amneris
5. Pasha Selim
6. Dr. Bartolo (in *Il Barbiere di Siviglia*)
7. Médée
8. Marquise de Berkenfeld
9. Crespel
10. Timur
11. Rigoletto
12. Rosalinde
13. Dorabella
14. Sarastro
15. Madeleine de Coigny
16. Rocco
17. Maria Stuarda
18. Alice Ford (name four)
19. Madame Larina
20. Scarpia
21. Minnie (name three)
22. Elisabetta de Valois
23. Desdemona
24. Juliette

Answers on page 209.

50. SERVANTS, SLAVES, AND COMPANIONS

Identify the operas in which these servants or slaves appear, name their various masters or mistresses, and briefly describe the ways in which the servants influence the outcome of the operas in which they appear.

1. Annina
2. Mariandl
3. Robin
4. Aida
5. Brangäne
6. Adele

7. Suzuki
8. Bersi
9. Carlo Gérard
10. Curra
11. Despina
12. Frantz
13. David
14. Monostatos
15. Antonio

Answers on page 211.

51. HOLY MEN AND WOMEN

Here is a list of religious figures who appear in various operas. For each person listed, identify the opera he or she appears in and summarize the influence the character has on his or her hero.

1. Zaccaria
2. Varlaam
3. High Priest of Dagon
4. Ramfis
5. Mme. de Croissy
6. Cardinal Brogni
7. High Priest of Baal
8. The Bonze
9. Athanaël
10. Rangoni
11. Frère Laurent
12. John of Leyden

Answers on page 213.

52. HI, MOM! HI, DAD!

Below are listed various operatic parents. Identify the child or children of each, and describe the parents' influence on the outcome of the operas involved.

1. Oroveso
2. Peter and Gertrude
3. Archibaldo
4. La Cieca
5. Mamma Lucia
6. Marcellina
7. Antonio
8. Rocco
9. Strominger
10. Erda
11. La Mère and Le Père
12. Simon Boccanegra
13. Marquise de Berkenfeld
14. Mamm'Agata
15. Azucena

Answers on page 214.

53. WHAT'S MY LINE?

While many operatic characters are aristocrats with a great deal of money to burn, others must hold down jobs or, if they are lucky, run businesses. Below is a list of job titles or professions. For each, name the operatic character who holds such a position, the opera, and the composer.

1. Actress in a major repertory company
2. Actress in a small traveling company
3. Street singer
4. Broommaker
5. Birdcatcher
6. Clown (name two)
7. Physician
8. Rabbi (name two)
9. Painter (name two)
10. Valet
11. Duenna
12. Barmaid
13. Soldier (name at least five)
14. Recruiting officer (name two)
15. Schoolmistress

Answers on page 217.

54. DISGUISES

Operatic characters often conceal their true identities in order to gain entrance to forbidden places. Can you identify the characters whose disguises are described below?

1. This chap pretends to be a monk in order to gain admission to a palace where a wedding is about to be performed. The wedding party doesn't come off quite as planned.
2. Although he is a handsome nobleman, he dresses up as a drunken soldier in order to be with his beloved.
3. He dresses up as a country girl in order to stay in a place from which he has been banished. His costume, however, does him little good.
4. This noble lady costumes herself as a humble servant girl and finds true love in an unlikely place.
5. These folks have a grudge against a certain fellow. They put on masks and are invited to a ball given by their enemy. At the ball, they accuse their host of unbecoming conduct.

6. He dresses up as his own lawyer in order to trap the man who has dressed up as our hero.
7. These two fellows assume the most outlandish disguises in order to test the constancy of their fiancées. Ultimately, they wish they hadn't done so.
8. He dresses up as a monk and follows his prey home from a town fair, then proposes an interesting exchange.
9. Although she is a popular figure in society, this young lady pretends to be a Parisian *grisette* in order to enjoy a night on the town.
10. In order to show off his power, this boastful fellow transforms himself into a rodent, only to be promptly captured and robbed by the very ones whom he sought to impress.

Answers on page 218.

55. ALIASES

Certain operatic characters use false names. Below is a list of such aliases. Identify each by his or her real name, and tell why these people took on phony identities.

1. Lindoro
2. Pereda
3. Andrea
4. Amelia Grimaldi
5. Enzo Giordan
6. The Wanderer
7. Padre Raffaele
8. Enrico
9. Marquis Renard
10. Tantris
11. Mariandl
12. Zdenko
13. Signor Fontana
14. Idia Legray
15. Mlle. Olga
16. Gualtier Maldé

Answers on page 218.

Basso Cesare Siepi was once asked by the Met's management to make a guest appearance in a gala New Year's Eve *Die Fledermaus,* enter-

taining at Prince Orlofsky's ball. Evidently, Siepi wasn't familiar with the Strauss operetta, for, told that the "ball" would be hosted by mezzo Regina Resnik, Siepi did not realize that Resnik would be playing a male, Prince Orlofsky. At the appointed moment Siepi strode onto the stage. He spotted Resnik at once but failed to notice her false moustache and masculine attire. He graciously bowed and kissed her hand. We will never know when Siepi became aware of the snickering or if he ever realized its cause.

56. WHO WEARS THE PANTS?

One of opera's most exotic conventions is the device of the travesti, *or trouser role, in which a male character is impersonated by a female. Guess the character, opera, and composer from the clues given below.*

1. This mischievous youth is constantly getting into scrapes. Even the threat of being shipped off to the army can't subdue him for very long.
2. The queen's page, he is falsely accused of treason and is cruelly tortured.
3. A crown prince, this character ascends the throne at the end of the opera, but history tells us his reign was short.
4. Too talkative for his own good, this foppish youth is tricked into betraying his master's disguise to a would-be assassin.
5. This young musician claims to live only for his art, but a pretty ankle (belonging to a bewitchingly high-voiced singer) turns his head.
6. This foolish boy taunts his master's rival, provoking a tragic consequence.
7. Sent to woo in place of another, this young fellow immediately falls in love with the object of the other man's affection.
8. This young stableboy remembers the name of his master's murderer.
9. Flowers wither at his touch—until he finds the way to beat the Devil.
10. In this version of one of the greatest love stories of all time, the star-crossed hero is sung by a mezzo-soprano.
11. A great lover's steadfast friend, this high-voiced chap helps sing the most famous tune in "his" opera.

12. This jaded nobleman likes practical jokes and loves to launch young actresses' careers.

Answers on page 220.

57. HOME WRECKERS

Opera plots abound with illicit love affairs. Below are listed the names of some operatic home wreckers. Identify the operas and composers, the respective lovers and the spouses whom they betray, and briefly describe the outcome of the affair.

1. Luigi
2. Werther
3. Turiddu
4. Enzo Grimaldo
5. Riccardo
6. Roberto Devereux
7. Alfred
8. Percy
9. Countess Geschwitz
10. Drum Major

Answers on page 220.

58. GOOD DREAMS . . . BAD DREAMS

Identify the dreamers of the dreams described here. Name the opera, its composer, and state the relevance of the dream to the outcome of the opera.

1. He dreams of a terrible vengeance at the hands of the woman he has betrayed.
2. In her dream she views a horrible transformation to be undergone by her husband.
3. This lady dreams of her own death at the hands of her children.
4. She dreams of one who will defend her from false charges of witchcraft.
5. She is frightened by a dream in which her closest relative is slain.
6. This character dreams of a crime she has committed.
7. A dream is reported that seems to implicate an adulterous couple.
8. A dream that leads to a miracle terrifies the title character of this opera.
9. A dream in which her lover is restored to her comforts this heroine.

10. This account of a nightmare is not only a comic classic, but a highly detailed and lifelike description of this phenomenon.
11. This man dreams that he has been changed into a donkey. (No, it's not based on a Shakespearean comedy!)

Answers on page 222.

59. LOCO EN EL COCO

Operatic mad scenes are often the dramatic and musical high points of the works they climax. Explain why the following characters go off their rockers, and identify the operas and composers.

1. Elvira
2. Ophélie
3. Lucia
4. Nabucco
5. Marguerite
6. Peter Grimes
7. Azucena
8. Imogene
9. Boris Godunov
10. Juana (a.k.a. La Loca)

Answers on page 223.

60. *SUICIDIO*

There are many operatic heroes and heroines who take their own lives. Guess the identity of these poor souls from the following brief descriptions. Name the character, opera, composer, and give as many details of the suicide as you can recall.

1. Her lover having just been killed in a natural disaster, this melancholy lady follows him to her own icy grave.
2. Her only love rejects her as a faithless fiancée, and he prepares to travel onward in the hope of finding eternal love. Desperate to prove her devotion, this girl offers her life as evidence of her loyalty.
3. The villain holds the hero and his mother in his power. To free them, the heroine must declare her love for her enemy. Rather than live up to her promise, this lady chooses an easier way out of her dilemma.
4. Believing his humble sweetheart faithless, this titled chap poisons a

carafe of water and drinks it, offering some to his unlucky beloved, who assures him—after it is too late—that she has never betrayed him.

5. Responsible for two accidental deaths in a short period of time, this fisherman is advised to make an end of his own life. He follows the advice.
6. Determined to be united with her man in spite of all opposition, this maiden eludes her captors and reveals herself to her lover at the moment of his death.
7. Having killed his faithless lover, this not-too-bright chap decides he can no longer cope with life, and wades out into a conveniently located sea to drown himself.
8. In this early version of a familiar opera that had its ending revised, this poor boy finds his long-lost sweetheart, only to have her slain by their sworn enemy a few moments later. In despair, he jumps off a cliff to his death.
9. Rather than reveal her hero's secret to a rival, this girl stabs herself for fear that torture might wring the magic word from her otherwise unwilling lips. Her death was the final triumph of a beloved composer.
10. This suicide is averted when the downcast lad with the rope in his hand is reminded of the magic powers he has in his own music.

Answers on page 224.

61. MURDERS MOST FOUL

Operatic characters are often a bloodthirsty lot. See how many of these singing killers you can identify from the following descriptions. For each, name the opera and composer too.

1. This lady combines chemistry with floristry in order to do in her romantic rival. Name her, her victim, the man they shared, and, of course, the method.
2. Once upon a time there lived a king who suspected that his daughter-in-law was unfaithful to her husband. The king took the situation into his own hands and dispensed with the naughty lady, and then devised a clever plot to punish the poor girl's lover. This plot backfired. Name the king, the lady, and tell how things went wrong.
3. This girl had a weak will and a big mouth, not to mention a short fuse. Betrayed by her lover, she tattles, and from this indiscretion

comes a killing. Who is she, who does she tell, and who gets bumped off?

4. This ruler comes home from a hard day's debauchery, is greeted by his stepdaughter in surprisingly pleasant fashion, goes inside his palace, and there receives an unpleasant surprise. Name the king, his daughter, and the "surprise."
5. A hero has been betrayed by his paramour and humiliated by his enemies. Calling for aid from a friend on high, the man punishes the wicked and accepts his own doom in the bargain. Name the hero, the victims, and the method.
6. A loyal friend jumps to the wrong conclusion and vows revenge. How does he get it and what happens to him?
7. A famous and beautiful lady who loved to cook, and often felt the need to kill, combined hobbies at a dinner party in a well-known Italian city. She finds out too late, of course, that she always hurts the ones she loves. Name the lady, the city, her intended victims–and her *unintentional* one.
8. Two big brothers argue over fee-splitting after a construction job. One kills the other. Who are they, what do they quarrel over, who kills whom, and then what happens?
9. This wily fellow found that his dessert was none too good for him. Name the villainous Roman and his after-dinner surprise.
10. The Scottish lady in question comes up with a unique, if tragic, way of annulling her marriage. What are the particulars?

Answers on page 225.

62. PRISONERS OF FATE

All too many operatic folk are thrown in jail for one reason or another. Can you remember why the characters listed here were imprisoned? Describe each character's eventual fate, and, as always, name the opera and composer.

1. Piquillo
2. Margherita
3. Manon Lescaut
4. Monterone
5. Duchess Elena
6. Don Carlo
7. Angelotti
8. Manon
9. Eisenstein
10. The Old Prisoner

Answers on page 227.

63. CAPITAL PUNISHMENT

Many operatic characters face execution in the course of an opera. From the brief descriptions given here, name the character, the reason for his or her execution, and the opera and composer.

1. This man loses his head, crying his beloved's name with his last breath.
2. This fellow is shot even as his lover plots their escape and future joy.
3. This man is beheaded, but not before he effects the death of the man who has ordered his execution.
4. She is executed in the presence of her loyal followers, having lost a vicious power struggle.
5. His beloved dead at his feet, this chap dies calling out a farewell to his mother.
6. She dies for the crime of another but is glad enough to do so.
7. These women go to their deaths calmly, singing a prayer.
8. Although his death is not actually shown in the opera, it is foretold in the libretto and described in the novel on which the opera is based. The character's very last words would undoubtedly serve to convict him in any court.
9. He is executed because the one person who can save him is held under guard and unable, therefore, to reach her sovereign.
10. He is beheaded, but the one who had wanted him killed is executed very shortly thereafter because of her shocking behavior.

Answers on page 229.

64. FINAL REQUESTS

Some of opera's doomed characters are allowed to voice one last request before meeting their fate. For each character listed below, give the request, and also name the opera and its composer.

1. Violetta
2. Dick Johnson
3. Mario Cavaradossi
4. Paolo Albiani
5. Werther
6. Amelia

7. Simon Boccanegra
8. Anna Bolena
9. Don Alvaro
10. Desideria

Answers on page 230.

It's hard to imagine today that Verdi's *La Traviata* was considered very raunchy stuff when it was first heard in 1853. Clara Louise Kellogg, one of the first American opera stars, often sang *La Traviata* using an English translation. However, Kellogg sought to "protect" her audiences from the true miseries of a courtesan's life, and therefore, whenever she thought that the English libretto was becoming too steamy, she lapsed into the original Italian, and the "smut" went harmlessly above the heads of her American audiences.

65. OPENING LINES

Below is a list of opening lines from operas. Identify the opera and its composer, and the character who sings these words, as well as the characters to whom they are addressed.

1. "Questo Mar Rosso mi ammollisce." (This Red Sea is freezing me.)
2. "Della mia bella incognita borghese" (As I was saying about my anonymous little middle-class beauty)
3. "Una vela! una vela!" (A sail! a sail!)
4. "Popolo di Pekino, la legge è questa." (People of Peking, this is the law.)
5. "All'erta, all'erta." (Be watchful.)
6. "Wie schön ist die Prinzessin" (How lovely the Princess is)
7. "Buona notte, mia figlia, addio, diletta." (Good night, my daughter, farewell, beloved.)
8. "Cinque . . . dieci. . ." (Five . . . ten. . .)

9. "Zu hilfe! Zu hilfe!" (Help! Help!)
10. "Rien!" ("Nothing!")
11. "Summertime, and the livin' is easy"
12. "Oh, just what I wanted. Thank you."
13. "Glou, glou, glou . . . je suis le vin." (Glug, glug, glug . . . . I am wine.)
14. Assez! assez!" (Enough! enough!)
15. "From Alexandria, this is the news"

Answers on page 231.

66. FAMOUS FIRST WORDS

Many operatic arias are introduced by recitatives, short, not always versified, lines that move the plot forward or set the scene for the aria that follows—the "connective tissue" of the operatic libretto. Below is a list of recitatives and aria cues. For each, identify the opera, its composer, the aria that follows it, and the character who sings the aria.

1. "Morir! Tremenda cosa!" (To die! A terrible thing!)
2. "Qui Radamès verrà!" (Radames will come here!)
3. "E Susanna non vien!" (And Susanna doesn't come!)
4. "Ti ringrazio Sonora." (I thank you, Sonora.)
5. "Quand je vous aimerai? Ma foi, je ne sais pas." (When will I love you? In faith, I do not know.)
6. "Ancor non giunse!" (He's not here yet!)
7. "Son giunta! Grazie a Dio!" (I am here! Thank God!)
8. "Perchè m'hai fatto segno di tacere?" (Why did you signal me to be quiet?)
9. "Recitar! mentre preso del delirio" (To perform! while I tremble with delirium)
10. "Ecco: respiro appena." (You see: I scarcely breathe.)
11. "Piangi? Perchè?" (You cry? Why?)
12. "In quali eccesi" (In what excesses)
13. "Sediziosi voci, voci di guerra!" (Seditious, warlike voices!)
14. "Ma perchè mai discendere scortesia?" (But why be so rude and unkind?)
15. "Vanne, lasciami; nè timor di me ti prenda." (Go away, leave me; don't fear for me.)

Answers on page 232.

67. DRAMATIC ENTRANCES

Below is a list of entrance lines of operatic characters. Identify the opera and its composer, the character who sings the line, and the person or persons being addressed.

1. "In questa reggia, or son mill'anni e mille, un grido disperato risonò." (In this palace, thousands of years ago, a desperate cry rang out.)
2. "Ein quel, ein quel!" (Get me something to drink!)
3. "Me voici." (Here I am.)
4. "La sacra Iside consultasti?" (Have you consulted holy Isis?)
5. "Flora, amici, la notte che resta d'altre gioie qui fate brillar." (Flora, my friends, the night remains for us to make merry.)
6. "Madre adorata, vieni." (Come, beloved mother.)
7. "Un' altra notte ancora senza vederlo." (Yet another night without seeing him.)
8. "Hojotoho! Hojotoho! Heiaha! Heiaha!" (war whoops)
9. "Son io dinanzi al re?" (Am I in the king's presence?)
10. "Ohimè, di guerra fremere, l'atroce grido io sento." (Alas, I hear terrible cries of war.)
11. "Wie du warst! Wie du bist!" (How you love! How you are!)
12. "I am sick and sullen."
13. "Non, monsieur! je ne suis demoiselle, ni belle." (No, sir! I am not a lady, nor am I beautiful.)
14. "Je viens célébrer la victoire de celui qui règne en mon coeur." (I am coming to celebrate in the victory of he who reigns in my heart.)

Answers on page 233.

68. LOVE DUETS

Below are the titles or opening lines of twenty-four operatic love duets. Name the opera, the composer, and characters who sing each.

1. "Pur ti riveggo" (To see you again)
2. "O nuit d'amour" (O night of love)
3. "Tu, tu, amore, tu" (You, you, beloved, you)
4. "Veranno a te sull'aure i miei sospiri ardenti." (My ardent sighs will come to you on the breeze.)

5. "Teco io sto." (I am here with you.)
6. "Già nella notte densa s'estingue ogni clamore." (Now in the dark night every noise is stilled.)
7. "Ist ein Traum." (This is a dream.)
8. "Bimba, bimba non piangere per gracchiar di ranocchi." (Sweetheart, sweetheart, do not weep about the croaking of a few frogs.)
9. "Un dì, felice" (One happy day)
10. "Decidi il mio destin" (Decide my fate)
11. "Va crudele, al Dio spietato." (Go, cruel woman, share my blood.)
12. "Principessa di morte! Principessa di gelo!" (Princess of death! Princess of ice!)
13. "O soave fanciulla" (O lovely girl)
14. "Il faut nous séparer." (We must part now.)
15. "Heil die Sonne" (Hail, o sun)
16. "O namenlose Freude!" (O nameless joy!)
17. "Pace, pace, mio dolce tesoro." (Let's make peace, my beautiful treasure.)
18. "Trinke, Liebchen, trinke schnell." (Drink, my darling, drink quickly.)
19. "Vicino a te s'aquieta l'irriquieta anima mia." (When I am near you, calm overtakes my rebellious spirit.)
20. "Io vengo a domandar grazia alla mia Regina." (I have come to ask a favor of my queen.)
21. "Perchè chiuso?" (Why was it locked?)
22. "Benvenuto, signore mio cognato." (Welcome, my brother-in-law.)
23. "É il sol dell'anima" (Love is the flame)
24. "Amaro sol per te m'era il morire." (Only because of you was death bitter to me.)

Answers on page 234.

69. *CABALETTE*

Bel canto, *the Italian phrase for "beautiful song," lent its name to the Italian operas of the late eighteenth and nineteenth centuries characterized by limpid, often embellished melodies. It was a format for composition followed to a greater or lesser extent by the great* bel canto *composers: Rossini, Donizetti, Bellini, and the young Verdi. The* bel canto scena *for a principal character consists of a longish, slow or moderately paced* cavatina, *in which the character expresses his mood or feelings—usually on the current status of his or her love life. The* cavatina *is followed by the* cabaletta, *an agitated, often brilliantly ornate final section of the aria that generally reflects a change of mood (sometimes a message is transmitted to the protagonist). Listed below are titles of* cavatina *sections of* bel canto *scenes. For each, name the composer, the opera, and the title of the subsequent* cabaletta. *Also identify the character who sings it and describe the dramatic context of the scene.*

1. "De' miei bollenti spiriti"
2. "Quando le sere al placido"
3. "Tacea la notte placida"
4. "Casta Diva"
5. "Vieni! t'afretta!"
6. "Ah! non credea mirarti"
7. "Ah fors'è lui che l'anima"
8. "Ah sì, ben mio"
9. "Qui la voce sua soave"
10. "Regnava nel silenzio"

Answers on page 236.

70. SELF-AWARENESS

The following phrases are used by operatic characters to describe themselves. Name the character, the person or persons being addressed, the opera, and the composer.

1. "Io non sono che un critico." (I am only a critic.)
2. "Io son l'umile ancella del Genio creator." (I am the humble handmaiden of creative genius.)
3. "In povertà mia lieta, scialo da gran signore . . . rime ed ini d'amore." (Happy in my poverty, I squander my poems of love like a gentleman of leisure.)
4. "Son lo spirito chi nega sempre tutto." (I am the spirit who denies everything, always.)
5. "Somehow I never could believe that life was meant to be all dull and gray."
6. "Io son la donna più lieta del Giappone." (I am the happiest woman in Japan.)
7. "I do not ask to be believed, but I believe."
8. "Ho il cor eccellente mi piace scherzare." (I'm goodhearted [but] I like to play tricks.)
9. "Sono il factotum della città." (I am the factotum of the whole city.)
10. "Io rea non sono!" (I am not guilty!)
11. "Sono un'ombra che t'aspetta." (I am a shadow that awaits you.)
12. "Son tranquilla e lieta." (I am quiet and happy.)
13. "La cosa bramata perseguo, me ne sazio e via la getto, volto a nuova

esca." (I pursue the craved thing, sate myself and cast it away, and seek new bait.)

14. "Non son più re, sono Dio!" (I am no longer King, I am God!)
15. "Fuggo, fuggo, son vil!" (I'm running away, I'm a coward!)
16. "Io non son che un povera fanciulla." (I'm only a poor girl.)
17. "Siam pentiti e contriti." (We're repentant and contrite.)
18. "Je ne suis que faiblesse et toute fragilité." (I am only weakness and fragility.)
19. "Quando m'en vo soletta per la via, la gente soste e mira." (Whenever I go out, all the people stop to admire me.)
20. "Io son dannata." (I am damned.)

Answers on page 237.

71. FAMOUS LAST WORDS

From which operas do the following quotations, all exit lines or curtain lines, come? Name the opera, composer, the character who speaks, and briefly summarize the situation.

1. "Non ode più!" (She hears no more!)
2. "Viva la morte! Insiem!" (Long live death! Together!)
3. "Ah! la maledizione!" (Ah! the curse!)
4. "Tout est fini. Noel! Noel!" (All is ended. Christmas! Christmas!)
5. "Mio padre!" (My father!)
6. "Notte d'orror!" (Night of horror!)
7. "E spenta!" (She is dead!)
8. "Cette bague autre fois tu me l'avais donnée,–tiens!" (This ring that you once gave me, take it!)
9. "Ah ma io ritorno a viver, o gioia!" (Ah, I am coming back to life, o joy!)
10. "Enrico, mi fai ribrezza!" (Enrico, you fill me with loathing!)
11. "Maria!"
12. "Madre! Ah, madre, addio!" (Mother, oh mother, good-bye.)
13. "Loge . . . Loge . . . Loge"
14. "Ja . . . ja"
15. "La commedia è finita!" (The comedy is finished!)

16. "Now it is my turn to wait."
17. "Seigneur, seigneur, pardonnez-nous!" (O God, forgive us!)
18. "Orest! Orest!"

Answers on page 237.

AND THEN WHAT HAPPENS? OPERA PLOTS AND PLOTTINGS

72. EXTRA! EXTRA! READ ALL ABOUT IT!

If there had been tabloid newspapers during the times in which various operas were set, the gory endings of these operatic works would have stimulated sensational headlines. Can you guess the operas that are referred to in the following imaginary headlines:

1. SPY STRANGLES MA—SINGER KILLS SELF
2. LONG-LOST BROTHER RETURNS—SIS DIES OF JOY
3. QUADRUPLE MURDERS/SUICIDE ROCK ROME
4. FUTURE RULER SLAYS GIRL FRIEND, RIVAL, SELF AS POP WATCHES
5. KING ORDERS STEPDAUGHTER KILLED
6. "I KILLED MY OWN BABY," SHRIEKS AGONIZED MOTHER
7. POP'S MURDER ENDS HAPPY HONEYMOON FOR BRIDE
8. WOULD-BE ROMANCER GETS DUMPED IN RIVER
9. HUBBY FUMES, WIFE RUNS OFF WITH OWN BROTHER
10. STRONG-MAN ACT BRINGS DOWN HOUSE
11. CHIEF WITNESS SAYS "I LIED"—TOO LATE TO SAVE CONDEMNED MAN
12. TERRORISTS SLAY DOZENS AT WEDDING
13. GENERAL STRANGLES WIFE, STABS SELF
14. ROYAL WEDDING (FINALLY) PLANNED IN CAPITAL

15. MIRACLE COMES TOO LATE TO SAVE PENITENT'S GIRL FRIEND
16. MAN, BOY MISSING—NEIGHBORS FEAR FOUL PLAY
17. MONASTERY'S DOUBLE MURDER SHOCKS TOWN
18. DUKE ESCAPES MURDER PLOT
19. COUNT KILLED, MYSTERY WOMAN SOUGHT
20. COMIC GOES NUTS—TWO DEAD
21. ARMY SPY SCANDAL—ONE SURRENDERS, TWO ESCAPE
22. EASTER PARTY ENDS IN TRAGEDY
23. END OF WORLD PREDICTED
24. "NO SEX, PLEASE, WE'RE BRITISH," QUIPS KING—WIFE DIES ANYWAY
25. RIOT THREATENS HOLIDAY CELEBRATION
26. CROWN PRINCE ASSASSINATED??? CHARGE COVER-UP
27. FIANCÉ CRUSHED IN FREAK ACCIDENT, WOMAN KILLS SELF
28. FIRE DESTROYS CELEB'S HOME—ARSON SUSPECTED
29. SON AXES MOM, STEPDAD AFTER FAMILY QUARREL
30. QUEEN EXECUTED AS KING REWEDS

Answers on page 240.

73. THE RAIN IN SPAIN

Weather sometimes has a bearing on operatic plots. From the meteorological events described below, identify the opera, its composer, and the characters affected.

1. A raging thunderstorm provides a fitting background for this hostile encounter.
2. Too much sun and too little water does in this glamorous heroine.
3. Taking refuge in a stranger's home during a storm changes this fellow's entire life, and not necessarily for the better.
4. It's so cold outside that this gentleman burns one of his own manuscripts in order to keep warm.
5. Waiting outside her beloved's home, hoping to catch a glimpse of him, this poor woman freezes to death.
6. A heat wave in the big city brings out the gossips, whose wagging tongues betray an adulterous neighbor.
7. Traveling through Spain barefoot during a blizzard, this girl reaches her destination more dead than alive.
8. A violent storm almost sinks this hero before he can make his first appearance.
9. This short rainshower has little bearing on the plot, but it does allow

the composer of the opera to create a brief, orchestral divertissement before bringing the plot to its happy ending.

10. This poor chap is not only tossed out into a snowstorm, he's shot as soon as the door is slammed behind him.

Answers on page 241.

74. LITTLE THINGS MEAN A LOT

Every opera fan knows that grandiose and supernatural props are often crucial to operatic plots–Wotan's spear, Alberich's Tarnhelm, *Tamino's magic flute, and the like. However, common household items can influence the outcomes of operas. Below is a list of some of these simple objects. Name the opera (and its composer) in which the object is found, and explain its significance to the plot.*

1. Four sheets of paper and some ink
2. A little table
3. A dime
4. A boy's sweater
5. A dinner knife
6. An American flag
7. A pair of earrings
8. An injured garden plant
9. A cup of coffee
10. A handkerchief
11. A lit match
12. A rosary

Answers on page 242.

There are many tales of operatic mayhem caused by props that were not in position or failed to work. A New York City Opera Violetta summoned Annina with a vocalized "ting-a-ling" when her bell was misplaced by the prop man. Caruso shot the Marquis of Calatrava with his fingers—shouting "Bang!"—to compensate for the gun that would not fire.

Murder weapons that didn't work have caused more hysteria in operas than an army of Figaros attacking a regiment of Bartolos with shaving cream. There is the celebrated Tosca who aimed too low

with her dinner knife, and Baron Scarpia thus met an embarrassing end, dying of a stab wound in his bottom. One corpulent Norma drew laughs from an audience when she ran to attack her children with a knife, showing the zeal with which one slices a baked ham during a midnight raid on the refrigerator. More recently there is the story of Luciano Pavarotti's being the first Riccardo at the Met who "died" of shock when Renato's gun misfired during a 1980 performance of *Un Ballo in Maschera.*

However, the ultimate death that didn't quite come off was the "suicide" of Renata Tebaldi's Tosca on New Year's Eve 1969. Tebaldi ran up to the parapet and sang a suitably dramatic "Scarpia avanti a dio!" but didn't jump off the "roof." The soldiers, some of whom appeared rather confused, simply closed ranks around Renata as the curtain, mercifully, fell. When asked about her new ending for *Tosca,* Tebaldi explained that the platform with the mattress that customarily awaits all Toscas had not been raised. "And if Rudolf Bing thinks I am going to jump fifty feet in the pitch dark just for him, he is crazy!"

75. HOT TIMES

Fires are often important operatic events. From the clues below, identify the opera, composer, and who or what gets burned by whom.

1. This ruler, himself governed by some shady religious figures, gathers all his enemies within his palace and has his own store of ammunition set on fire, thus incinerating his foes along with his friends.
2. Setting his own ship on fire seems the only way to escape from his beloved's husband, so this hero puts his vessel to the torch, neatly accomplishing his exit and providing an exciting "curtain" for this scene of the opera.
3. A folk dance around a campfire provides a rare, peaceful interlude in this opera that portrays passion, deceit, love, and violent hate.
4. This fire punishes a couple who evoke the wrath of a primitive culture because they have been lovers.
5. These poor souls are set on fire by local religious leaders and un-

willingly provide entertainment of a cruel sort for a king and his court.

6. These flames abruptly end the career of a famed party-giver and lover. They are the handiwork of an unexpected guest.
7. This fire has been lit for the purpose of turning some guests into lunch. In a sudden turnabout, the hostess is cooked instead!
8. If you went about burning the wrong victims at the stake in order to avenge a great injustice, you'd end up as cracked as which character in what opera?
9. Probably the biggest bonfire of all time, this blaze takes care of just about everybody and expunges a world filled with guilt and lust. Only three creatures, apparently, survive.
10. This question is about a fire that does *not* occur in an opera about a historical character who in all other accounts was burned at the stake, but here dies in battle. Who is the character and what is the opera?

Answers on page 243.

76. HOLIDAYS

Certain opera plots are influenced by holidays of one sort or another. See how many of the special occasions listed below you can associate with an opera. Name the opera, its composer, and briefly outline the significance of the holiday in the operatic plot.

1. Christmas Eve (name three)
2. Easter
3. Midsummer Night
4. All Hallows' Eve
5. Viceroy's birthday
6. Passover
7. Good Friday
8. Carnival (name three)
9. Feast of San Gennaro
10. Feast of the Assumption

Answers on page 245.

77. WINE, PERSONS, AND SONG

Operatic plots are often affected by the actions of characters who drink more than is good for them or drink at the wrong time from the wrong glass. Below are a number of descriptions of liquor-related incidents in opera. Identify the characters, the opera, the composer, and note how the drink plays a role in the outcome of the opera.

1. This chap has a few too many while celebrating a religious holiday and finds himself at a loss when confronted by a rival.
2. She promises to meet him at her favorite night spot, where she will dance and drink her favorite wine with him *if* he does her a little favor.
3. Whiling the time between acts of a Mozart opera, this romantic fellow starts to talk about his amorous past. His friends ply him with drink until he loses track of the present, misses the end of the opera—and another chance at happiness.
4. She invites some neighborhood rowdies to a party and serves poisoned wine. Overplaying her hand, this lady kills one guest too many.
5. He offers her wine for fortitude. As she puts the glass aside, she finds a way out of a horrible dilemma.
6. Taking a drink after a tiring journey, this heroic type is made to lose his memory, with earth-shattering results.
7. Suffering the effects of a rough joke, he shivers as he sips his sherry. The drink warms him up, as demonstrated by a brilliant orchestral effect, but the wine dulls his senses and he is duped yet another time.
8. This ardent man plies his sweetie with wine, hoping to remove all her scruples. All he gets for his trouble is a case of mistaken identity and spends the night not with her, but by himself in a drafty cell.
9. Sharing a dinner laid out for two others, this shy maiden is encouraged by her guest to drink too much wine, with unfortunate results.
10. While exchanging pleasantries and clinking glasses with a young guest at a dinner party, this girl begins to wonder if she should abandon her racy friends and settle down with one steady fellow.

Answers on page 246.

78. CRIMES MAJOR AND MINOR

For each of the operas listed below, name the crimes committed therein, and identify the criminals and the victims.

1. *Boris Godunov*
2. *Don Carlo*
3. *Le Prophète*
4. *Madama Butterfly*
5. *La Gioconda*
6. *Manon Lescaut*

7. *Das Rheingold*
8. *Simon Boccanegra*
9. *Lulu*
10. *Billy Budd*
11. *Lucia di Lammermoor*
12. *Die Fledermaus*

Answers on page 247.

79. HIDING PLACES

Below is a list of places in which, for whatever reasons, operatic characters hide. For each, identify the character who hides and what he or she is hiding from, and briefly indicate the outcome. Of course, name the opera and its composer.

1. A closet in a palace
2. Behind a tree
3. A well in a garden
4. A loft
5. A laundry basket
6. Behind a gravestone
7. A chapel
8. Behind a partition
9. Hidden in a crowd of sports fans
10. A cave
11. A trapdoor leading to a basement
12. A closet in a home

Answers on page 249.

80. GIFTS

Operatic characters do their share of giving and receiving. Can you remember what gifts the characters below receive? As usual, name the opera and the composer.

1. What does the Mikado give Cio-Cio-San's father?
2. What token is given by Elvino to Amina?
3. What does Arlecchino bring to Colombina?
4. What does Arabella give to Mandryka?
5. Name the present received by Manon from de Brétigny.
6. What does Hans Sachs give to Beckmesser?
7. What is given by La Cieca to Laura Adorno?
8. What is the first present that Rodolfo buys for Mimi?
9. What does Brünnhilde give to Sieglinde?

10. Do you remember what Adriana Lecouvreur gives to Maurizio, and what he does with the gift?
11. What is given to Desdemona by her husband?
12. What does Prince Orlofsky give to Adele?
13. What does Mario Cavaradossi give to his friend Angelotti?
14. What does Ernani give to Silva?
15. The ever present Dapertutto offers aid to Hoffmann by giving the poet this item. What is it?

Answers on page 250.

81. MEMBERS OF THE WEDDING

Wedding celebrations or plans often figure prominently in opera. From the descriptions given below, identify the opera and composer, the characters being married, and briefly describe the aftermath of the weddings.

1. Although it is her wedding day, and she dearly loves her husband-to-be, this bride arranges a rendezvous with an old admirer, to take place on her wedding night.
2. The groom marries the bride after a rather brief courtship. It is a double wedding in which the groom's former fiancée marries the bride's brother. The ex-fiancée is bewildered and unhappy about the whole state of affairs, and she, her new husband, and another relative vow vengeance on this man who wronged her.
3. This wedding celebration is interrupted when a passing gentleman forces his attentions on the bride.
4. This couple's wedding night is spoiled because the bride reneges on a promise that she had made.
5. An act of political terrorism breaks up this wedding party.
6. The bride stalls this ceremony because the beau she jilted isn't around for her to gloat over.
7. This ardent couple share a brief, secret wedding ceremony that proves to be the calm before the storm.
8. Soldiers rescue this reluctant bride whose past, when revealed, shocks her mother-in-law elect.
9. The bride discovers, on the night before her wedding, that her fiancé is making love and telling state secrets to her hated rival.
10. An eager bridegroom receives a terrible surprise when, as soon as the

marriage contract is signed, his new wife changes from demure maiden to raging hussy.

11. Her wedding is halted because the groom has run off with an aging noblewoman. The abandoned bride suffers a tuneful nervous breakdown.
12. As soon as she becomes engaged to the man she loves, this princess learns that she will have to marry her lover's mean old father instead.

Answers on page 252.

82. STOP ALL THAT SINGING AND LET US DANCE!

The French formula for grand opera always included an interlude of ballet. Sometimes, the ballet was used to further the plot, although it was often a divertissement presented for the entertainment of the characters in the opera, as well as for the audience. From the descriptions given here, identify the opera in which each ballet occurs. Incidentally, not all of these works are French.

1. A tense situation between two rivals for a certain man's affections is temporarily interrupted when this ballet, in which the Judgment of Paris is depicted, is presented. The dancer who plays Paris, knowing on which side his bread is buttered, presents his patroness with Paris's golden apple at the conclusion of the ballet.
2. A political uprising is halted long enough for some skaters to frolic about the scene in a charming dance in which ice skating is simulated.
3. A victory celebration is crowned by the appearance of a number of exotic dancers from the ranks of the conquered.
4. A queen is paid tribute in this ballet, generally cut from a rather lengthy opera, in which the dancers portray pearl fishers. (Hint: This is *not* from an opera by Bizet.)
5. A murder is announced shortly after this ballet (representing the metaphorical struggle between night and day) is performed for the assembled guests of a vengeful nobleman.
6. In this ballet, the sensual delights of the netherworld are shown to this opera's protagonist in order to make him forget about the pregnant girl he left behind.
7. In this operatic account of a Biblical event, a lusty crowd of pagans

dances its way through an orgiastic ritual, unaware of the fate in store for them when Jehovah steps in.

8. A lavish party is the scene for all kinds of amorous antics. These are interrupted when a ballet troupe arrives to waltz for all the guests, whose minds, one would think, are geared to anything but such spectator sports as ballet-watching.
9. In a version of this opera not always performed, the delights of bacchanalian revels are graphically portrayed to the strains of some of a composer's headiest music. When the sung action begins, the hero "wants out," and one wonders why he wishes to leave.
10. This solo dance is meant to be performed by the singer who portrays the character who must dance. It is not unknown, however, for the vocalist to withdraw in favor of a dancer when the character begins to dance in this chilling scene that leads to the dramatic climax of the opera.

Answers on page 253.

83. GETTING THERE IS HALF THE FUN

Name the opera that features the appropriate mode of transportation listed below. Name the character who avails himself or herself of this form of travel.

1. A barge
2. A ship with blood-red sails
3. A boat drawn by a fowl
4. A cart driven by a ram
5. A broomstick
6. A goat cart
7. A train
8. A spaceship
9. A bus
10. The subway
11. A fishing boat
12. A warship
13. Two feet for a very long walk
14. A battered truck
15. A sleigh

Answers on page 254.

84. FARAWAY PLACES

Name the operas that take place (at least in part) in the exotic locations listed on the following page. Don't forget the composer.

1. India
2. Bohemia (name two)
3. Hell
4. Venice (name at least three)
5. Peru
6. Palestine
7. Gaul
8. Mexico (name three)
9. Lithuania
10. Frankfurt (name three)
11. Scotland
12. Manhattan (name two)

Answers on page 255.

85. CRUEL AND UNUSUAL

Opera plots abound with murders, suicides, and assorted torture and mayhem. While most lyric methods of dealing death blows are fairly straightforward–pistols, swords, and the like–some characters meet their ends in remarkably imaginative fashion. Can you remember how each of the characters named below was put to death or otherwise harmed? Name the operas, composers, and describe the circumstances.

1. Manfredo
2. Rachel
3. Cecilia
4. Queen of the Night
5. La Cieca
6. Giuseppe Hagenbach
7. Lisa
8. Antonia
9. Loris Ipanoff's brother
10. Lakmé
11. Glauce
12. John of Leyden and Fidès

Answers on page 256.

A POTPOURRI

86. OPENING NIGHTS

1. Gounod's *Faust* was the first opera to be performed at the Metropolitan Opera House. Who sang the role of Marguerite that night?
2. What was the language of that first Met *Faust*?
3. What was the first opera produced by the New York City Opera and who sang the title role?
4. How many important singers can you name who made Metropolitan Opera debuts on opening nights? Give their roles, too, if you can.
5. What opera opened the Metropolitan Opera's first season at Lincoln Center? Give the names of composer, librettist, director, designer, choreographer, and at least five singers. How about the conductor?
6. What opera opened the first full season of the Chicago Lyric Opera? Who sang the title role?
7. A famous operatic feud was ended moments after the opening night of the Metropolitan's 1968–69 season. Who sang, and who was feuding with whom?
8. La Scala of Milan always opens on the same date. Coincidentally, this date has negative connotations to Americans. What is the date?

9. Enrico Caruso sang every opening night at the Metropolitan Opera between 1903 and 1920—except one. To what artist did Caruso concede the honor, and what was the opera?
10. Can you name the program with which the rebuilt La Scala opened after World War II? Can you name the conductor and at least three singers?

Answers on page 259.

87. OPERA HOUSES AROUND THE WORLD

What do you know about these famous opera houses and their history?

1. Two Italian operas by an Austrian composer had their world premieres at this Eastern European opera house. Name the theater, the operas, and the composer.
2. A soprano, famed more for her beautiful face than for her voice, managed this opera house for one season and nearly bankrupted the company. Name the soprano and the opera house.
3. Now known as the Salle Favart, this theater, under another name, was the first to present one of the most popular operas of all time. Name the theater, the opera, and its composer.
4. Which of Verdi's operas was his first work to be performed at La Scala?
5. Puccini's *La Bohème* had its first performance at this Italian opera house in a city better known for its industrial output than for its artistic interests. This theater lay in ruins for years after World War II and reopened with a production of a rarely done work, staged by two famous singers. Name the opera house, the work with which it reopened in 1973, and the singers-turned-directors who staged it.
6. Which opera house opened its doors with a performance of a French opera sung in Italian, then performed its entire repertory in German for the seven years that followed?
7. Which Verdi opera was composed for the opera house in St. Petersburg, Russia?
8. Who were the three codirectors who organized the Chicago Lyric Opera?
9. This theater in a beautiful city was the location for Renata Tebaldi's American debut. Name the opera house, the opera, the year of Tebaldi's debut, and her leading man in that performance.

10. When Joan Sutherland made her second appearance at this theater, she was hardly noticed, due to the brevity of her role and the presence of another fabulous soprano in that performance. Name the theater, opera, and *prima donna* of that evening.
11. This tiny and beautiful opera house, in one of the playgrounds of Europe, was the scene of the first performance of a Puccini opera. Name the house and the opera.
12. Which two major opera houses were destroyed by Allied bombing raids during World War II? Can you give the dates of the reopening of these rebuilt houses?
13. This European opera house has created a famous production of a "standard repertory" that departs radically from the work's original libretto. Name the opera house and the opera.
14. Name the city whose opera house boasts the most difficult to please group of opera buffs in the world.
15. Giulio Gatti-Casazza managed which two great opera houses?
16. This ancient outdoor amphitheater is the home of lavish summertime performances of *Aida.* Name the theater and give its location.
17. Which two Puccini operas had their premieres at La Scala? Name the leading sopranos and conductors of each performance, and briefly describe how each work was received.
18. *La Traviata* was created by Verdi for this opera house, but it was not initially a success.
19. Rolf Liebermann left one theater, which he had managed successfully for many years, in order to take on the challenge of restoring a fabled opera house to its former glory. From where was Liebermann lured, and where did he go?
20. This annual summer music festival was the scene of Renata Scotto's first international success. Name the festival, the opera sung by Scotto, and the special circumstances surrounding the performance.

Answers on page 260.

La Scala's *loggioni,* the regulars who occupy the balconies night after night, are quick to pounce upon an erring singer who loses control of a high note. Carlo Bergonzi, returning to La Scala as Radames

after an absence of a few years, cracked the high B flat at the end of "Celeste Aida" and was savagely booed. The diminutive master from Busseto did not lose his nerve and continued the performance with a Radames that ranked with his work fifteen years earlier. Bergonzi won a rare point from La Scala's claque: after a particularly beautiful phrase in the Nile scene, an apologetic voice wafted down from the gallery, *"Perdonateci, Carlo!"* (Forgive us!)

88. FROM PAGE TO STAGE

Here is a list of eight novels that have been adapted for opera. For each, name the opera and its composer, and the author of the original novel.

1. *Ivanhoe*
2. *The Wings of the Dove*
3. *Great Expectations*
4. *Don Quixote*
5. *The Gambler*
6. *The Bride of Lammermoor*
7. *War and Peace*
8. *L'Histoire de Manon Lescaut* (name three)

Answers on page 262.

89. PLAY VERSUS OPERA

Below is a list of plays and novels on which were based some well-known operas. Match the work of literature to the opera it inspired. Name the author of the original work and the composer of the opera.

1. *Much Ado About Nothing*	a. *Lodoletta*
2. *Le Réveillon*	b. *Mignon*
3. *Kabale und Liebe*	c. *Peter Grimes*

4. *Le Roi S'Amuse*	d. *Les Contes d'Hoffmann*
5. *Two Little Wooden Shoes*	e. *Béatrice et Bénédict*
6. *Scènes de la Vie de Bohème*	f. *La Traviata*
7. *La Dame aux Camélias*	g. *Rigoletto*
8. *The Borough*	h. *Die Fledermaus*
9. *Le Philtre (Il Filtro)*	i. *Luisa Miller*
10. *Angelo, Tyran de Padoue*	j. *La Bohème*
11. *Wilhelm Meister*	k. *L'Elisir d'Amore*
12. *Spring's Awakening*	l. *La Gioconda*
13. *Counsellor Crespel*	m. *Lulu*

Answers on page 262.

90. LIBRETTISTS

Most of us can name the composers of our favorite operas, but can we readily recall those unsung heroes who provided the words? Name the librettists for the following works:

1. *Aida*	7. *I Vespri Siciliani*
2. *La Bohème*	8. *Così Fan Tutte*
3. *I Pagliacci*	9. *Tannhäuser*
4. *La Gioconda*	10. *Carmen*
5. *Nabucco*	11. *Turandot*
6. *Andrea Chénier*	12. *Rigoletto*

Answers on page 263.

The city of Parma, Italy, is famous—perhaps notorious is more appropriate—for its hypercritical opera buffs who sit in judgment in the *galleria* and pounce on any and every mistake a singer might make. As recently as Christmas 1979, the booing and jeering sufficiently unnerved an experienced soprano that she canceled the final act of *La Traviata* rather than face the enraged audience. My favorite

Parma story concerns a performance of *I Pagliacci* that was given in the early 1950s. Halfway through the prelude, the baritone singing Tonio stepped out through the curtain to sing the Prologue. Tonio's first words are "Si puo?" (May I speak?) The audience, as one, roared "No!" And there ended the shortest performance of *I Pagliacci* ever attempted!

91. RECORD COLLECTORS I

1. Name the nine operas recorded by the Metropolitan Opera and released on Columbia Records between 1947 and 1954. Name principal singers and conductors.
2. Who conducts the famous EMI/Angel *Tosca* with Maria Callas, Giuseppe di Stefano, and Tito Gobbi?
3. Who are the two artists who share the role of Wotan in the Solti *Ring* cycle on Decca/London? In which operas do they each sing?
4. Leontyne Price has recorded the role of Leonora in *Il Trovatore* three times. Name her principal colleagues and the conductors on each recording.
5. Name six operas recorded by the New York City Opera.
6. A father and son team may be heard on the 1979 London/Decca recording of *I Pagliacci.* Who are they, and what role does each sing?
7. For which company were Caruso's first recordings made?
8. There was a major cast change made only days before Arturo Toscanini entered Studio 8-H of New York's RCA Building to conduct what became his final operatic broadcast and recording. For which role was there a hasty substitution? Who replaced whom?
9. Magda Olivero recorded only two complete operas. Name them, the roles she sings, and her principal colleagues in each.
10. Dusolina Giannini, a famous soprano of the 1920s (and mother of the film star Gian Carlo Giannini), is best remembered as the protagonist in the first complete recording of which ever popular Verdi opera?
11. Soprano Kiri Te Kanawa recorded two tiny roles for Decca/London before she achieved stardom. Identify the roles and the operas, and identify the stars on those sets.

12. What is José Carreras's first complete operatic recording?
13. There is an exciting recording in German of highlights from Verdi's *La Forza del Destino* released by German EMI. Who are the Leonora and Alvaro on that set? What is the German title of *La Forza*?
14. What was the special memento found in each copy of the 1966 RCA release *Opening Nights at the Met*?
15. Who sang the baritone and soprano leads in the first recording of Verdi's *Nabucco*? What label released this performance?
16. Jussi Bjoerling's indisposition forced the cancellation of a recording of this opera midway through the sessions. Name the opera and Bjoerling's eventual replacement.
17. Name six complete operatic roles recorded by Zinka Milanov.
18. Name ten roles sung by Maria Callas that are available solely on pirated recordings (live, in-house, or broadcast tapes later transferred to disc).
19. Who was the artist Birgit Nilsson replaced in the Angel/EMI recording of *La Fanciulla del West*?
20. How many complete operas did Franco Corelli and Renata Tebaldi record together commercially?
21. Name the artist who, on two separate occasions, recorded three leading roles in an opera in which such casting would be physically impossible in an actual performance. Name the opera and the roles in question.
22. Name two complete operatic recordings in which Birgit Nilsson, Renata Tebaldi, and Jussi Bjoerling appear together.
23. What trick was perpetrated on the listener by the producers of the Flagstad/Suthaus *Tristan und Isolde*?
24. Pietro Mascagni conducted a 1940 recording of his opera *Cavalleria Rusticana.* Who sang the roles of Santuzza, Turiddu, and Mamma Lucia in this performance?

Answers on page 263.

Opera fans can be quite cruel when singers are not in voice. One evening at the Met several years ago, a once popular American soprano had more than her share of problems singing Liù in *Turan-*

dot. Her performance of "Signore, ascolta" marked a low point in her career, and she was loudly booed by members of the audience. The lady withdrew after Act I. Before Act II began, a stage manager walked in front of the gold curtain and announced, "Miss Lucine Amara will sing Liù for the rest of tonight's performance, because Miss M— is unable to sing anymore tonight." At this, there was heard one loud, clear voice from somewhere in the theater saying, "You can say *that* again!"

92. RUDOLF BING

The twenty-two years of Rudolf Bing's administration at the Metropolitan Opera (1950–72) were often marked by controversy but remain notable for much excitement and great singing. How much do you know about Sir Rudolf and his career?

1. What was Bing's principal operatic credit prior to coming to the Metropolitan?
2. Whom did Bing replace as general manager?
3. Name the four important artists who made their debuts on Bing's first Met opening night. Also name the opera and the role sung by these four artists.
4. Which great soprano, whom the previous Met management had let go, did Bing reengage during his first season?
5. One of the Bing regime's great triumphs was an idiomatic English version of *Die Fledermaus.* Who were the coauthors of the translation?
6. What was the first work to be given its American premiere at the Met during the Bing years?
7. Why did Bing dismiss Maria Callas from the Met?
8. Birgit Nilsson sang her second Met Isolde opposite three Tristans—a different ailing colleague in each act. Name the three tenors.
9. Bing fired one noted tenor because he balked at signing a contract. Who was the tenor?
10. Bing engaged the son of a great tenor, whom he had admired years earlier, for a comic role in an operetta revival. Name the guest artist, who is, incidentally, a noted stage and screen star.

11. Which two operas were staged by Alfred Lunt during the Bing administration?
12. Why did Bing banish standees from the Met for one performance?
13. Who infuriated Bing on the occasion of the closing gala concert at the old Metropolitan Opera, and why?
14. Name three very important singers who did *not* appear at the Met during Bing's regime.
15. One of Bing's early seasons saw the farewell performance of Kirsten Flagstad. What was her final role at the Met?
16. Bing allowed a famous Salome to sing one performance of Musetta in *La Bohème.* Who was she?
17. A famous soprano once listed Rudolf Bing as a "dependent" on her United States federal income tax return. Who was she?
18. Name the unknown soprano who made her Met debut on three hours' notice during Bing's first season. This lady became an authentic "overnight star" and is still a member of the Metropolitan Opera.
19. What was the opera sung at the Met to mark the close of Bing's official tenure?
20. Where did Bing go after leaving the Met?

Answers on page 266.

Marilyn Horne once confided to a radio audience her method for getting balky conductors to employ *tempi* that suit her. Early in her career, Horne was singing Musetta in San Francisco. During rehearsals the mezzo found that her maestro was taking "Quando me'n vo'soletta" at a frighteningly fast tempo. At the next rehearsal Horne began her aria at a speed that threatened to break the sound barrier. Down went the baton. "Oh, no, *signorina,*" clucked the conductor. "You're singing *much* too fast. Let's try again, slowly." "I'm dreadfully sorry," purred the relieved Horne. For the rest of the engagement, this Musetta never had to worry that her waltz would be over too quickly!

93. FAMOUS OPERATIC CONDUCTORS

Identify the conductors from the clues given below.

1. He conducted the first performance at the Metropolitan Opera in 1883. (Hint: His brother sang the tenor lead that night.)
2. One of his first musical assignments was playing second cello at the world premiere of Verdi's *Otello.*
3. He was one of Verdi's favorite maestri.
4. He "discovered" Maria Callas when she was an unknown singer struggling to make a career in Italy.
5. He conducted the opening night of the new Metropolitan Opera House.
6. Wagner repaid him for brilliantly conducting his early operas by stealing his wife from him.
7. She was the first woman to conduct an opera at the Met.
8. Having been a cofounder of the Chicago Lyric Opera, he left with another member of that company's original triumvirate to create the Dallas Civic Opera.
9. Shortly before his eightieth birthday, he conducted what has become a famous recorded performance of one of his own operas.
10. This conductor has for many years piloted his own plane, created his own music festival, reinterpreted many operas by Wagner and Verdi, and counts, among his protégés and discoveries, such artists as René Kollo, Helga Dernesch, Anna Tomowa-Sintow, and flutist James Galway.
11. This famous composer spent several years as a principal conductor at the Metropolitan Opera early in this century.
12. He was the first conductor to lead a complete recording of *Der Ring des Nibelungen.*
13. Once the director of the Bolshoi Theatre, this celebrated exile is also a fine cellist and frequently provides the piano accompaniment when his soprano wife concertizes.
14. Considered an heir to Toscanini, this brilliant young maestro, who left behind prized broadcast recordings of only a few operas and symphonic works, died in an aircrash in 1956.
15. This renowned specialist in Beethoven and Mozart fled the Nazis to America, conducting at the Met for several seasons before retiring to California.
16. He celebrated his eighty-fifth birthday conducting *Die Frau ohne Schatten.*

17. His specialty is the *bel canto* repertoire, and being married to a famous soprano has undoubtedly helped his career.
18. A master of the French repertoire, he had a concert hall in Montreal named for him.
19. Although this iconoclast once stated to an interviewer that he'd like to see all the world's opera houses burned down, in recent years he has had a number of triumphant productions at Bayreuth and Paris.
20. Less than five years after his debut as a last-minute substitute in a very great theater, this conductor became musical director of this company.
21. He conducted the recording of *Tosca* with Maria Callas that many consider to be the finest of all *Tosca* recordings.
22. A close friend and great interpreter of Richard Strauss, this conductor and artistic administrator lived the last years of his life tainted with the stigma of his pro-Nazi activities.
23. As celebrated for his wit as for his abilities as a conductor, this beloved *maestro* enriched the Met's World War II years with his mastery of the French repertoire, and later led a highly successful recording of *La Bohème.*
24. Famous for his Wagner, this conductor led a renowned *Ring* cycle at La Scala shortly after the end of World War II.
25. He brought international renown to the once strictly regional New York City Opera.
26. The former head of both the Royal Opera and the Chicago Symphony, he resigned under fire from his position as musical director of the Metropolitan in 1974.
27. Himself the son of a famous conductor, he has made a name for himself in many European theaters as a major conductor.
28. He was the first American ever to conduct at La Scala, Milan. (Can you name the opera, the year, and the prima donna?)

Answers on page 268.

Late in his career, Arturo Toscanini was invited to dine at the home of a retired soprano, once the most beautiful and popular Carmen, Butterfly, and Zaza of the Met. Toscanini returned from the meal in one of his vilest rages. A friend innocently asked the maestro if he had enjoyed the meal. "Damn that stupid woman," ranted Tosca-

nini. "For twenty-five years we slept together, and she still can't remember that I hate fish!"

94. SATURDAY AFTERNOONS AT THE MET

So many Americans were first attracted to opera through the weekly live broadcasts from the Metropolitan Opera House that it's fitting to include a series of questions about these beloved programs.

1. Two great Wagnerian sopranos made unheralded debuts at the Metropolitan within five years of one another on Saturday broadcasts. They debuted in the same role. Who were they, and what role did they share?
2. Maria Callas sang only one role broadcast from the Met. Name it.
3. A famous singer was stricken with an acute (but fortunately not serious) illness while singing an aria during a broadcast. Who was the artist and what was the aria?
4. A now celebrated baritone flew to New York from Milan on less than a day's notice in order to replace a famous colleague who was forced to cancel. Name the newcomer, the opera he sang, and the singer whose illness started the crisis.
5. What was the first role that Joan Sutherland broadcast from the Met? Who was her tenor?
6. What was the first opera to be broadcast complete, live from the Met? When did this broadcast take place?
7. Name the sponsor of the Met broadcasts.
8. Who was the beloved soprano who shared hosting duties with Met commentator Milton Cross for several years during the 1940s?
9. What was the first opera to be broadcast from the new Met at Lincoln Center?
10. Jan Peerce, Zinka Milanov, and Richard Tucker were honored with ceremonies marking their twenty-fifth anniversaries at the Metropolitan Opera. What role did each sing at these commemorative performances? Identify the year of each anniversary.

Answers on page 268.

During the intermission of an opera broadcast, a small group of singers was taking part in a round-table discussion about life on the operatic stage. A question was raised about the practice of canceling performances. One singer, a lady known as much for her claws as for her voice, said, "Well, whenever I feel that I cannot do justice to the music, I will cancel." Her colleague, a baritone highly respected for incisive wit, responded, "Then, my dear Miss —, you must have to cancel nearly every night!" The lady managed to swallow most of her outraged gasp, and the program concluded.

95. OPERA ON THE SILVER SCREEN

Although there has never been a totally satisfactory film made of an opera, the lyric theater has fascinated filmmakers since the early days of motion pictures. Test your knowledge about filmed opera.

1. Name three silent versions of operas.
2. A 1953 Italian film of *Aida* featured Sophia Loren in the title role. Who sang Aida on the soundtrack? Can you name the other singers and the conductor?
3. A nonoperatic treatment of *Salome,* starring Rita Hayworth, was born in the Hollywood of the mid-1940s. Although a few of the Wilde-Strauss plot devices were in evidence, much had been changed. What significant alterations of the story were there?
4. Who starred in a nonmusical version of *Madama Butterfly* in a Hollywood film from the 1930s?
5. In the film *Interrupted Melody,* a biography of soprano Marjorie Lawrence, another famous soprano did the singing for the movie's operatic sequences. Who was she?
6. Everyone knows that Mario Lanza played and sang Enrico Caruso in

the film *The Great Caruso.* Can you name the two well-known sopranos who sang with Lanza in the film?

7. Years before he actually sang in the United States, a beloved tenor was introduced to American audiences in a film in which he sang one of his most famous roles. Name the tenor, the opera, and the soprano costar.
8. Maria Callas appeared in one film. Although she did no singing, the film was a treatment of which of her great operatic roles?
9. Risë Stevens never got to make a film of her most famous role, Carmen, but she did make several movies. Name her best-known film and her costar in it, one of America's most popular singers.
10. There is a beautiful film of an actual performance of *Der Rosenkavalier* from a major European festival. Do you know the names of the conductor, and the singers who portrayed the Marschallin, Octavian, and Baron Ochs in that performance?
11. In the spring of 1982, American audiences were introduced to a virtually unknown American soprano by means of a French film in which she played an opera star and sang an aria. Shortly after the film opened, the soprano made her debut with the New York City Opera. Name the artist, the film in which she appeared, the aria she sang in the film, and her debut opera role.

Answers on page 269.

96. RECORD COLLECTORS II

1. This artist recorded the role of Kate Pinkerton in two EMI performances of *Madama Butterfly,* made fifteen years apart–first with Dal Monte and Gigli, later with de los Angeles and di Stefano. Who is she?
2. Name four supporting roles recorded by Fiorenza Cossotto at the start of her career.
3. Tullio Serafin's conducting of this recording caused a rift in his once cordial relationship with Maria Callas. Name the opera and the stars, and state the reason for Callas's ire.
4. Who are baritone Tito Gobbi's costars on his recording of *Il Tabarro?* Name the soprano, tenor, and conductor.
5. José Carreras has recorded the role of Mario Cavaradossi in *Tosca* twice. Who are the artists who sing Tosca and Scarpia with Carreras on each recording? Who conducts, and on which labels do these recordings appear?

6. The Metropolitan Opera recorded three complete operas for RCA. Identify the operas, their principal singers, and the conductors.
7. Name the first seven Verdi operas recorded at La Scala by Deutsche Grammophon. Name the principals and conductors.
8. Name three noncomic roles recorded by *basso buffo* Fernando Corena.
9. For what reason has the 1970 Bolshoi recording of *Eugene Onegin* become an embarrassment to the Soviet Union?
10. Name Maria Callas's only complete opera *not* sung in Italian. Identify the language, costars, and conductor.
11. Who sings the title role in Renata Tebaldi's *first* recording of *Andrea Chénier*?
12. Leonard Warren and Astrid Varnay recorded for RCA a duet from a Verdi opera they performed together in New York. Name the opera.
13. Herva Nelli was a favorite of a very important conductor in the later years of his career. She recorded five Verdi works under his direction. Name the conductor and the music in question.
14. Birgit Nilsson sings Brünnhilde in two commercial recordings of the *Ring*. Who sing Wotan and Siegfried with her in each recording?
15. Which three heroines of Offenbach operettas has Régine Crespin recorded?
16. Who conducts these much-prized early operatic recordings starring Renata Tebaldi: *Otello; Aida; Tosca; La Bohème; Madama Butterfly;* and *Il Trovatore?*
17. Giulietta Simionato sang the brief role of the Countess de Coigny on a recording of *Andrea Chénier.* Who sang the three leading roles on that set, and who conducted?
18. What was Luciano Pavarotti's first complete operatic recording? Who were his soprano and mezzo colleagues? (Each received billing *above* Pavarotti's.)
19. Who sang Calaf opposite Maria Callas's Turandot on the EMI recording?
20. Leontyne Price's first *Aida* recording was originally meant for another soprano who canceled because of illness. Whom did Price replace?

Answers on page 270.

97. OLD VIENNA

1. In what city does *The Merry Widow* take place?
2. In *The Gypsy Baron,* what is the secret that surrounds the heroine, Saffi?

3. Who composed *The Czar's Princess?*
4. What country is meant by the title *The Land of Smiles?*
5. In *The Merry Widow,* which character is in love with Valencienne?
6. Who is Valencienne's husband?
7. Name the famous stage and film star who starred in the Metropolitan Opera's *The Gypsy Baron* in 1959? (Hint: He is the son of a famous tenor.)
8. What is the name of the Viennese theater that specializes in operetta?
9. Returning to *The Merry Widow,* what is the name of the famous song for Hanna, early in Act II?
10. Identify the following ten characters by the operettas in which they appear, the composer, and a brief description.

    a. Prince Orlofsky
    b. Mi
    c. Giuditta
    d. Sándor Barinkay
    e. Loulou, Froufrou, Joujou
    f. Frosch
    g. Count Wittenburg
    h. Sonja
    i. Gabrielle
    j. Bella Giretti

11. Where does Prince Danilo, of *Merry Widow* fame, like to spend his evenings?
12. Which of Johann Strauss's operettas was created posthumously from his previously published music?
13. Who composed *Two Hearts in 3/4 Time?*
14. Name the six operettas recorded by EMI/Angel in the 1950s that comprised that company's "Champagne Operetta Series." Who sang the soprano and tenor leads in all six works?
15. Who were the noted Broadway playwright and lyricist who adapted *Die Fledermaus* for the celebrated Metropolitan production and recording?
16. In *The Land of Smiles,* what makes Lisa decide to leave China and return to Vienna?
17. *Die Fledermaus* was the source of a popular Broadway musical of the 1940s. What was it, and who was the leading lady?
18. In which Hollywood version of a Viennese favorite did Maurice Chevalier play the leading man?
19. From which operetta does the "Du und Du" waltz come?
20. A performance of *Die Fledermaus* was televised live from London's Royal Opera on New Year's Eve 1977. Name the conductor, the Eisenstein, and the Rosalinde. In what language was it sung?
21. Can you name three Broadway musicals that have entered the repertoire of the Vienna Volksoper?
22. For which tenor did Lehár compose *The Land of Smiles?*

23. In the Decca/London "gala" *Die Fledermaus* recording, during the interpolated celebrity concert in Act II, what pieces were performed by the following artists: Renata Tebaldi, Birgit Nilsson, Jussi Bjoerling, Leontyne Price, Ljuba Welitsch, Giulietta Simionato, and Ettore Bastianini?
24. Which famous Salome was also a Metropolitan Rosalinde?

Answers on page 272.

98. THEY HAD SOME SONGS TO SING, O

Gilbert and Sullivan are worth a book of their own, but this brief quiz is included as a tribute to the importance of the G & S repertoire.

1. The first G & S opera was composed as a curtain-raiser for another work. Name this other piece, and the G & S work in question.
2. Who was Richard D'Oyly Carte?
3. For each of the characters listed here, identify the operetta in which they appear.
   - a. Dick Deadeye
   - b. Rose Maybud
   - c. Colonel Fairfax
   - d. Luiz
   - e. John Wellington Wells
   - f. Jack Point
   - g. Cousin Hebe
   - h. Angelina
   - i. Strephon
   - j. Prince Hilarion
   - k. Mad Margaret
   - l. Peep-bo
   - m. The Lord Chancellor
   - n. Josephine
   - o. Ruth
4. What is Little Buttercup's real name?
5. In *Iolanthe,* a reference is made to Captain Shaw. Who was Captain Shaw, and in what song is the reference made?
6. Name the London theater built for Gilbert and Sullivan's works.
7. Which of Verdi's plots was a constant target for William Gilbert's satire?
8. Name three other works by Arthur Sullivan.
9. Why did Queen Victoria knight Sullivan but not Gilbert?
10. Which of the G & S operas almost had its world premiere in the United States?
11. Which is the only G & S opera *not* to open with a chorus? How does it open?

12. Which is the only G & S work in three acts?
13. After a period of animosity that followed the composition of *The Gondoliers,* Gilbert and Sullivan collaborated on two more works, neither of which is frequently performed. Name them.
14. Who was the principal comedian of the last years of the D'Oyly Carte Opera?
15. For each song title listed here, name the operetta from which it comes and the character who sings it.
    a. "Braid the raven hair"
    b. "Sorry her lot who loves too well"
    c. "Never mind the why and wherefore"
    d. "When I went to the bar as a very young man"
    e. "The magnet and the silver churn"
    f. "When Frederick was a little lad"
    g. "When first my old, old love I knew"
    h. "I stole the prince"
    i. "I know a youth"
    j. "I cannot tell what this love may be"
16. Who was the only D' Oyly Carte star to re-create his most famous role in a Hollywood version of the G & S opera? Name the opera and the role.

Answers on page 273.

99. WOMEN'S WORLD

The questions below concern women who have influenced opera in another capacity than that of star soloist.

1. This lady ran a musical salon in nineteenth-century Milan and was a close confidante of Giuseppe Verdi. What was her name?
2. This scholarly Englishwoman has had a number of operas produced in recent years. She has chosen as subjects such varied material as the misadventures of a lovelorn monarch, a little-known Henry James novel, and an English classic. Who is she?
3. For more than forty years, this dynamic broadcasting czarina ran the Metropolitan Opera broadcasts with a will of iron and the skill of a major general. Name her.
4. Who was the first woman to conduct at the New York City Opera?
5. The daughter of a great composer, she married another musical giant and shared his musical as well as ideological beliefs. Name her and her father.

6. Conductor/director Sarah Caldwell is the founder of which opera company?
7. A female impresario was responsible for the United States debut of Maria Callas. Name the woman and her company.
8. A woman who conducts as well as produces opera has been responsible for important concert revivals of such operas as *L'Africaine, Kátya Kabanová,* and *Tancredi* at New York's Carnegie Hall. Who is she, and what is the name of her company?
9. This Englishwoman has directed many productions at Milan's La Scala and at the Metropolitan Opera. Name her.
10. This former actress, who married a multimillionaire, provided the impetus for the salvation of the Metropolitan Opera when that company faced financial ruin during the Great Depression. She was the founder of the Metropolitan Opera Guild. What was her name?
11. The daughter-in-law of a famous composer who died years before she was born, this woman ran a great music festival for many years but was barred from continuing in that capacity after World War II due to her unrepentant Nazi sympathies. Name her. Where was this woman born?
12. This woman, a music critic for a major American daily, has caused many an artist, as well as impresario, to tremble at her wrath. Who is she, and with which major newspaper has she been associated?
13. This temperamental wife often made life difficult for her husband, a renowned composer. He paid tribute to his fiery spouse, who was, incidentally, a singer of much renown, by composing an opera that affectionately made fun of their conjugal life. Name the lady, her husband, and the opera.
14. Although she had a brief but brilliant career as a soprano, this lady made her finest contribution to opera by loving and sustaining Giuseppe Verdi for half a century, first as an admirer of his music, later as mistress and wife. What was her name?

Answers on page 275.

Jussi Bjoerling was such a wonderful singer that audiences forgave his less than dynamic acting and his occasional straying from the directions in the libretto. A *Manon Lescaut* that Bjoerling sang in the early 1950s was made memorable by his impromptu change in stage direction. Pleading fatigue, Bjoerling whispered to his "dy-

ing" soprano in Act IV that he would not go off and search for water for her, as called for in the libretto. The obliging soprano wandered offstage herself and returned with the prop cup filled with water. More memorable still was a performance of *Tosca,* in which Bjoerling performed in spite of severe back pain. Not wishing to overexert himself, Bjoerling became the first Cavaradossi in the opera's history to die on his feet in front of the firing squad!

100. OFF THE BEATEN PATH

Answer the following random questions, which deal with esoteric pieces of operatic information.

1. Name a Polish opera.
2. Name four Wagnerians from Finland who have been active in the past twenty years.
3. What is soprano Zinka Milanov's real name?
4. To whom belonged the last three solo voices ever heard on stage at the old Metropolitan Opera House?
5. Who starred in the Hollywood film about an opera singer, entitled *One Night of Love?*
6. Which well-known soprano openly denounced Luciano Pavarotti during a television broadcast?
7. Who was the Wagnerian soprano who starred in a musical comedy by Rodgers and Hammerstein? Name the show, too.
8. What was the first operatic "novelty" performed at the old Metropolitan in 1883? What was the first "standard" opera to be performed at the new Met in 1966?
9. Mary Martin, prompted and harassed by the late Noel Coward, once performed a hilarious rendition of a beloved aria on a classic TV show, "Together with Music." Name the aria.
10. Ezio Pinza starred in a short-lived television situation comedy in the early 1950s. Do you recall its name?
11. What was the name of the self-styled artist's agent who sued Maria Callas, having her served with a subpoena as she stepped off the stage after a performance of Puccini's *Madama Butterfly* in Chicago?

12. Who are three great sopranos born in Australia?
13. Which well-known French opera had its first performance in Vienna in a German translation?
14. Who is the famous soprano who was a mere chorister in the 1937 Berlin recording of Mozart's *The Magic Flute*?
15. Name two composers, celebrated in their own right, who created libretti for other composers to set?
16. Who were Puccini's coauthors of the libretto for his *Manon Lescaut*? (None of them received billing on the libretto, by the way.)
17. A soprano some consider to be the finest "Italian" soprano of the twentieth century was born in Connecticut. Who is she?
18. Name an opera based on a motion picture script.
19. Who was the operatic composer responsible for coaxing soprano Magda Olivero out of her premature retirement in 1951?
20. The daughter of the owner of Milan's Hotel Ritz, where Verdi died, was married to one of Verdi's successors as a composer of popular operas. Who was he?
21. What was the opera that was staged at the Vienna State Opera the night that Allied bombers practically destroyed that theater?
22. Name two books written by the late Francis Robinson, for nearly thirty-five years the principal raconteur (and assistant manager) of the Metropolitan Opera.
23. Which is the German opera whose most famous aria, sung by the tenor, is almost invariably sung in Italian, while its second most famous number, for soprano, is a German version of an English folksong?
24. What was the name of the nineteenth-century social club that set the rules for performances at the Paris Opéra?
25. Who are Ruben Ticker, Pincus Perlmutter, and Janet Angelovich?
26. Soprano Dorothy Kirsten was the protégée of which very famous singer?
27. Cesare Siepi appeared in two unsuccessful Broadway musical comedies. Coincidentally, the characters he portrayed in both plays had the same occupation. Name the two shows, and state the business that Siepi's two characters engaged in.
28. Who were two opera singers who had foods named for them? What are the two dishes in question?
29. Who was the Metropolitan star arrested on false charges of espionage, furnished by a jealous colleague, during World War II?
30. Who was the first American ever to sing at the Bolshoi? What role did this artist perform?

31. Name two composers who reorchestrated Mussorgsky's *Boris Godunov.*
32. Name the artist who performed no less than seven roles in the world, London, and American premieres of Britten's *Death in Venice* opposite the formidable Peter Pears, the opera's doomed protagonist.

Answers on page 275.

A wonderful Canadian tenor, internationally admired for his work in such roles as Peter Grimes and Otello, was singing Tristan in the American South. During Tristan's arduous third-act monologue, this singer, known for his temper, could no longer control his irritation at the audience's noisy display of respiratory ailments. In midphrase, he leapt from Tristan's deathbed, stalked to the footlights, and, shaking his fist at the audience, ordered them to "Shut up your damned coughing!" Having vented his righteous anger, he stamped back to Tristan's cot and continued the scene.

101. DON'T BELIEVE EVERYTHING YOU READ I

True or false?

1. *Carmen* was Bizet's first opera.
2. Puccini adapted his opera *Tosca* from a play by Victorien Sardou.
3. Two Verdian characters share the name Iago. Iago is, of course, the villain in *Otello.* However, in *Ernani* the title character has a henchman also named Iago.
4. Gustav Mahler conducted at the Metropolitan Opera for several years during the first decade of the twentieth century.
5. In Verdi's *Il Trovatore,* Azucena's final revelation to Count di Luna is that she is the count's mother.

6. Maria Callas was first introduced to American opera fans because of a film she made of *Medea.*
7. In Verdi's *Falstaff,* the librettist Boito grafted a famous speech from Shakespeare's *Henry IV, Part 1* onto the libretto he fashioned from the bard's *The Merry Wives of Windsor.*
8. In Puccini's *Madama Butterfly,* the heroine is cursed for marrying a foreigner and renouncing her religion by her father, a Buddhist priest.
9. José Carreras was "discovered" by Joan Sutherland when he sang a small role in an opera in which she starred in London in 1970.
10. Three composers who produced operas based on *Manon Lescaut* were Massenet, Puccini, and Leoni.
11. Placido Domingo sang for several seasons in Tel Aviv, relearning his roles in Hebrew.
12. Ezio Pinza appeared in a Broadway musical with Ethel Merman.
13. The recitatives in *Carmen* were composed not by Bizet, but by Ernest Guiraud, after Bizet's sudden death.
14. Bruno Walter conducted the first performance at the rebuilt La Scala, after the damage done by Allied bombers had been repaired.
15. The first opera ever televised from the new Metropolitan Opera at Lincoln Center was Puccini's *La Bohème,* starring Renata Scotto and Luciano Pavarotti.
16. In *Die Götterdämmerung,* Siegfried is drugged and tricked into marrying Sieglinde.
17. Beniamino Gigli died onstage at the Metropolitan during a performance of Verdi's *La Forza del Destino.*
18. In Rossini's Cinderella opera *La Cenerentola,* the heroine's wicked stepmother is named Griselda.
19. The answers to the three riddles posed by Turandot to Calaf in Puccini's opera are, respectively: Sangue (blood), Speranza (hope), and Turandot, herself.
20. Richard Strauss and poet Hugo von Hoffmansthal collaborated on the following operas: *Elektra, Der Rosenkavalier,* and *Ariadne auf Naxos.*
21. Richard Strauss's *Ariadne auf Naxos,* in its original format, was performed as part of a production of Molière's play *Le Médecin Malgré Lui.*
22. Teresa Stratas deserves a place in any operatic book of world records for having sung such diverse roles as Gretel in Humperdinck's opera, and the title role of Berg's shocker *Lulu.*
23. Beverly Sills is married to Julius Rudel, whom she replaced as general director of the New York City Opera in 1979.

24. Puccini himself conducted his opera *La Fanciulla del West* on the occasion of its world premiere at the Met in December 1910.

Answers on page 278.

102. OPERATIC SCAVENGER HUNT

Can you supply the information called for by the following questions?

1. Name two soprano heroines who die of consumption.
2. Name two soprano characters who kill themselves rather than let villainous baritone characters make love to them.
3. Name a mezzo-soprano gypsy who appears in a nineteenth-century French opera who is *not* a "bad girl."
4. Name four tenor characters in Italian opera who murder their wives or lovers. (Give the beloveds' names, too.)
5. Name two Bellini heroines who have mad scenes but who regain their wits at the end of their respective operas.
6. Who are three operatic fathers who are responsible for the deaths of their children? (Give the children's names, too.)
7. Who are five villains who are apprehended at the end of the works in which they appear? Who are the characters who catch them?
8. Name three operas that have masked balls (excluding Verdi's work, of course).
9. Name two German operas based on Shakespearean plays. (Name the plays, too.)
10. Which American opera is based on a play by Chekhov?
11. Who are two tenor characters who die shortly after leading drinking songs?
12. Supply the names of six operatic characters who are beheaded. In which operas do they appear?
13. Name two soprano characters who have happy marriages to bass characters. (Name the husbands and operas, too.)
14. Who are three operatic characters who kill their own brothers?
15. Name three malevolent high priests.
16. Name five baritones who are "good guys."
17. Name five evil soprano characters.
18. Name two operatic wives who strike their husbands.

19. Who is an operatic doctor who ought to be sued for malpractice?
20. Name five operas set in the United States.
21. Name three operas by Mascagni excluding *Cavalleria Rusticana* and *L'Amico Fritz.*
22. Name three operas based on plays by Eugène Scribe.
23. Name three Verdi operas with libretti by Francesco Maria Piave.
24. Name four German opera singers who fled Nazi Germany and settled in the United States.

Answers on page 279.

103. DON'T BELIEVE EVERYTHING YOU READ II

True or false?

1. Verdi's first opera was *Nabucco.*
2. The first singer to perform the title role in Puccini's *Turandot* was Rosina Storchio.
3. Beethoven composed four overtures to his only opera, *Fidelio.*
4. Renata Tebaldi recorded Cilea's *Adriana Lecouvreur* in 1946, with Arturo Toscanini conducting.
5. Although Victoria de los Angeles recorded *Carmen* in 1959, she did not actually sing the role onstage until November 1978, when she appeared in a production of Bizet's opera in Newark, New Jersey.
6. Tenor Carlo Bergonzi began his career as a baritone.
7. Francesco Cilea, composer of *Adriana Lecouvreur* and *L'Arlesiana,* was a noted musicologist.
8. Don Giovanni briefly allows Donna Elvira to think that he is coming back to her, but it is Elvira's maid who really interests him.
9. Puccini once considered composing an opera about Marie Antoinette.
10. In 1955 Leontyne Price became the first black artist to sing at the Metropolitan Opera.
11. Alfredo Catalani, composer of *La Wally,* also composed an opera based on Murger's *Scènes de la Vie de Bohème.* Puccini stole the idea of the opera from the unfortunate Catalani.
12. Sir Georg Solti spent several years as musical director of the Royal Opera House Covent Garden.
13. One of Verdi's principal librettists was Lorenzo da Ponte.

14. On the first night of Rudolf Bing's administration at the Met, Cesare Siepi, Delia Rigal, Fedora Barbieri, and Lucine Amara made their debuts in Verdi's *Don Carlo.*
15. During Maria Callas's time at La Scala, the head of that opera house was Giovanni Battista Meneghini.
16. Puccini once remarked that his favorite Tosca was Rosa Ponselle.
17. The original cast of Carlisle Floyd's *Susannah,* as produced by the New York City Opera, included Norman Treigle as Blitch and Beverly Sills as Susannah.
18. A vicious feud between Jan Peerce and Zinka Milanov made backstage at the Met a war zone whenever they appeared together in the 1950s.
19. The great Italian mezzo-soprano Giulietta Simionato began her career at La Scala singing such minor roles as Mamma Lucia in Mascagni's *Cavalleria Rusticana.*
20. Donizetti composed a revised version of his French *opéra comique La Fille du Régiment* and called it *Die Regimentstochter.*
21. Verdi composed *Aida* for Jenny Lind.
22. Enrico Caruso sang the role of Dick Johnson in Puccini's *La Fanciulla del West* in that opera's world premiere performance, at the Royal Opera, London, in 1910.
23. Verdi revised his opera *Stifellio* and called it *Jérusalem.*
24. Boris Christoff once had a real swordfight onstage during a performance of *Don Carlo* at the Rome Opera.

Answers on page 281.

104. OUT IN THE COLD

Below are a dozen groups of four—titles of operas, names of characters, singers, or companies. Three items in each group share a common characteristic. Select the one item that is different from the others and explain why.

1. Eboli, Fenena, Amneris, Federica.
2. *Le Nozze di Figaro, Suor Angelica, Turandot, Das Rheingold* (two possibilities).
3. *Norma, I Puritani, Il Pirata, La Sonnambula.*

4. Ernani, the Duke of Mantua, Enzo Grimaldo, Chevalier des Grieux.
5. Carmen, Mignon, Dalila, Preziosilla (two possibilities).
6. Scarpia, Adriana, Luisa Miller, Gennaro.
7. Mimi, Madeleine de Coigny, Leonora di Vargas, Violetta.
8. The Metropolitan Opera, the Royal Opera House, La Scala, Paris Opéra.
9. *Falstaff, Don Carlo, Un Ballo in Maschera, Il Trovatore* (two possibilities).
10. Mary Garden, Grace Moore, Patrice Munsel, Dorothy Kirsten (two possibilities).
11. *Linda di Chamounix, Parisina d'Este, Emilia di Liverpool, Elisabetta Regina d'Inghilterra.*
12. Leporello, Mariandl, Despina, Figaro (two possibilities).

Answers on page 283.

105. RECORD COLLECTORS III

1. What was the first opera to be recorded in the new digital process? Name the label, conductor, and cast.
2. Fiorenza Cossotto, known primarily for her Verdi and *verismo,* recorded a Mozart role in a delightful performance of a great comedy. Name the role, the conductor, and Cossotto's colleagues.
3. Name five sopranos who have recorded *The Merry Widow* in English.
4. Who sings Pollione opposite Callas's Norma in the soprano's first recording of Bellini's opera?
5. When Boris Christoff recorded the death of Boris Godunov for the first time, which soon-to-be-famous soprano sang the brief lines of the czar's little boy?
6. Who sings the title role in the only commercial recording of Spontini's *La Vestale?*
7. What is the only complete opera recorded commercially by Anita Cerquetti, the ill-fated soprano whose promising career lasted only a few seasons? Who are her colleagues on this set?
8. Who is the only artist who has recorded all three soprano roles in Puccini's *Il Trittico?*

9. Who is the celebrated soprano whose recording debut was as the bloody child in the RCA recording of Verdi's *Macbeth*?
10. Tenor Jon Vickers has recorded Florestan in *Fidelio* on two occasions. Who were the sopranos and conductors on each set?
11. Martina Arroyo recorded Elena in Verdi's *I Vespri Siciliani* for RCA as a last-minute replacement for an ailing colleague. Whom did Arroyo replace?
12. Name the soprano who has recorded both Mimi and Musetta in *La Bohème.*
13. Elisabeth Schwarzkopf sang in the chorus of a famous opera recording made in Berlin in 1939, on the eve of World War II. Name the opera and conductor.
14. The brief role of the Italian tenor in *Der Rosenkavalier* has attracted several great tenors on records. Name the tenors who sing the cameo role in the following recordings:
    a. Bernstein–CBS
    b. von Karajan–EMI/Angel
    c. De Waart–Philips
    d. Solti–Decca/London
15. One of Maria Callas's complete operatic recordings was not released for several years until the soprano could be persuaded to allow its distribution. Name it.
16. Who was the extraordinarily gifted producer of the first stereophonic recording of the *Ring*?
17. A famous interpreter of Salome sings a cameo role on a beloved recording of another Strauss opera. Name the soprano, the role, and the conductor of the performance.
18. Name the two Verdi operas that, as of 1982, have never received commercial recordings.

Answers on page 284.

106. ULTIMATE WAGNER

1. How many solo parts are there in Wagner's *Der Ring des Nibelungen*?
2. List, in order of appearance, every character in the *Ring.* (Note: Do not list characters again that appear in more than one section.)

Answers on page 285.

107. OPERA PIX

1. (ABOVE LEFT) Not the winner of the von Karajan look-alike contest. Who is this worthy artist and for which role is he costumed?

2. (ABOVE RIGHT) Vatever Lola vants, Lola gets! Who is this temptress?

3. This diminutive artist gave the Metropolitan Opera its most controversial opening night in its history. Who is she, and what is the role she sang?

4. Who is this tenor?

5. This lovely, angel-faced lady has, as of 1982, sung more performances at or with the Metropolitan Opera than any other soprano in the company's history. Who is she, and for which of her roles is she costumed in this picture?

6. Name this operatic Valentino. In what role is he pictured?

7. Identify this southern belle whose voice rang out in music by Verdi, Strauss, Wagner, Berg, and Barber.

8. What is the name of Madame Tebaldi's poodle?

9. What were these two doing on the night of January 31, 1955?

10. Who are these comic conspirators?

11. Who are these two aristocratic singers and in what opera are they performing?

12. (OPPOSITE) Who is Caruso's lady friend, and what opera are they performing? (Hint: Opera is a forgotten sequel to what was once a very popular opera.)

13. Name this Biblical hero and opera's greatest tenor who is portraying him.

14. King for a day! Who is the regal artist and which autocrat is he portraying?

15. Identify these stars who seem quite pleased with the love duet they have just sung.

16. Who are these performers, and what opera are they singing?

17. An operatic duo worth selling one's soul to hear! Who are they, and what are they singing?

18. Who is that lady in black?

19. Can you identify four famous artists in this Triumphal Scene?

20. Identify these two singers and the opera.

21. Identify this singer.

22. Identify this singer and the character he's portraying.

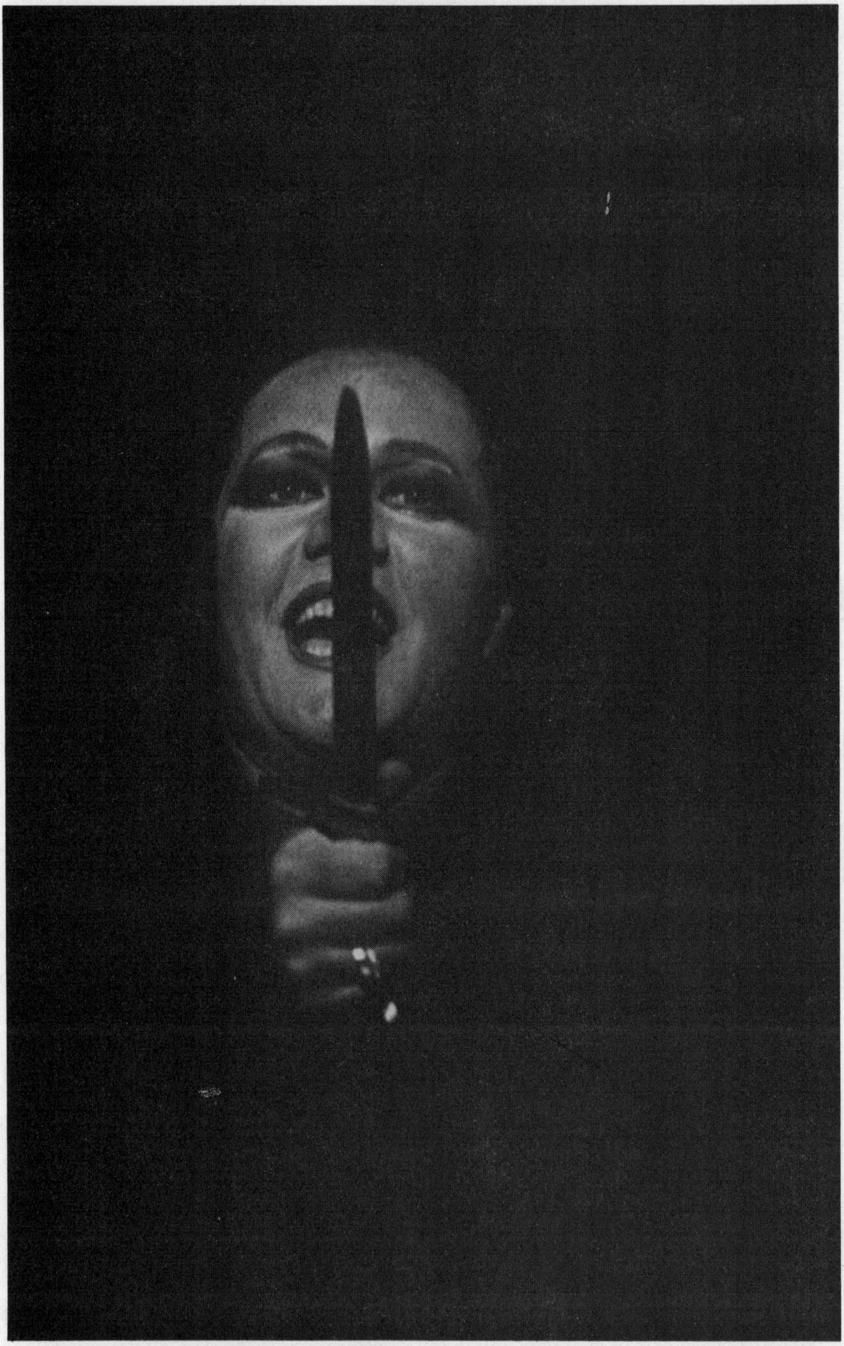

23. Who is the lady with the shiv?

24. Name this singer and the character she's portraying.

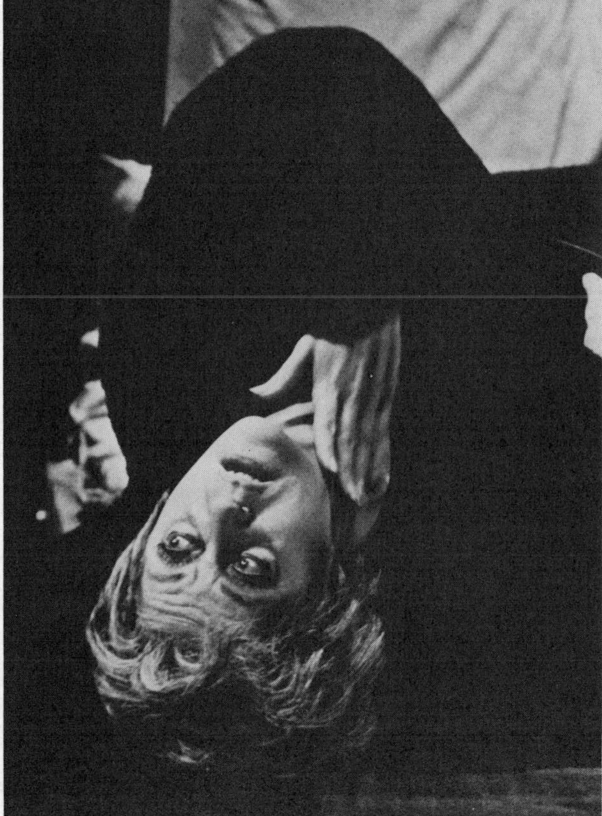

25. Who is this soprano and what has just happened to her?

26. (ABOVE LEFT) A brief role but an unforgettable moment in American music history–who is she?

27. (ABOVE RIGHT) Name this singer and his role.

28. Who is this Rosina?

29. Name this singer and the character he's portraying.

30. Who is this strange-looking soldier? The opera he is singing is remembered for only one aria. Name the singer, the opera, the composer, and the aria.

31. Who is this king?

32. The only comic role in this artist's vast repertoire. Identify the singer and the character he's portraying.

33. Singing powerful enough to shatter all the clichés about tenors. . . . Who is he and what role is he singing?

34. Name this singer and the character he's portraying.

35. A "classical" hero as sung by one of today's classiest heroic voices. Name the singer and the role.

36. Identify the singer and the role.

37. Identify the singer and the role.

38. A comic role with a tragic significance for the singer shown here. Identify the singer and his role, and explain the "tragic significance."

Answers on page 286.

THE ANSWERS

COMPOSERS AND THEIR OPERAS

1. AMERICAN OPERA

1. Gian Carlo Menotti was born in Italy but became an American citizen, although he currently resides in Scotland. Menotti's *Amahl and the Night Visitors,* commissioned by the National Broadcasting Company, was the first opera to have its inaugural performance on television.
2. Callas declined the invitation to sing Vanessa in Samuel Barber's opera of that name. The honor was given to Eleanor Steber after Sena Jurinac, who had agreed to sing the role, canceled a few weeks before the premiere, which took place on January 15, 1958, at the Metropolitan Opera. Miss Steber scored one of the greatest successes of her long and notable career.
3. Sills starred in the New York City Opera premiere (and many subsequent revivals) of Douglas Moore's *The Ballad of Baby Doe.*
4. Blitzstein was working on an opera based on the case of Sacco and Vanzetti.
5. Beeson's *Lizzie Borden* does not, unfortunately, feature a chorus of "Lizzie Borden took an ax . . ."

6. Miller's *The Crucible* was adapted into a melodious and dramatically powerful opera by Robert Ward.
7. The answer, of course, is *Porgy and Bess.* George Gershwin composed the music, while the libretto was written by Ira Gershwin and DuBose Heyward. Three stars of the original 1935 production were Todd Duncan (Porgy), Anne Brown (Bess), and John W. Bubbles (Sportin' Life). In 1952 soprano Leontyne Price received international acclaim in a revival of the work in which she sang Bess opposite the Porgy of William Warfield (whom she subsequently married and divorced). The production played on Broadway and toured Europe and the Soviet Union.
8. Hanson's opera, now more or less forgotten, is *Merry Mount.*
9. Traubel debuted in the May 2, 1937, premiere of *The Man Without a Country,* composed by Walter Damrosch, based on the story by E. E. Hale.
10. Eugene O'Neill's *Mourning Becomes Electra* was the basis for Marvin David Levy's 1967 opera of the same name. Its world premiere as the second America opera to be created during the Met's inaugural season at Lincoln Center served as the vehicle for Evelyn Lear's Met debut.
11. Powers sang Madame Flora (also called Baba) in *The Medium* by Menotti.
12. A crucial tenor-soprano duet, accompanied by the IRT, is found in *The Saint of Bleecker Street.*
13. Menotti's *The Mother of Us All* was set to music by Virgil Thomson. The "Mother" in question is Susan B. Anthony.
14. *Susannah,* by Carlisle Floyd, is a version of *Susannah and the Elders,* set in the rural South. It was first performed at Florida State University, Tallahassee, in 1955. Phyllis Curtin (Susannah) and Norman Treigle (Olin Blitch) were the two stars of the New York City Opera's production in 1957.
15. *Miss Havisham's Fire* by Dominick Argento, is based on material taken from *Great Expectations. A Christmas Carol,* by Gregory Sandow, is adapted from Dickens's perennial yuletide favorite.
16. Menotti's libretto for *Vanessa* was set to music by Samuel Barber. Rosalind Elias, who had been singing *comprimario* roles at the Met since her debut there in 1954, found herself in demand for leading roles in opera houses throughout the world after she created the role of Erika, Vanessa's troubled niece.
17. *Mourning Becomes Electra* had music by Marvin David Levy. Evelyn Lear was Lavinia, Marie Collier was Christine, Sherrill Milnes was Adam Brant, and John Reardon was Orin in the original production.

The staging by Michael Cacoyannis (the director of the film *Zorba the Greek*) was more admired than was Levy's score.
18. *The Tender Land* is Copland's only opera.
19. *The Trial of Mary Lincoln* and *The Seagull.*
20. Emperor Jones (in Louis Gruenberg's opera based on the Eugene O'Neill play) and the title role in Deems Taylor's *Peter Ibbetson.*

2. ENGLISH OPERA

1. Henry Purcell is considered the first English composer of opera. His two best-known operas are *Dido and Aeneas* and *The Fairy Queen.*
2. Britten's *The Turn of the Screw* is based upon Henry James's novel.
3. Paul Bunyon.
4. *The Midsummer Marriage.*
5. Thea Musgrave is Britain's best-known living woman composer. Two of her operas are *Mary, Queen of Scots* and *A Christmas Carol.*
6. The Sadler's Wells Opera has metamorphosed into the English National Opera.
7. The D'Oyly Carte Opera used the wonderful old Sadler's Wells Theatre as its home base.
8. Sir Peter Pears.
9. One learns in that opera's prologue that Grimes's first apprentice died of dehydration when Grimes's fishing boat is stalled in a becalmed sea.
10. The American baritone Theodor Uppman.
11. The Royal Opera shares Covent Garden with the Royal Ballet.
12. Sir Colin Davis.
13. The Royal Opera, Welsh National Opera, English National Opera, Scottish Opera, and English National North.
14. Benjamin Britten composed *Gloriana* for Her Majesty's coronation. The opera dealt with her namesake, Elizabeth I.
15. Marie Collier replaced Callas as Tosca, an assignment that boosted her career, sadly cut short by Collier's untimely death in 1971.
16. Shuard was a celebrated Turandot.
17. Sir Peter Pears, Sir Geraint Evans, Dame Eva Turner, and Dame Janet Baker.
18. Tadzio, the young boy to whom the opera's protagonist is fatally attracted, is a mute role played by a dancer.

19. International stars whose home base is the ENO include Norman Bailey, Rita Hunter, Ann Howard, Valerie Masterson, Alberto Remedios, and Josephine Barstow.
20. Francesco Paolo Tosti and Franco Leoni were resident Italian composers in London at the turn of the century.
21. Alberto Remedios.
22. Gwyneth Jones and Margaret Price.
23. Britten composed for Pears the title role in *Peter Grimes,* Vere in *Billy Budd,* Aschenbach in *Death in Venice,* and Quint in *The Turn of the Screw.*
24. Glyndebourne Festival.
25. *Sir John in Love* and *Hugh the Drover.*
26. *A Village Romeo and Juliet.*

3. FRENCH OPERA

1. Two of Thomas's operas are *Mignon* and *Hamlet.*
2. Verdi composed *Don Carlo, Les Vêpres Siciliennes,* and *Jérusalem* for the Paris Opéra.
3. The librettists for *Carmen* were Henri Meilhac and Ludovic Halévy. They based their work upon the novella by Prosper Mérimée.
4. Le Théâtre des Italiens.
5. Poulenc's *Dialogues des Carmélites,* Massenet's *Thérèse*, Giordano's *Andrea Chénier,* and John Eaton's recent American opera, *Danton and Robespierre.*
6. The first Mélisande was Mary Garden.
7. a. Zuniga, in Georges Bizet's *Carmen,* is the officer who is one of Don José's principal rivals for Carmen's attention.
   b. Spalanzani, in Jacques Offenbach's *Les Contes d'Hoffmann,* is the inventor whose creation, Olympia, captures Hoffmann's heart.
   c. Philine, in Ambroise Thomas's *Mignon,* is the flighty actress who is not terribly kind to the heroine.
   d. Siebel, in Charles Gounod's *Faust,* is the youth who adores Marguerite.
   e. Blanche is the heroine of Francis Poulenc's *Les Dialogues des Carmélites.*

f. Charlotte is the already promised object of Werther's melancholy passion in Jules Massenet's *Werther.*

g. De Brétigny is the officer who becomes Manon's protector after des Grieux has been spirited away in Massenet's opera.

h. Schlémil is the unfortunate admirer of Giulietta in *Les Contes d'Hoffmann.* He loses his shadow to Giulietta and his life in a duel with Hoffmann.

i. Mercedes is Carmen's fortune-telling friend in Bizet's opera.

j. Rachel is the foster daughter of Eleazar in Jacques Halévy's *La Juive.*

k. Leila is the heroine of Bizet's opera *Les Pêcheurs de Perles.*

l. Cassandre is the prophetess daughter of the Trojan King Priam in Hector Berlioz's *Les Troyens.*

m. Athanaël is the sex-crazed monk who attempts to reform a courtesan in Massenet's *Thaïs.*

n. Abimelech is the Hebrew-baiter whom Samson kills early on in Camille Saint-Saëns's *Samson et Dalila.*

o. Nicklausse is Hoffmann's devoted companion in Offenbach's opera.

8. *Louise* and its sequel, *Julien.*
9. Camille Saint-Saëns composed *Henri VIII.*
10. The world premiere took place at La Scala, Milan, in January 1957.
11. Sybil Sanderson.
12. Aix-en-Provence and Orange.
13. Debussy was working on *La Chute de la Maison Usher.* The long-lost manuscript was given its first performance in 1979 at the Juilliard School of Music.
14. *La Périchole, La Vie Parisienne,* and *La Grand Duchesse de Gerolstein.*
15. *Le Coq d'Or* is a Russian opera by Nikolai Rimsky-Korsakov. The other operas are, respectively, the work of Edouard Lalo, Giacomo Meyerbeer, and Jules Massenet.
16. Wilfred Pelletier was a renowned Canadian operatic conductor.
17. The old Comique is now known as the Salle Favart.
18. Hoffmann's loves are: Olympia, the doll; Giulietta, the courtesan; Antonia, the young girl; and Stella, the prima donna.
19. a. Sung by the title character in Massenet's *Werther.*

    b. Sung by Olympia in Offenbach's *Les Contes d'Hoffmann.*

    c. Sung by the newly blinded Samson in Saint-Saëns's *Samson et Dalila.*

    d. Sung by Micaela in Bizet's *Carmen.*

    e. Sung by the title character in Thomas's *Mignon.*

f. Sung by Marguerite in Gounod's *Faust.*
g. Sung by Valentin in Gounod's *Faust.*
h. Sung by Chimène in Massenet's *Le Cid.*
i. Sung by Rodrigo in *Le Cid.*
j. Sung by the title character in Massenet's *Cendrillon.*
k. Sung by Marguerite in Berlioz's *La Damnation de Faust.*
l. Sung by the title character in Rossini's *William Tell.*
m. Sung by des Grieux in Massenet's *Manon.*
n. Sung by the title character in Offenbach's comic opera *La Périchole.*
o. This is otherwise known as Lakmé's "Bell Song" in Leo Delibes's *Lakmé.*

20. *Les Martyrs* is a French opera by Gaetano Donizetti. Its Italian version is *Poliuto* and, as such, was a 1960 La Scala vehicle for Maria Callas, Franco Corelli, and Ettore Bastianini.

4. GERMAN OPERA

1. Two of Lortzing's operas are *Zar und Zimmermann* and *Der Wildschütz.*
2. Otto Nicolai composed this opera, based on Shakespeare's *The Merry Wives of Windsor.*
3. *Margarete* is the German title for Frenchman Charles Gounod's *Faust.* This opera has always been popular in Germany, but Germans took exception to the excessively sentimental and unintellectual qualities of this work and therefore renamed it after Faust's unlucky mistress in order to distinguish the opera from Goethe's play.
4. Beethoven's *Fidelio* had its premiere at Vienna's Theater an der Wien on November 20, 1805.
5. Ernestine Schumann-Heink's supposed immolation took place at the Metropolitan Opera.
6. Georg Büchner wrote the play *Woyzeck.* The spelling of Berg's opera is different because of a typographical error in his edition of the play.
7. Wozzeck's tormentors include the Captain, the Doctor, and the Drum Major. The Captain degrades and badgers Wozzeck, the Doctor subjects him to weird experiments, and the Drum Major not only steals Marie, Wozzeck's common-law wife, from him, but brutally attacks the poor man as well.
8. *Martha* is the work by which most people remember Flotow. Its

popular tenor aria is best known in its Italian translation "M'appari tutt'amor," for it was in that language that Enrico Caruso recorded it.

9. Max and Agathe are the lovers in Carl Maria von Weber's *Der Freischütz.*
10. This aria is from Carl Maria von Weber's *Oberon.* More commonly known as "Ocean, thou mighty monster," Maria Callas's recording of this is the only aria she recorded in English.
11. Friedrich Cerna, a musicologist and expert in Berg's music, completed the third act of *Lulu.*
12. Berg's widow claimed that Berg had communicated with her from beyond the grave. In his visits, the composer allegedly told his wife not to allow anyone to tamper with his notes. Frau Berg's death made her objections academic, and Cerna reported no visitations from ghosts, friendly or otherwise, during his work on Berg's score.
13. The world premiere of the completed *Lulu* took place at the Paris Opéra in February 1979. Pierre Boulez conducted, and Teresa Stratas sang Lulu.
14. Rudolf Bing, the former general manager of the Metropolitan Opera, performed the role of the whip-cracking trainer of the young lord in the 1973 production.
15. The opera is *Lear,* the composer is Aribert Reimann, and the artist who sang the title role was Dietrich Fischer-Dieskau.

5. ITALIAN OPERA

1. *Il Barbiere di Siviglia* (this is the assumed name of Almaviva) and *L'Italiana in Algeri.*
2. *Il Duca d'Alba.*
3. Mayr was Donizetti's mentor.
4. Ponchielli (composer of *La Gioconda*) was the teacher of Giacomo Puccini.
5. The elder Verdi ran a humble inn and general store in the village of Le Roncole.
6. Catalani's two best-known operas are *La Wally* (for whose heroine Toscanini named a daughter) and *Lorelei,* which did *not* inspire Anita Loos's heroine of that name.
7. *Il Giuramento* shares its source, Victor Hugo's *Angelo, Tyran de Padoue,* with Ponchielli's *La Gioconda.*
8. Riccardo Zandonai's *Francesca da Rimini.*

9. The composer was Fr. Licino Refice, the opera was *Cecilia,* and the diva was Claudia Muzio.
10. a. Arrigo Boito's *Mefistofele,* sung by Faust.
    b. Giuseppe Verdi's *Luisa Miller,* sung by Rodolfo.
    c. Pietro Mascagni's *L'Amico Fritz,* sung by Suzel.
    d. Amilcare Ponchielli's *La Gioconda,* sung by La Cieca.
    e. Mascagni's *Cavalleria Rusticana,* sung by Alfio.
    f. Gaetano Donizetti's *L'Elisir d'Amore,* sung by Nemorino.
    g. Vincenzo Bellini's *La Sonnambula,* sung by Amina.
    h. Umberto Giordano's *Andrea Chénier,* sung by Carlo Gérard.
    i. Gioacchino Rossini's *L'Italiana in Algeri,* sung by Isabella.
    j. Riccardo Zandonai's *Francesca da Rimini,* sung by Francesca.
11. The censors rejected *Un Ballo in Maschera* as it originally stood because it involved the assassination of a European monarch.
12. a. Giordano's *Andrea Chénier*
    b. Verdi's *Macbeth*
    c. Mascagni's *Cavalleria Rusticana*
    d. Bellini's *Norma*
    e. Verdi's *Nabucco.* (This, the chorus of Hebrew slaves, is practically the second national anthem of Italy.)
13. a. Gaetano Donizetti
    b. Umberto Giordano
    c. Giuseppe Verdi
    d. Gaetano Donizetti
    e. Pietro Mascagni
    f. Riccardo Zandonai
    g. Vincenzo Bellini
    h. Amilcare Ponchielli
    i. Both Mascagni and Arrigo Boito wrote operas based on the exploits of Emperor Nero of Rome.
    j. Wolfgang Amadeus Mozart
    k. Giacomo Puccini
    l. Gioacchino Rossini
14. Verdi pondered Shakespeare's *King Lear* for years, but he could never satisfy himself with the work he did on this project.

6. RUSSIAN OPERA

1. Mussorgsky wrote the libretto and the music for *Boris Godunov.*
2. Nikolai Rimsky-Korsakov and Dimitri Shostakovich reorchestrated

Boris Godunov. Rimsky-Korsakov's version is still the most frequently performed, as he brightened the austere orchestral palette of the original version. Shostakovich's *Boris* is occasionally performed. In 1974 the Metropolitan Opera gave *Boris* in its original version, orchestrated by Mussorgsky. The Bolshoi, however, continues to produce *Boris* in the Rimsky-Korsakov version.

3. Each of the two operas is based on poems by Pushkin.
4. a. The show is *Kismet.*
   b. *Kismet*'s score was taken, in large part, from the Polovetsian Dances.
   c. The Broadway team of Robert Wright and George Forrest created *Kismet.*
   d. The hit song is "Stranger in Paradise."
   e. Richard Kiley, better known for his work in *Man of La Mancha,* sang "Stranger" in the original Broadway production, but Tony Bennett made the hit record.
5. Tatyana, the overly sensitive young heroine of *Eugene Onegin,* sends a declaration of love to Onegin, whom she has only just met. The cynical Onegin rejects Tatyana's proffered love. Years later, at a ball in Moscow, Onegin meets Tatyana, now married to Prince Gremin. All at once Onegin realizes that he has always loved Tatyana. Singing in the same melody as that of Tatyana's Letter Scene, he begs her to leave Gremin. Although Tatyana acknowledges her own love for Onegin, she refuses to desert her husband, leaving Onegin to his own despair.
6. *War and Peace*'s American premiere took place not in an opera house, but on television as part of the old NBC Opera Company series.
7. The three Bolshoi stars who made the deepest impression in America are Elena Obraztsova, Yuri Mazurok, and Vladimir Atlantov. Although Obraztsova and Mazurok have since sung in Chicago, San Francisco, and at the Met, tenor Atlantov has had to cancel his subsequent American visits for mysterious reasons. Because of international politics, no Soviet singers have appeared in the United States since 1980.
8. Bolshoi soprano Galina Vishnevskaya was the first Soviet soprano to appear at the Met. She made her debut as Aida in 1960, singing that role and the title role in *Madama Butterfly* in Russian while her colleagues sang in Italian. In 1975, after Vishnevskaya and her husband Mstislav Rostropovich had left the Soviet Union, Vishnevskaya returned to the Met for a performance of *Tosca,* this time singing in Italian.
9. The first version of *Boris Godunov* had no love interest and no sizable role for a woman. Mussorgsky amended this by adding the "Polish

act," in which the pretender Dmitri dallies with a Polish princess, Marina, whom the Jesuits have persuaded to seduce Dmitri into bringing Roman Catholicism into Russia. The role of Marina contains a solo aria, and duets with the bass, Rangoni (a Jesuit priest), and with the tenor, Dmitri.

10. Prokofiev composed an opera based on Dostoevsky's *The Gambler.*
11. *The Czarevitch*, by Franz Lehár, is a Viennese operetta; *The Czar's Bride* is an opera by Rimsky-Korsakov; *A Life for the Czar* is by Mikhail Glinka.
12. Lisa's first suitor is the baritone Prince Yeletsky, who, unlike Herman, has a beautiful and romantic aria to sing in Act II.

7. *AIDA*

1. Phtha.
2. Amneris (in Act II, scene 1) tells Aida that Radames has been killed in the war between Egypt and Ethiopia. When Aida becomes distressed, Amneris cries out that she has been lying, and Radames is really alive. Aida is overjoyed, and Amneris immediately pounces upon her rival for Radames's heart.
3. Teresa Stolz was the first Aida. Although the truth has never been established, Stolz is believed to have been Verdi's mistress for many years in spite of the presence of Verdi's wife, Giuseppina Strepponi, to whom Verdi was apparently devoted.
4. *Aida* originally began with a full overture. While preparing the Italian premiere of the opera, he discarded that piece in favor of the brief prelude heard ever since.
5. In the score of *Aida,* Verdi instructs the tenor to sing the high B flat that ends the aria "ppp," or, very, *very* softly. Since many tenors won't and most can't take that note on anything less than a *fortissimo,* Verdi sanctioned that change, providing that the tenor repeated the last three words, "Vicino al sol," one octave lower, quietly. Richard Tucker opted for this ending on the famous Toscanini recording of the opera. More recently, Placido Domingo has performed this version of "Celeste Aida."
6. In that film, Sophia Loren acted the part of Aida, while Renata Tebaldi did the singing.

7. Radames plans to take his men through the gorge of Napata (in Italian, *la gola di Nàpata*).
8. The cast of the RCA recording included Herva Nelli (Aida), Eva Gustavson (Amneris), Richard Tucker (Radames), and Giuseppe Valdengo (Amonasro).
9. Callas, singing Aida in 1951, interpolated a high E flat at the very end of the Triumphal Scene. The audience went wild. Re-engaged for Aida the following year, Callas again sang the high E flat, this time joined by tenor Mario del Monaco.
10. Antonio Ghislanzoni.

8. *CARMEN*

1. A letter, a little money to add to his pay, "and yet another thing worth more than money and which a good son will surely value higher," a kiss given by his mother to Micaela to be passed on to José.
2. The girls quarrel after Carmen makes some insulting references to her colleague, who has recently acquired a donkey. Carmen tells her that she should have bought a broom to ride instead.
3. Manuelita.
4. *Les Pêcheurs de Perles* was composed in 1863. *Carmen,* composed in 1875, turned out to be Bizet's final work, as he died three months after the opera's first performance.
5. The directors of the Opéra-Comique were afraid that their middle-class subscribers would be offended by a heroine who not only got herself murdered but actually smoked on stage. It was these timid souls who insisted on the invention of Micaela, the sweet, virtuous hometown sweetheart of Don José, to act as a foil to the unwholesome Carmen.
6. El Dancaïro is the boss. In the Opéra-Comique version of *Carmen* he is constantly reprimanding his loquacious subordinate, El Remendado.
7. Ernest Guiraud, the New Orleans-born friend of Bizet, composed music for the badly truncated recitatives that replaced *Carmen*'s spoken dialogue when the work was performed at the Vienna Opera. The recitatives successfully transformed *Carmen* into a "grand opera" and, for the first century following *Carmen*'s appearance, formed the stan-

dard version of the opera. Only recently have major international theaters restored the original spoken dialogue.

8. Escamillo lets José live, saying that his business is to slaughter beef, not men. José repays this generosity by attacking Escamillo after he has turned his back on José.
9. Early critics claimed Bizet had imitated Wagner in *Carmen,* mentioning the use of the "fate motif" that punctuates Carmen's various adventures.
10. Geraldine Farrar, the most celebrated Carmen of the first two decades of this century, first sang the role of Micaela.

9. *CAVALLERIA RUSTICANA*

1. Santuzza has been excommunicated because of her affair with Turiddu and because, one supposes, she has become pregnant with Turiddu's baby.
2. Gemma Bellincioni was the first Santuzza.
3. Turiddu is once again in love with his old flame, Lola, who, unfortunately for all concerned, has become the wife of Alfio, the village teamster.
4. Alfio says that he is afraid that the beverage would turn to poison in his breast.
5. Turiddu asks Lucia to bless him, as she did when he went off to be a soldier. Then he begs his mother to pray for him. Finally, he makes her promise that, in case he should not return, she will be like a mother to Santuzza.
6. "A te, la mala Pasqua, spergiuro!" (An evil Easter to you, betrayer!) In view of the fact that Turiddu is murdered by Alfio a short time later, Santuzza's curse is fulfilled in no uncertain terms!

10. *MADAMA BUTTERFLY*

1. The short story on which Belasco based his play was written by John Luther Long (1861–1927).

2. Under the terms of Pinkerton's lease, the agreement is to run for 999 years but is cancelable on one month's notice. This latter point is identical to the "escape clause" on Pinkerton's marriage contract.
3. Butterfly shows him a jar of rouge. With an unparalleled show of hypocrisy, the blasé Pinkerton registers displeasure, and the compliant bride throws the makeup away.
4. At the moment of Butterfly's first entrance, a solo violin quotes Musetta's Waltz from *La Bohème.* The anti-Puccini claque that had smuggled itself into the theater seized upon this detail as a reason for one of many noisy demonstrations that wrecked the first night.
5. This recording, made by RCA Victor (later reissued by EMI/Angel), starred Toti dal Monte as Butterfly and Beniamino Gigli as Pinkerton.
6. Pinkerton promises that he will return to his bride "when the robins return," meaning, one assumes, the following spring. Since three springs have passed before Sharpless visits Butterfly to attempt to break the news of Pinkerton's remarriage and imminent arrival, Butterfly asks him if, in America, the robins nest less frequently than in Japan. Sharpless is embarrassed by this and teaches Butterfly a new English word when he disclaims all knowledge of ornithology.
7. The opera is set in Nagasaki.
8. First, Puccini divided the two scenes of the original second act into two separate acts. This gave the fidgety members of future audiences a break. Second, the composer removed an aria in Act I from Pinkerton's role but made amends by adding "Addio, fiorito asile" for the tenor to sing in Act III. Third, Puccini omitted the brief supporting role of Butterfly's mother from the first act. The character still appears, but since she has no lines to sing, the role is almost always assigned to a chorus member. Fourth, Puccini further shortened the first act wedding scene by excising a vignette during which an uncle of Butterfly's named Yakuside gets very drunk.
9. The sopranos are Renata Tebaldi, Victoria de los Angèles, and Renata Scotto. Tebaldi's two Pinkertons are Giuseppe Campora and Carlo Bergonzi; de los Angeles sings with Giuseppe di Stefano and Jussi Bjoerling; Scotto's pair of Pinkertons are Carlo Bergonzi and Placido Domingo.
10. Butterfly is wooed by the wealthy Prince Yamadori.
11. Notwithstanding the best efforts of many set designers and lighting experts, there are no fireflies to be found in Japan, rendering their appearance during the love duet for Butterfly and Pinkerton highly unlikely.
12. Butterfly demands that Sharpless leave her house when he urges her to forget Pinkerton and marry her rich suitor, Prince Yamadori.

11. *I PAGLIACCI*

1. Originally, Tonio speaks the final line. Once, however, a now forgotten Canio usurped the line, and it has remained a tenor property ever since. However, in his film of *I Pagliacci,* von Karajan gave the line back to Tonio.
2. The famous last words are: "La commedia è finita!"
3. Leoncavallo based *I Pagliacci* on an actual case tried in the court of the composer's magistrate father.
4. Nedda's lover is Silvio.
5. Tonio counsels Canio to calm down and bide his time, predicting (correctly, as it turns out) that the man will attend the evening's performance of Canio's troupe of players and reveal himself.
6. Placido Domingo has sung *Cavalleria Rusticana* and *I Pagliacci* on the same evening in London in 1976, in San Francisco in 1976, and in New York (at the Met) in 1978.

12. *DER RING DES NIBELUNGEN*

1. Alberich must renounce love.
2. Wotan and Fricka are worried because Wotan has promised the goddess Freia as payment to the two giants, Fasolt and Fafner, who have built Valhalla for the gods.
3. Freia's special talent is caring for the tree that produces magic apples that keep the gods eternally youthful. Without Freia and her fruit, the gods will grow ancient immediately.
4. Alberich makes himself invisible by means of the *Tarnhelm,* a magical cap of loosely woven chain mail that allows its wearer to assume any shape (or lack thereof) that he chooses.
5. Valhalla.
6. In the Solti *Ring,* Flagstad sings Fricka in *Das Rheingold.*
7. Hunding.
8. The possessive Hunding is in no position to prevent Siegmund and Sieglinde from running off because Sieglinde poured a sleeping potion into Hunding's nocturnal libation.

9. According to the libretto of *Die Walküre,* Fricka travels in a cart drawn by a ram.
10. Siegmund is honored when Brünnhilde describes to him the hero's welcome that will await him in Valhalla, but he refuses to consider going there unless Sieglinde goes with him, which, as things turn out, is out of the question. Siegmund's defiance is not effective, for Wotan aids Hunding in the duel between the two men, and Siegmund dies.
11. Initially, Wotan wants to put Brünnhilde asleep on her rock, to be awakened by the kiss of the first man who happens by. After much pleading from his daughter, Wotan agrees to surround Brünnhilde with magic fire, which only a brave, heroic type could penetrate.
12. Before Brünnhilde leaves Sieglinde, she tells her that she, Sieglinde, will bear Siegmund's child, and she gives her the pieces of Siegmund's sword, "Nothung," which was shattered by Wotan and Hunding.
13. Unlike its three sister musical dramas, *Siegfried* has some moments of humor and a happy ending. Siegfried and Brünnhilde live happily ever after until the first act of *Die Götterdämmerung.*
14. The magic of the blood enables him to understand the language of the Forest Bird, thereby enabling him to find the hidden *Tarnhelm,* and helping him to divine the real meaning behind Mime's deceitful words.
15. Siegfried kills Mime because the Forest Bird has told Siegfried that the dwarf who had raised him will now try to kill him in order to have the cursed ring for himself.
16. Siegfried learns of Brünnhilde's existence from the Forest Bird.
17. The Wanderer, who appears in *Siegfried,* is actually Wotan, who has come down from Valhalla to enter into the human drama that has overtaken the ring, once the plaything of Rhinemaidens, gods, and dwarves.
18. Between *Das Rheingold* and *Siegfried,* or, to be exact, between *Das Rheingold* and *Die Walküre,* Wotan and Erda have produced a litter of Valkyries, warrior maidens who serve Wotan & Co.
19. The Norns, daughters of the surprisingly prolific Erda, are spinning the rope of fate. The rope breaks, which means that the world, as the *Ring* characters know it, will soon end.
20. This piece is called Siegfried's Rhine Journey.
21. Waltraute visits her sister Brünnhilde in a vain attempt to get the ring of the Nibelung, which, in spite of its jinxed history, Siegfried has given to Brünnhilde as a wedding ring.
22. The *Ring* libretti were sketched backward because Wagner originally contemplated doing one opera—more or less *Die Götterdämmerung.*

Then, mired in mythology, he realized that a first opera, giving background, would be necessary. Hence came the idea for *Der Junge Siegfried.* Ultimately, he conceived the grand tetralogy as we know it today.

23. Wagner wrote his own libretti.
24. Hagen, who has been conspiring evilly throughout *Die Götterdämmerung,* has drugged Siegfried into forgetfulness and has had him marry Hagen's half sister, Gutrune. Now, as a ruse for gaining possession of the ring, Hagen gives Siegfried a drink that will bring back his memory. Siegfried soon begins expounding upon his love for Brünnhilde, and Hagen stabs him in the back for "treachery."
25. Brünnhilde's horse, which she calls for in order to ride into the flames of Siegfried's pyre at the climax of the Immolation Scene, is named Grane.
26. Five highlights would include the Entrance of the Gods into Valhalla, the Ride of the Valkyries, Forest Murmurs, Siegfried's Rhine Journey, and Siegfried's Funeral March.
27. Andrew Porter, the South African-born music critic for *The New Yorker,* has written the excellent new English version of the *Ring.*
28. Fricka is angry at Siegmund because Fricka is the goddess of marriage, and Siegmund has not only broken up Hunding's home, but has also committed incest.
29. Wotan is Siegmund's father.
30. Brünnhilde is a half sister to Siegmund and Sieglinde.
31. This sounds (and is) highly unorthodox and complicated, but Brünnhilde is actually Siegfried's aunt.
32. Her first words are "Heil du Sonne" (Hail to you, O Sun).
33. Seeing his very first woman (actually, he only gets to meet four other females, Gutrune and the Rhinemaidens) Siegfried exclaims: "Das ist kein Mann" (That's *not* a man!).
34. *Die Götterdämmerung* is the only *Ring* opera that uses a chorus, and an all-male one at that. The men are used in the Act II sequence known as Hagen's Gathering of His Vassals.
35. The "neo-Bayreuth" style of spare, symbolic sets and subdued lighting was developed by Wieland Wagner, the composer's grandson, who ran the Bayreuth Festival from 1951 until his death in 1966.
36. Birgit Nilsson, Kirsten Flagstad, Régine Crespin, Astrid Varnay, and Helen Traubel all sang Brünnhilde and Sieglinde. Of these five, only Crespin did not go on to sing the *Siegfried* and *Götterdämmerung* Brünnhildes.
37. Helen Traubel, a great singer on anyone's list, was an especially prized

Brünnhilde during the war years, when Flagstad and various other European artists were unavailable.

38. Pierre Boulez was the conductor of the badly received 1978 Bayreuth *Ring.*
39. Von Karajan first staged his own *Ring* at the Salzburg Easter Festival. The Metropolitan Opera bought his concept, but von Karajan personally directed only *Das Rheingold* and *Die Walküre* in New York.
40. Rita Hunter is the British Wagnerian who has sung the *Ring* in two languages. Hunter was Birgit Nilsson's "cover" when the Metropolitan produced *Die Götterdämmerung* in 1974. Days before the premiere, Nilsson broke her shoulder when, in a freak accident, part of the set collapsed under her during a rehearsal. Nilsson managed the premiere but withdrew from the nationwide radio broadcast several days later. Although millions were disappointed by the cancellation, Hunter did a fine job of substituting.
41. Nilsson and Caballé sang a "joint" *Walküre* at Barcelona's Teatro Liceo in 1977. Richard Cassilly was the fortunate tenor.
42. Callas sang Brünnhilde at the Teatro La Fenice, Venice, with Tullio Serafin conducting.
43. Toscanini's soloists in *Die Walküre,* Act I, scene 3, and *Die Götterdämmerung* Dawn duet were Helen Traubel and Lauritz Melchior.
44. In the von Karajan *Ring* recording, Dietrich Fischer-Dieskau sings the *Rheingold* Wotan, while Thomas Stewart is heard in *Die Walküre* and as the *Siegfried* Wanderer.
45. Von Karajan's two Brünnhildes are Régine Crespin in *Die Walküre* (interestingly, Crespin doubles as Sieglinde in Solti's *Walküre*), and Helga Dernesch, a one-time von Karajan protégée, is heard in the two subsequent operas.
46. Joan Sutherland may be heard as the Forest Bird in Solti's *Siegfried.*
47. The Met's Brünnhilde during the 1950s was American-born Margaret Harshaw.
48. Astrid Varnay, Swedish-born but raised in the United States, enjoyed a series of triumphs at Bayreuth during the 1950s, including her Brünnhilde under the baton of Hans Knappertsbusch, a performance that has found its way onto Cetra Opera Live records.
49. The curse pronounced on the ring by the dwarf Alberich, who is understandably bitter because Wotan has stolen it from him, is that it will bring death to all who own it until it is returned to the Rhinemaidens. As often happens in opera, the curse works!

13. *DER ROSENKAVALIER*

1. The Marschallin often refers to Octavian as Quinquin, while he calls her Bichette.
2. Ochs von Lerchenau.
3. Leopold is Ochs's bumptious valet and confidant. Ochs implies to the Marschallin that Leopold is Ochs's illegitimate son. In the Act III farce staged to embarrass Ochs, Annina, pretending that Ochs is her long-lost husband and father of a large brood of urchins, calls him "Leopold."
4. She tries to assuage Octavian's hurt feelings by saying that he may ride alongside her carriage when she is driven through the Prater later on in the day. Of course, by the end of that day, Octavian will have fallen blindly in love with Sophie, and the Marschallin will sadly relinquish him to the younger woman.
5. She calls for her little servant to take the silver rose to Octavian, who will act on behalf of Ochs by presenting the rose to Sophie.
6. At first Ochs seems a little put out, but then he encourages Octavian to make love to Sophie, to "break her in" for Ochs. This horrifies Sophie and so offends Octavian that he challenges Ochs to a duel.
7. The irate Faninal, who wishes to marry off his daughter to a titled person, even if he is as boorish as Ochs, tells Sophie that if she doesn't marry the baron, he will place her in a convent.
8. The Marschallin is sung by Elisabeth Schwarzkopf; Octavian by Sena Jurinac; Sophie by Anneliese Rothenberger; Ochs by Otto Edelmann. The conductor is Herbert von Karajan.
9. The Marschallin is sung by Lotte Lehmann; Octavian by Maria Olszewska; Sophie by Elisabeth Schumann (recreating her world premiere performance); Ochs by Richard Mayr. The conductor is Robert Heger.
10. Annina has brought Ochs the *billet-doux* from "Mariandl" (Octavian dressed as the Marschallin's maid) setting up a tryst, and Ochs, while overjoyed by this development, is so stingy that he does not tip her. This makes Annina more eager than ever to undo Ochs.
11. The Marschallin tells Ochs that his supposed marriage to Sophie will never happen. Then, when Ochs starts to make allusions to the Marschallin's affair with Octavian, the Marschallin firmly tells Ochs to put the entire matter out of his mind and to go home and never refer to the incident again. As for Sophie, who chatters nervously as

Octavian presents her to the Marschallin, the latter advises her not to talk so much, saying that Sophie is so pretty that she need not bother with making so much conversation.

12. Mahomet is sent back to look for Sophie's fallen handkerchief, which he finds as the curtain falls.

14. *TOSCA*

1. The play, *La Tosca,* was written by Victorien Sardou, and Sarah Bernhardt had one of her greatest successes touring in the title role.
2. Puccini had a penchant for stealing the ideas and wives of other men. He became enamored of *La Tosca,* but the rights were owned by Alfredo Franchetti. Ricordi, guessing that a Puccini *Tosca* would be a bigger success than one by Franchetti, went with Puccini to visit the unfortunate man. Together, the two convinced him that the play was too violent for successful transition to opera. Franchetti agreed to relinquish his option, and Puccini immediately snapped it up.
3. The unwitting model for Mario's religious artwork is La Marchesa d'Attavanti, Angelotti's sister, who does not herself appear in the opera, but is significant to the plot for several reasons. Her frequent visits to church are meant to conceal her real purpose–arranging her brother's escape. The marchesa leaves a key to her family's private chapel, as well as some women's clothing with which Angelotti can disguise himself. Also, the marchesa is vital to the plot because she provides, by virtue of her beauty, the bait with which Scarpia triggers Tosca's jealousy. Scarpia produces a fan left behind by the fleeing Angelotti and suggests to Tosca that the marchesa herself left it behind, fleeing with Tosca's lover, Mario.
4. Angelotti escapes from the Castel Sant' Angelo, a notoriously grim and brutally administered prison.
5. Tosca returns to the church to give Mario the bad news that she has been summoned to sing for Queen Caroline of Rome, to celebrate the supposed defeat of Napoleon. Scarpia, at the church to investigate Angelotti's escape from prison, seizes the opportunity to poison Tosca's mind against her lover and to use her as an unwitting spy, hoping that she will lead him to Angelotti, Mario's friend.
6. Puccini eventually came to dislike Tosca's Act II aria, "Vissi d'arte."

He felt that the introspective prayer held back the action and cooled the suspense.

7. Scarpia asks which road Tosca would like to travel, and she replies, "The shortest." Scarpia suggests Civitavecchia, the major highway leading from Rome, and Tosca approves.
8. In an early production of *Tosca* in Vienna, soprano Maria Jeritza, who came to be Puccini's favorite Tosca, tripped while dodging Scarpia's attentions and found herself face down on the floor as her cue to sing the aria drew near. Therefore, the beautiful Jeritza sang the aria from that extraordinary position and has been emulated by many Toscas since.
9. The premiere performance was plagued by undercurrents of political unrest and professional jealousy on the part of the composer's rivals. Although no bombs were tossed inside the opera house, the opening scene was interrupted when sounds of fracas in the foyer reached the auditorium. Angry latecomers were being refused entry, and their shouts so unnerved the conductor, Leopoldo Mugnone, that he stopped conducting and barricaded himself in his dressing room until he was assured by the management that no saboteurs were present, at which time the performance resumed.
10. The music for the offstage cantata in the second act was composed by Puccini's father. The elder Puccini, a locally famous organist and composer, died when Puccini was a young child. He studied his father's compositions and conferred immortality on this piece by making use of it in *Tosca.*

15. *LA TRAVIATA*

1. *La Traviata*'s first performance was given in 1853 at the Teatro La Fenice in Venice.
2. Two reasons for the opera's initially cool reception were that the audience was surprised and displeased by the then contemporary settings and costumes (for years afterward the opera was given in eighteenth-century costumes) and the fact that the obese soprano singing Violetta was a most unlikely consumptive.
3. Baron Douphol.
4. The party guests include Douphol, Flora, the Marquis d'Obigny, Gastone, Alfredo, and Dr. Grenvil.

5. This aria is sung by the temporarily joyous Alfredo in Act II.
6. Papa Germont wants to break up Violetta and Alfredo because the scandal of Alfredo's living with a courtesan threatens the marriage plans of Alfredo's sister and her seemingly snobbish fiancé.
7. Germont figures out Alfredo's plans when he sees the invitation to Flora's party, which Alfredo has read and thrown to the ground as he runs off in despair.
8. Germont sings "Di sprezzo degno sè stesso rende chi pur nell'ira la donna offende" (He who, even in anger insults a woman, is worthy only of disdain). These words are surprising since Germont's own first words to Violetta accused her of "ruining" his son.
9. Maria Callas sang Violetta, Giuseppe di Stefano sang Alfredo, and Ettore Bastianini sang Germont. The production was designed and staged by Luchino Visconti, and conducted by Carlo Maria Giulini.
10. Toscanini's cast included Licia Albanese as Violetta, Jan Peerce as Alfredo, and Robert Merrill as Germont.
11. Violetta's outburst happens shortly after Alfredo returns to her, and although she wishes to leave with him immediately, she finds that she is not strong enough even to dress herself.
12. Violetta's last delirious words are "Ah! Ma io ritorno a viver! O gioia!" (But I am returning to life! Oh joy!).

16. I'VE HEARD THAT BEFORE

1. In the final scene of Mozart's *Don Giovanni,* Don G is giving a party. A stage band entertains, playing tunes from two non-Mozartean operas, allowing Leporello to make a few topical allusions. Finally, the band strikes up Mozart's own "Non più andrai" from *Le Nozze di Figaro.* Leporello, recognizing the tune, quips, "I've heard that one too often!"
2. In Puccini's *Il Tabarro* the bargebound Giorgetta and her stevedore lover Luigi listen to a song vendor hawk a song about the love of Mimi and Rodolfo. Sure enough, the orchestra, in *Il Tabarro*'s one humorous moment, briefly plays a bit of "Sì. Mi chiamano Mimì" from *La Bohème.*
3. In the prologue to Offenbach's opera, Hoffmann and his friend Nicklausse arrive at Luther's tavern after an act of *Don Giovanni.* Nicklausse sees that his subservient attitude toward Hoffmann, and the

latter's condescension toward him, make him into a nineteenth-century Leporello. Therefore, Nicklausse sings a few bars of Leporello's "Notte e giorno faticare."

4. In the third act of *Die Meistersinger von Nürnberg,* Wagner slips the famous "Tristan chord" into the scene in which Sachs realizes that he must help Walther win Eva's hand. As the music echoes Wagner's tragic work, Sachs alludes to the story of King Marke, Tristan, and Isolde to his young friends.
5. In the first act of *Madama Butterfly,* at the point of Cio-Cio-San's first entrance, Puccini quotes Musetta's Waltz from *La Bohème.* It is totally unmotivated and probably was an unconscious quote by the composer.

17. WAGNER I

1. Wagner's first opera, more or less neglected in his own day and in ours, was *Die Feen,* which had its American premiere in a concert performance by the New York City Opera on February 24, 1982.
2. Wagner's first wife was Minna.
3. The critic was Eduard Hanslick. Wagner mercilessly caricatured Hanslick in the character of Beckmesser, the comic villain in *Die Meistersinger von Nürnberg.*
4. The first version of *Tannhäuser* is known as the Dresden version. The revision is called the Paris version. The principal difference is that in the Paris version, the bacchanal that opens the opera (the Venusberg scene) is expanded to accommodate the ballet that was *de rigueur* at the Paris Opéra during the nineteenth century. Also, the orchestral coloration is more sensual and the character of Venus is more fully developed than in the Dresden version.
5. King Ludwig II of Bavaria was a staunch supporter and financial "angel" of Wagner.
6. Wagner's second wife was Cosima Liszt von Bülow. She was the daughter of Franz Liszt. When Wagner met her, she was married to the conductor Hans von Bülow, an early champion of Wagner's music.
7. Mathilde Wesendonck was a close friend of Wagner's. She wrote the poems that Wagner set to music in his Wesendonck Lieder.

8. Themes from *Tristan und Isolde*'s love music are heard in the Wesendonck Lieder.
9. George Bernard Shaw was the writer, and the book is *The Perfect Wagnerite.*
10. The several Wagnerian operas that treat this theme include *Die Walküre,* in which Wotan is forced by pressure from his wife Fricka to allow his son Siegmund to die at Hunding's hands. In *Die Götterdämmerung* the evil dwarf Alberich appears to his son, the equally hideous Hagen, to urge him on to recapture the ring. In *Tristan und Isolde,* King Marke's feelings toward Tristan are, initially, those of a father for a son, and, indeed, it has often been argued that Tristan actually *is* Marke's son. Finally, Lohengrin, one learns, has been consecrated to a life as a Knight of the Grail by his father, Parsifal (*Lohengrin*).
11. Wagner learned about the legend of *The Flying Dutchman* while on a miserable, storm-wracked ocean voyage, during which sailors recounted the tale to the composer.
12. Rysanek has been particularly well received as Senta in *The Flying Dutchman* and as Sieglinde in *Die Walküre.* She is also known for her performances as Elsa in *Lohengrin,* and as Elisabeth in *Tannhäuser.*
13. The composer was Engelbert Humperdinck, best known for *Hansel and Gretel.* The few bars that Humperdinck composed for *Parsifal* were never performed. They were discarded before the premiere because the stage machinery had been improved to the point where the scene change could be accomplished before Wagner's own music ended.
14. Wagner composed the *Siegfried Idyll,* a tone poem made up of themes from the *Ring,* as a present for Cosima upon the birth of their son Siegfried.
15. a. Melot is the aide to King Marke in *Tristan und Isolde.* He fatally wounds Tristan in a duel after Marke and his retainers have discovered Tristan and Isolde making love.
    b. Henry is the king in *Lohengrin.*
    c. Wolfram is the noble friend of both Tannhäuser and Elisabeth in *Tannhäuser.* Based on a real medieval poet, Wolfram sings the famous "Evening Star" aria.
    d. Erik is the huntsman who loves Senta in *The Flying Dutchman.* His inopportune appearance at the wedding of Senta to the Dutchman indirectly causes Senta's death.
    e. Fafner is the crueller of the two giants in *Das Rheingold.* He and his brother Fasolt have built Valhalla for the gods. The two giants quarrel over possession of the ring of the Nibelung, included as

part of the ransom for Freia, the goddess whom the two giants were promised as payment for their work. Fafner kills Fasolt and takes the ring for himself.

f. Mary is the older woman who keeps a watchful eye on Senta and the other young girls in *The Flying Dutchman.*

g. Pogner is one of the Mastersingers in Wagner's only comedy. He offers his daughter Eva in marriage to the winner of the Mastersingers' song contest. Fortunately, the young man to whom Eva has lost her heart, Walther von Stolzing, wins!

h. Waltraute is one of Brünnhilde's sister Valkyries. Her role in *Die Walküre* is brief, but in *Die Götterdämmerung* Waltraute makes a crucial appearance in Act I when she urges Brünnhilde to return the ring that Siegfried has given her to its rightful owners, the Rhinemaidens.

i. Woglinde is a Rhinemaiden. She appears in *Das Rheingold* and *Die Götterdämmerung.*

j. Brangäne is Isolde's servant in *Tristan und Isolde.* Brangäne complicates matters when, although Isolde has called for a death potion for her and Tristan to imbibe, the well-meaning Brangäne substitutes a love potion.

16. a. These words are cried out by Parsifal as he breaks away from Kundry's attempts to seduce him. His realization of Amfortas's terrible suffering prevents him from falling into Klingsor's power. (*Parsifal*)

b. With these words Lohengrin begins his revelation of who he is and why he has come to Brabant. (*Lohengrin*)

c. These rapturous words are sung by Sieglinde to her newly discovered twin brother Siegmund as they prepare to leave Hunding's hut. (*Die Walküre*)

d. These are the first words uttered by the Dutchman as he steps ashore for the first time in seven years. (*The Flying Dutchman*)

e. These are the opening words of Isolde's "Liebestod." (*Tristan und Isolde*)

f. These nonsensical words are cooed by the Rhinemaidens as they frolic about in the deceptively tranquil opening of *Das Rheingold.*

g. These are the first words of Elisabeth's entrance aria in *Tannhäuser.*

h. Tristan sings these words to Isolde as part of their love duet. (*Tristan und Isolde*)

i. These words open Adriano's aria in *Rienzi.*

j. These hostile words are addressed by Fricka to Wotan in *Die Walküre.*

17. Klingsor was not "pure" like the other knights and, in his desperation, castrated himself in a futile attempt to root out his sexual obsessions.
18. Kundry, we learn in her scene with Parsifal, was a contemporary of Christ. She laughed at Him on His way to the Cross, and was condemned by God to wander incessantly in a kind of living Hell.
19. *Parsifal.*
20. The composer died in Venice in 1883.

18. WAGNER II

1. Tenor René Kollo.
2. Soprano Lillian Nordica.
3. Siepi's only Wagnerian role so far has been Gurnemanz in *Parsifal,* which he sang with great success at the Met in 1970.
4. Tristan is served by the fiercely loyal if not terribly bright Kurwenal.
5. Tristan originally introduced himself to Isolde, when he came to claim her as King Marke's bride, as "Tantris."
6. Herzelaide is Parsifal's mother, as Kundry tells us. However, she does not make an appearance in the opera.
7. Price has yet to sing a Wagnerian role, although once she was announced for Elsa at the Boston Symphony's Tanglewood concert series in 1965. She withdrew and was replaced by Lucine Amara at the performance and on the subsequent recording.
8. Anna Russell has delighted audiences for years with her satirical monologues on Wagner, especially on the *Ring.*
9. Arturo Toscanini's Wagner was at least as fine as his Verdi.
10. In the third act of *Die Meistersinger von Nürnberg*, the elderly Sachs realizes that although he loves Eva, he cannot hope to compete for her love against Walther, and he alludes to the legend of Tristan as the orchestra echoes King Marke's monologue from the latter work.
11. The Mastersingers include: Hans Sachs, Veit Pogner, Kunz Vogelgesang, Konrad Nachtigall, Sixtus Beckmesser, Fritz Kothner, Balthasar Zorn, Ulrich Eisslinger, Augustin Moser, Hermann Ortel, Hans Schwarz, and Hans Foltz.
12. Only *Die Meistersinger von Nürnberg* is "naturalistic"; there are no spells, potions, gods, or miracles.

13. Reginald Goodall has led the English *Ring* performances.
14. Melba, misunderstanding a comment by Jean de Reszke, who had suggested that she sing the Forest Bird in *Siegfried,* insisted on attempting Brünnhilde, in that opera. One disastrous performance at the Metropolitan taught Melba to stay away from Wagner.
15. Grace Bumbry was the first black artist to sing at the Bayreuth Festival (1961). She sang Venus in *Tannhäuser,* hence the nickname.

19. MOZART

1. Mozart's first opera was *La Finta Semplice,* composed when he was eleven.
2. Fiordiligi and Dorabella are sisters.
3. a. This is from *Don Giovanni* and is sung by Don Ottavio.
   b. This is Papageno's famous song in *The Magic Flute.*
   c. This angry *arioso* is sung by Count Almaviva in *Le Nozze di Figaro.*
   d. This *romanza* belongs to Ferrando in *Così Fan Tutte.*
   e. This little duet is sung toward the end of *Le Nozze di Figaro* by Figaro and Susanna.
   f. This charming piece is a duet for Pamina and Papageno in *The Magic Flute.*
4. a. *La Clemenza di Tito*
   b. *Idomeneo*
   c. *Le Nozze di Figaro*
   d. *Don Giovanni*
   e. *The Magic Flute* (Astrafiammante is the Queen of the Night's other name!)
   f. *Così Fan Tutte*
5. Milanov's one Mozart role was Donna Anna in *Don Giovanni.*
6. *Le Nozze di Figaro* and *Don Giovanni* were first performed in Prague.
7. *Der Schauspieldirektor (The Impresario).*
8. "Dalla sua pace" and "Non mi dir."
9. Clemens Krauss was better known for his Richard Strauss than for his Mozart.
10. *Der Rosenkavalier* is intended as a salute to *Le Nozze di Figaro,* while *Die Frau ohne Schatten* is an homage to *The Magic Flute.*
11. Don Ottavio proposes to the still grieving Donna Anna. She agrees to marry him after another year of mourning for her slain father has

passed; Donna Elvira announces that she shall retire to a convent; Masetto and Zerlina simply declare that they are going home to supper; while Leporello says that he is heading for the inn, hoping to find a new, better master.

12. Sarastro sentences Monostatos to a sound thrashing for his wickedness.
13. Constanze in *The Abduction from the Seraglio* is a gallant portrait of Frau Mozart.
14. Feodor Chaliapin was not known to sing Mozart.
15. Callas often sang Constanze's "Martern aller Arten" in Italian as "Tutte le torture."
16. Joseph Losey directed the film version of *Don Giovanni.* Loren Maazel conducted; Don Giovanni was sung by Ruggero Raimondi; Donna Anna was sung by Edda Möser; Elvira was sung by Kiri Te Kanawa; while Teresa Berganza portrayed Zerlina.
17. Lunt staged an unforgettable *Così Fan Tutte* at the Metropolitan in 1952. From then on, this opera was a frequent adornment of the Met's stage.
18. Bergman changed Pamina's lineage, making her not only the Queen of the Night's daughter, but Sarastro's as well, thus more clearly motivating Sarastro's removal of the girl from her mother's clutches.
19. The Glyndebourne Festival in England, and Austria's Salzburg Festival were initially best known for their Mozart performances. More recently the repertories of both festivals have broadened considerably.
20. Cherubino's love song is "Voi che sapete."
21. *Mitridate, Rè di Ponto.*
22. Da Ponte created the libretti for *Don Giovanni, Così Fan Tutte,* and *Le Nozze di Figaro.*
23. Freemasonry is the moral basis for *The Magic Flute.*
24. Baker is highly regarded for her work in *La Clemenza di Tito.*
25. Chagall's 1967 settings and costumes for the Metropolitan Opera's *The Magic Flute* are ranked among the painter's finest achievements.

20. PUCCINI RARITIES

1. Giacomo Puccini was born in Lucca, Italy, on December 22, 1858.
2. Puccini's opera *La Rondine* was published by Sanzogno.

3. Rosa Raisa.
4. Torre del Lago, Italy.
5. Blanche Bates starred as Cio-Cio-San in the Broadway and London companies of *Madame Butterfly,* a play by David Belasco, based on a story by John Luther Long.
6. Puccini stole the idea of an operatic setting of Henri Murger's novel, *Scènes de la Vie de Bohème,* from Ruggiero Leoncavallo, the composer of *I Pagliacci.* Leoncavallo's *Bohème* was produced nearly two years after Puccini's opera, and even the presence of Caruso in the cast (as Marcello) did not prevent the opera from being overshadowed by the all but perfect Puccini version.
7. *La Fanciulla del West* and the three works that form *Il Trittico: Il Tabarro, Suor Angelica,* and *Gianni Schicchi* were given their first performances at the Met.
8. Puccini paid this compliment to Enrico Caruso, who, as Puccini began the interview, responded to the composer's question "Who are you?" by quoting, in song, the appropriate lines from Rodolfo's aria "Che gelida manina": "Chi son, son un poeta." (Who am I? I am a poet.)
9. The original cast of *La Fanciulla del West,* which had its world premiere in December 1910 at the Metropolitan, included Emmy Destinn as Minnie, Enrico Caruso as Johnson, and Antonio Scotti as Rance. Arturo Toscanini conducted.
10. The libretti for *La Bohème, Tosca,* and *Madama Butterfly* were written by Giuseppe Giacosa and Luigi Illica.
11. The fiftieth anniversary *La Bohème* was performed in New York City on February 3 and 10, 1946, in Studio 8-H of the RCA Building, and broadcast over the NBC network to commemorate the first performance of that work on February 1, 1896. The cast included the following artists: Rodolfo was sung by Jan Peerce; Mimi was sung by Licia Albanese; Marcello was sung by Frank Valentino; Musetta was sung by Anne McKnight; Colline was sung by Nicola Moscona; Schaunard was sung by George Cehanovsky; Alcindoro/Benoit were sung by Salvatore Baccaloni. The conductor was Arturo Toscanini, who had conducted at the work's premiere at the Teatro Reggio, Turin. This anniversary performance is still available on the RCA Victrola label.
12. Hungarian playwright Ferenc Molnár turned down Puccini's bid for the rights to the play *Liliom,* saying that he wanted the popular drama to be remembered as a play by Molnár rather than as an opera by Puccini. A generation later, Molnár's mind was changed by a bid from

Richard Rodgers and Oscar Hammerstein, who transformed *Liliom* into the musical play *Carousel.*

21. VERDI

1. Verdi was born in the Italian village of Le Roncole.
2. Antonio Barezzi.
3. Viva Vittorio Emmanuele, Re d'Italia–Long live Victor Emmanuel, King of Italy. This slogan, chanted by opera fans who were also supporters of a united Italy, infuriated the Austrian and Papal governors of the various Italian states during the 1840s and 1850s.
4. Verdi composed *Don Carlo, Les Vêpres Siciliennes,* and *Jérusalem* (a revised version of *I Lombardi*) to French libretti for performance at the Paris Opéra.
5. *I Masnadieri.*
6. Sant'Agata.
7. The author of the libretto's revisions was Arrigo Boito. The principal addition to the score was the council chamber scene (Act I, scene 2), from which the ensemble beginning "Plebe! Patrizi!" is considered by many to be the opera's most brilliant moment.
8. The *Requiem* was composed in honor of Alessandro Manzoni, the nineteenth-century Italian novelist and patriot, whose most famous work is *I Promessi Sposi.*
9. Francesco Maria Piave. He provided texts for several other Verdi operas including *La Traviata* and *Simon Boccanegra.*
10. "Stornello," "In solitaria stanza," and "Lo spazzocammin."
11. Arturo Toscanini.
12. "Va pensiero, sull'ali dorate" from *Nabucco.*
13. In *Nabucco,* the role of Abigaille was first sung by soprano Giuseppina Strepponi, who became Verdi's second wife.
14. Baritone Victor Maurel.
15. *The Hymn of Nations,* as adapted by Toscanini, was played by the NBC Symphony Orchestra, with Jan Peerce as tenor soloist.
16. Verdi passed up *La Tosca* because he thought himself too old to compose a new opera.
17. He died in the Hotel Ritz in Milan.
18. The Verdi home for elderly musicians, in Milan, was established by Verdi's estate.

22. VERDI RARITIES

1. Griselda is the heroine of *I Lombardi;* Federica is Luisa's rival in *Luisa Miller;* Fenena is the younger, better-natured sister of Abigaille in *Nabucco;* Odabella plots her Hun enemy's death in *Attila.*
2. "La mia letizia infondere" is heard in *I Lombardi,* and is sung by the tenor hero, Oronte.
3. Silva offers Ernani a cup of poison or a dagger. Ernani chooses the dagger.
4. The libretto of *Nabucco* was written by the poet, Temistocle Solera.
5. The soprano aria "La luce langue" in Act II of *Macbeth* is much better known than "Trionferai," which it replaced when Verdi revised the opera.
6. Verdi's *Il Corsaro* is based on the play *The Corsair* by Byron.
7. *Un Giorno di Regno* is set in Poland.
8. The aria "Me pellegrina ed orfano" was intended for Cordelia in *King Lear,* but was given to Leonora in *La Forza del Destino.*
9. The song "In solitaria stanza" later became Leonora's "Tacea la notte placida" in *Il Trovatore.*
10. a. Amelia is actually the long-lost daughter of the title character in *Simon Boccanegra.*
    b. Abigaille is the daughter (revealed eventually as the foster daughter) of the title character in *Nabucco.*
    c. Nannetta is the Verdi-Boito transfiguration of Shakespeare's Anne Page. In Shakespeare's *The Merry Wives of Windsor,* Anne is the daughter of Master and Meg Page. In Verdi's *Falstaff,* Master Page has been eliminated, and Nannetta is the daughter of Master and Alice Ford.
    d. Gilda is the daughter of the title character in *Rigoletto.*
    e. Leonora is the ill-starred daughter of the Marquis of Calatrava in *La Forza del Destino.*
11. *Otello* contains Verdi's only true "drunk scene." Iago and Roderigo make Cassio tipsy in Act I, in order to disgrace Cassio in the Moor's eyes.
12. Shakespeare's *Henry V,* which contains an account of the death of Sir John Falstaff, was not a source for Verdi's final opera. The "Honor Monologue" was lifted from *Henry IV, Part 1.* Schiller's *Die Räuber* became *I Masnadieri,* and the Duke of Rivas's *La Fuerza del Sino* became *La Forza del Destino.*

OPERA STARS AND SUPERNOVAS

23. BARITONES

1. Leonard Warren fell dead onstage at the Metropolitan Opera on the night of March 4, 1960, midway through the aria "Urna fatale" in *La Forza del Destino.* The baritone had apparently suffered a stroke.
2. Robert Merrill
3. Tito Gobbi
4. Ettore Bastianini
5. Victor Maurel
6. Lawrence Tibbett
7. Cornell MacNeil. The fracas occurred during a performance of Verdi's *Un Ballo in Maschera.* The claque booed the soprano, and unjustly, in MacNeil's opinion. As a protest, he quit the opera midway.
8. Walter Berry (once married to Christa Ludwig)
9. John Reardon (*Dough-Re-Mi* in 1960)
10. Antonio Scotti
11. Piero Cappuccilli
12. Sherrill Milnes
13. Robert Weede (*The Most Happy Fella*)

14. Richard Mayr
15. Sir Geraint Evans
16. George London
17. Robert McFerrin
18. Erich Kunz
19. Renato Capecchi
20. Dietrich Fischer-Dieskau
21. Sesto Bruscantini (once married to Sena Jurinac)
22. Gabriel Bacquier
23. Richard Stilwell
24. George Cehanovsky (married to Elisabeth Rethberg)
25. Cyril Ritchard, straight from his famous characterization of Captain Hook in the musical version of *Peter Pan* that had starred Mary Martin, staged Offenbach's *La Périchole* at the Metropolitan Opera, and he cast himself as the lecherous, if sentimental, Peruvian viceroy, Don Andres.

24. MEZZOS

1. Risë Stevens
2. Elena Obraztsova
3. Giulietta Simionato
4. Minnie Hauk
5. Ernestine Schumann-Heink
6. Louise Homer
7. Fiorenza Cossotto
8. Frederica von Stade
9. Ebe Stignani
10. Shirley Verrett
11. Regina Resnik
12. Christa Ludwig
13. Irina Archipova
14. Cloe Elmo

25. SOPRANOS

1. Kirsten Flagstad
2. Geraldine Farrar
3. Leontyne Price
4. Eleanor Steber (*Vanessa*)
5. Victoria de los Angeles
6. Lotte Lehmann
7. Renata Tebaldi
8. Zinka Milanov
9. Anna Moffo
10. Joan Sutherland

11. Shirley Verrett
12. Elisabeth Schwarzkopf
13. Lillian Nordica
14. Lucine Amara
15. Birgit Nilsson
16. Montserrat Caballé
17. Leonie Rysanek
18. Rosa Ponselle
19. Grace Moore
20. Maria Callas
21. Beverly Sills
22. Mado Robin
23. Renata Scotto
24. Luisa Tetrazzini
25. Anna Russell

26. TENORS

1. Franco Corelli
2. Placido Domingo
3. Ramón Vinay
4. Lauritz Melchior and Lily Pons
5. Richard Tucker and Jan Peerce
6. Giovanni Martinelli (sang the emperor in *Turandot* in Seattle in 1963)
7. Richard Tauber
8. Mario Lanza
9. Michele Molese (at the New York City Opera, during a performance of *Un Ballo in Maschera* in 1974)
10. Leo Slezak
11. Jussi Bjoerling
12. Robert Rounseville
13. Mario del Monaco
14. Luciano Pavarotti
15. Beniamino Gigli sang the role of Turiddu in the 1941 recording of Pietro Mascagni's *Cavalleria Rusticana.*
16. Jan Kiepura
17. Jon Vickers
18. Nicolai Gedda
19. John McCormack
20. Carlo Bergonzi
21. Alfredo Kraus (born in the Canary Islands)
22. James McCracken
23. Giuseppe di Stefano
24. Enrico Caruso

27. LUCINE AMARA

1. The San Francisco Opera.
2. In San Francisco the soprano was known as "the Cinderella soprano" because she rose from chorister to featured artist within one year.

3. The conductor whose early faith in Amara was borne out was the late Pierre Monteux.
4. Amara's five Met openings were: 1950–*Don Carlo* (Celestial Voice); 1951–*Aida* (Priestess); 1955–*Les Contes d'Hoffmann* (Antonia); 1957–*Eugene Onegin* (Tatyana); 1971–*Don Carlo* (Celestial Voice, sung as a special favor to the retiring Rudolf Bing, who invited four members of his first *Don Carlo* opening night cast to recreate their roles on the occasion of Bing's final opening night–the other artists were Robert Merrill, Cesare Siepi, and Jerome Hines).
5. Amara's commercially released operas include *I Pagliacci* (1951) in which she sings Nedda opposite Richard Tucker's Canio, with Fausto Cleva conducting; *La Bohème* (1955)–Musetta, with Victoria de los Angeles, Jussi Bjoerling, and Robert Merrill, conducted by Sir Thomas Beecham; *I Pagliacci* (1962)–Nedda, with Franco Corelli and Tito Gobbi, Lovro von Matačić conducting; *Lohengrin* (1965)–Elsa, with Sándor Kónya, Erich Leinsdorf conducting.
6. The roles include Micaela in *Carmen,* the title role in *Aida,* Tatyana in *Eugene Onegin,* the Countess in *Le Nozze di Figaro,* Pamina in *The Magic Flute,* Antonia in *Les Contes d'Hoffmann* and Nedda in *I Pagliacci.* Pamina, Tatyana, and Antonia, incidentally, were recorded in English.
7. Amara may be heard singing with Lanza in *The Great Caruso* (1950).
8. In 1975 Amara literally jumped into *La Forza del Destino,* replacing the ailing Martina Arroyo in the role of Leonora, midway in the Convent Scene.
9. *La Bohème* (Mimi and Musetta); *Aida* (Priestess and Aida); *Turandot* (Liù and Turandot); *Carmen* (Frasquita and Micaela); *The Magic Flute* (First Lady and Pamina).
10. Geraldine Farrar sang 517 performances at the Met.

28. MONTSERRAT CABALLÉ

1. Caballé was virtually unknown in the United States when she made her debut with the American Opera Society in New York, singing the title role in Donizetti's *Lucrezia Borgia* as a last-minute replacement for Marilyn Horne.

2. Caballé has stated in interviews that as a young child she dreamed of becoming a ballet dancer.
3. Kolodin described the soprano's Desdemona as having been so dull that Otello probably strangled her out of sheer boredom.
4. Caballé's husband is the recently retired tenor Bernabé Martì.
5. Caballé and Martì recorded Bellini's *Il Pirata* for EMI/Angel.
6. Cabellé's discovery was a twenty-four-year-old tenor named José Carreras, who sang with her at the Teatro Liceo in Barcelona.
7. Caballé has sung Liù to Nilsson's Turandot at the Metropolitan, and Sieglinde to Nilsson's *Walküre* Brünnhilde at the Teatro Liceo in Barcelona.
8. Caballé has sung the Marschallin in *Der Rosenkavalier,* Salome, and the title role in *Ariadne auf Naxos.*
9. Caballé sang her first Turandot at La Scala in 1976. Although scheduled to sing in the opening performance of that production, the soprano caused a scandal when she canceled her appearance moments before the second act (in which Turandot makes her first singing appearance) was to begin.
10. Caballé is notorious for her many "sudden" indispositions. A British writer for *Opera* magazine once quipped that "Mme. Caballé has gone into semiretirement, and thus will be available for only a few cancelations each season."
11. Caballé has canceled appearances in the Metropolitan's opening nights of *Don Carlo* in 1971 and of *I Vespri Siciliani* in 1975.
12. Caballé's two Rossini heroines on disc include *Elisabetta Regina d'Inghilterra* and Mathilde in *William Tell. Elisabetta* is on the Philips label. *Tell* is an EMI/Angel release.

29. MARIA CALLAS

1. Ponchielli's *La Gioconda* at the Verona Arena in 1947.
2. Renata Tebaldi.
3. Title role in *Madama Butterfly* in Chicago in 1955.
4. Toy.
5. Bellini's *I Puritani* with Giuseppe di Stefano, Rolando Panerai, and

Nicola Rossi-Lemeni, conducted by Tullio Serafin; Donizetti's *Lucia di Lammermoor* with Giuseppe di Stefano and Tito Gobbi, conducted by Serafin; Puccini's *Tosca,* with di Stefano and Gobbi, conducted by Victor de Sabata.

6. Norma, Lucia, Tosca, and Violetta (*La Traviata*).
7. Callas and Bjoerling appeared together in a Chicago production of *Il Trovatore.*
8. Paolina in Donizetti's *Poliuto,* with tenor Franco Corelli and baritone Ettore Bastianini.
9. Cherubini's *Médée;* Donizetti's *Anna Bolena* and *Poliuto;* Bellini's *Il Pirata* and *I Puritani;* Gluck's *Alceste;* Giordano's *Fedora;* Spontini's *La Vestale;* and Verdi's *Macbeth.*
10. Verdi's *Macbeth.* Callas was replaced by Leonie Rysanek.
11. Carmen, Mimì in *La Bohème,* and the title role in Puccini's *Manon Lescaut.*
12. Callas was replaced by Renata Scotto in the role of Amina in Bellini's *La Sonnambula.*
13. Both singers were appearing at a benefit concert at the Teatro Municipal in Rio de Janeiro. Supposedly, the two artists agreed not to give any encores, but Tebaldi received a prolonged ovation and therefore decided to sing an encore.
14. "It is like comparing champagne to cognac. No–with Coca-Cola."
15. Giovanni Battista Meneghini.
16. Rosina in *Il Barbiere di Siviglia* and Fiorilla in *Il Turco in Italia,* both by Rossini.
17. The title roles in *Fidelio* and *Madama Butterfly.* Callas did not want to sing *Fidelio* in English and feared she was too heavy to sing Cio-Cio-San onstage.
18. Giuseppe di Stefano.
19. Tokyo, Japan, in 1974.
20. *Norma,* in Paris, in July of 1965.
21. Tullio Serafin; Elvira de Hildago.
22. *Medea,* directed by Pier Paolo Pasolini. (This was a dramatic version, not the Cherubini opera.)
23. Isolde, Brünnhilde in *Die Walküre,* and Kundry in *Parsifal.* She sang them in Italian.
24. Impresario Sol Hurok, Callas's own concert manager, died suddenly on the afternoon of March 5, 1974, only a few hours before Callas and Giuseppe di Stefano were to appear at Carnegie Hall, marking the soprano's first New York appearance since 1965.
25. The title role in *Lucia di Lammermoor.* Baritone Enzo Sordello, sing-

ing the role of Enrico, offended Callas by holding the last note in their duet longer than Callas. She complained to the management, which promptly sacked Sordello.

30. ENRICO CARUSO

1. Ruggiero Leoncavallo, composer of *I Pagliacci,* penned "La Mattinata" especially for Caruso to record.
2. Caruso made his Met debut as the Duke of Mantua in Verdi's *Rigoletto* in 1903.
3. "Over There" by George M. Cohan in 1917.
4. "Vecchio zimarro" (the Cloak Aria) from Puccini's *La Bohème.*
5. Caruso was arrested in 1908 at the monkey house in New York's Central Park Zoo after a woman complained that he had pinched her. The case never came to trial, as the woman disappeared. Caruso's friends worried that the adverse publicity would hurt the tenor's American career, but the opposite was true, and Caruso was given a warm reception at the Metropolitan when he sang his first performance after the incident.
6. The opera was *Tosca* and the role was Mario Cavaradossi.
7. Baritone Tito Ruffo and Caruso were not on good terms. Their recording of the duet "Si pel ciel marmoreo giuro!" from Verdi's *Otello* makes one wish that they had worked together more often.
8. The Duke of Mantua in *Rigoletto;* Riccardo in Verdi's *Un Ballo in Maschera;* Enzo in Ponchielli's *La Gioconda;* Ferrando in Donizetti's *La Favorita;* Chevalier des Grieux in both Massenet's *Manon,* and Puccini's *Manon Lescaut.*
9. Rosa Ponselle.
10. Caruso and Farrar were recording the love duet from the first act of Puccini's *Madama Butterfly.* Farrar's Butterfly replied to Caruso's Pinkerton, when the latter sang "Ti serro palpitando" (I hold you trembling) by singing "He had a highball" instead of "Si per la vita" (Yes, for life). The two phrases have the same number of syllables. Caruso giggled, rendering his next line unintelligible. The recording survives and exists in several Caruso/Farrar anthologies.

31. FRANCO CORELLI

1. Ancona, Italy. It is a small and picturesque city not far from Venice.
2. He studied with the late Giacomo Lauri-Volpi.
3. Corelli sang the role of Pierre in the La Scala premiere of Prokofiev's *War and Peace.*
4. Placido Domingo.
5. Corelli starred in a film of *Tosca.* His on-screen Tosca was Franca Duval, while Tosca's voice was that of Maria Caniglia.
6. *Tosca, Aida,* and *Turandot.*
7. *La Bohème, Tosca, Andrea Chénier, La Gioconda,* and *Adriana Lecouvreur.*
8. Corelli's lost *verismo* outing with Callas was Giordano's *Fedora.*
9. Corelli's wife Loretta sang under the name Loretta di Lelio. She can be heard on the Cetra recordings of *Aida,* in which she sings the Priestess, and *La Favorita* as Ines. She also sings the role of Tebaldo on the EMI/Seraphim *Don Carlo.*
10. Corelli's stunt was intended to silence a member of the audience who had booed him.
11. Corelli announced violent intentions against Alan Rich, critic for the old *New York Herald-Tribune* and *New York* magazine.
12. Corelli's atypical ventures into Handel include *Giulio Cesare* and *Hercule.*

32. GIUSEPPE DI STEFANO

1. Among the operas that di Stefano and Callas performed together were *Tosca, La Traviata, Rigoletto, Un Ballo in Maschera, I Puritani,* and *Lucia di Lammermoor.*
2. *La Bohème* and *Manon Lescaut.*
3. Di Stefano's involvement in Viennese operetta consisted of a production of Lehár's *Land of Smiles*, which he sang at the Vienna Volksoper, and then on a tour that included Canada and the United States in 1967–68. His role was that of the partially Westernized Prince Soo-Fong.

4. Di Stefano and Tebaldi, along with Cesare Siepi, began to record Boito's *Mefistofele* for Decca. The tenor had by that time developed severe vocal problems, and he left the project after recording the opera's first and second acts, and the epilogue. The recording was remade with Mario del Monaco singing Faust. The outtakes with di Stefano lay in Decca's vaults for more than a decade but were issued as "Highlights from *Mefistofele*" in 1972.
5. Di Stefano's nickname is "Pippo."
6. There was a record ad in that playbill, proclaiming Franco Corelli to be the greatest tenor in the world. Di Stefano was not amused.
7. Risë Stevens.
8. Renata Tebaldi sang both *Adriana Lecouvreur* and *Fedora* with him in Chicago. For the Cilea opera, they were joined by Giulietta Simionato and Tito Gobbi for what is certainly the most lavishly cast *Adriana Lecouvreur* in that work's history.
9. Five of the tenor's French roles were Don José in *Carmen,* the title role in *Faust,* des Grieux in Massenet's *Manon,* the title role in that composer's *Werther,* and the title role in Offenbach's *Les Contes d'Hoffmann.*
10. Di Stefano sang the tenor part in Verdi's *Requiem.* His colleagues included soprano Herva Nelli, mezzo Fedora Barbiere, and bass Cesare Siepi.
11. His final appearance at the Met was in 1965, singing Offenbach's Hoffmann.
12. The *Otello* was performed in San Jose, California, in 1965. Marcella Pobbe was Desdemona, and Tito Gobbi sang Iago.

33. PLACIDO DOMINGO

1. Domingo sang several seasons at the Tel Aviv Opera. He sang many roles in Hebrew.
2. Domingo, changing his natural timbre to that of a baritone, sang Rodrigo "to himself" as Carlo.
3. In 1961 Domingo appeared with the Fort Worth (Texas) Opera in Donizetti's *Lucia di Lammermoor.* The Lucia that night was Lily Pons.
4. Domingo scored his first really important success singing the title role in Ginestera's *Don Rodrigo* at the New York City Opera in 1966.

5. Domingo was offered his La Scala contract for the role of Ernani in Verdi's opera at the suggestion of Richard Tucker, who was unable to accept that engagement.
6. Domingo has occasionally conducted performances at the City Opera and the Vienna State Opera.
7. Lohengrin, and Walther in *Die Meistersinger von Nürnberg.*
8. Domingo appeared as one of Doolittle's barroom companions in the Mexican production of *My Fair Lady.* He can be heard singing "With a Little Bit of Luck" (in Spanish) on the original cast album of that production.
9. Domingo first sang *Otello* at the Hamburg Opera in September 1975. James Levine conducted, and the cast included Katia Ricciarelli as Desdemona and Sherrill Milnes as Iago.
10. At the first New York City Opera performance of Donizetti's *Roberto Devereux,* soprano Beverly Sills, as Queen Elizabeth I, got so carried away that the slap she dealt Domingo, who sang Devereux, loosened some dental work. (This was an accident and neither suggested nor caused hard feelings between the two artists.)

34. TITO GOBBI

1. Gobbi's home base in Italian opera has always been the Rome Opera.
2. Gobbi's Wagnerian roles included the Herald in *Lohengrin,* and the roles of the Watchman and Pogner in *Die Meistersinger von Nürnberg.*
3. Gobbi's brother-in-law is Bulgarian bass Boris Christoff, who is married to Gobbi's wife's sister. The two men are renowned for their recorded work in Verdi's *Simon Boccanegra* and *Don Carlo.* In *Don Carlo,* Gobbi and Christoff performed the roles of Rodrigo and King Philip II, respectively, while in *Boccanegra* Gobbi sang the title role while Christoff sang Fiesco.
4. Gobbi's performance of the title role in Berg's *Wozzeck* in a guest engagement at La Scala was a success with the critics, but it did not endear Gobbi to that theater's backstage circles.
5. Gobbi sang Scarpia opposite Renata Tebaldi at the Metropolitan Opera in New York in 1964 and opposite Maria Callas at Covent Garden in London and at the Met in 1965.
6. Gobbi was one of Tullio Serafin's protégés, a select group of singers

that included, among others, Rosa Ponselle, Maria Callas, Renata Tebaldi, and Joan Sutherland.

7. Gobbi's first credit as a stage director was Verdi's *Simon Boccanegra.* Curiously, although the Royal Opera House Covent Garden was the first company to invite Gobbi to stage an opera, the baritone received Chicago's invitation shortly thereafter, and the American production predated the British engagement by several months.
8. Gobbi appeared in film versions of *Il Barbiere di Siviglia, Rigoletto,* and *I Pagliacci.* The *I Pagliacci* film is notable in that Gobbi played both baritone roles, Tonio and Silvio. The on-screen Nedda (her voice was dubbed) was the future star Gina Lollobrigida.
9. Gobbi first studied with tenor Giulio Crimi.
10. Maria Callas and Gobbi appeared in *Tosca* together only a dozen times. Their mutual success, coupled with the two recordings they made together of this opera, has made it seem as if they performed *Tosca* together many times.
11. Gobbi is a highly regarded painter.
12. These three Puccini roles were recorded with Renata Scotto (*La Bohème*), Victoria de los Angeles (*Madama Butterfly*), and Margaret Mas (*Il Tabarro*).

35. LUCIANO PAVAROTTI

1. He was born on October 26, 1934, in Modena, Italy.
2. Soprano Mirella Freni.
3. Rodolfo in *La Bohème.*
4. Joan Sutherland
5. He taught physical education in a boys' school.
6. Bellini's *Beatrice di Tenda* for Decca/London.
7. Tonio in Donizetti's *La Fille du Régiment,* which he sang in February 1972. Tonio's aria, "Pour mon âme," with its nine high C's, electrified the audience when Pavarotti sang it, and his career rocketed after that.
8. Renata Scotto.
9. Manrico in *Il Trovatore* at the San Francisco Opera (September 1975) with Joan Sutherland, Elena Obraztsova, and Ingvar Wixell, and Mario in *Tosca* in Chicago (Fall 1977) with Carol Neblett.
10. The American Express Card.

36. LEONTYNE PRICE

1. Laurel, Mississippi.
2. February 10, 1927.
3. Tosca, Mme. Lidoine in Poulenc's *Les Dialogues des Carmélites,* and Donna Anna in Mozart's *Don Giovanni.*
4. In San Francisco, as Tosca.
5. Leonora in *Il Trovatore,* Liù in *Turandot,* and Cio-Cio-San in *Madama Butterfly.*
6. Bess in Gershwin's *Porgy and Bess* in 1952.
7. Price sang at Lyndon B. Johnson's inauguration in 1965.
8. Lulu Shoemaker.
9. Baritone William Warfield.
10. Puccini's *La Fanciulla del West* (1961) singing Minnie, with Richard Tucker and Anselmo Colzani; Barber's *Antony and Cleopatra* (1966–opening night of the new Met at Lincoln Center) singing Cleopatra, with Justino Diaz and Jess Thomas; the title role in Verdi's *Aida* (1969) with Tucker, Irene Dalis, and Robert Merrill.
11. Leonora in Verdi's *Il Trovatore.*
12. The title role in Richard Strauss's *Ariadne auf Naxos* in San Francisco in 1977.
13. Herbert von Karajan.
14. Amelia in Verdi's *Un Ballo in Maschera.*
15. In 1963 Price sang the title role in Verdi's *Aida* with the La Scala company in Moscow.

37. RENATA SCOTTO

1. Scotto made her debut at La Scala in 1955, singing the "trouser" role of Gualtiero in Catalani's *La Wally.* The title role was sung by Renata Tebaldi.
2. When Cherubini's *Médée* was performed at La Scala in 1957, Scotto sang the ill-fated Glauce, and Callas sang the title role.
3. Some of Scotto's *verismo* roles include La Gioconda, Tosca, Giorgetta (in Puccini's *Il Tabarro*), Manon Lescaut, and Adriana Lecouvreur.

The strenuous role of Butterfly has long been in Scotto's repertoire, and many consider it to be Scotto's best role.

4. Scotto is married to Lorenzo Anselmi. Anselmi was formerly the concertmaster of the La Scala orchestra, but now he handles the management of his wife's career.
5. Scotto's colleagues on that *Lucia* set were Giuseppe di Stefano (Edgardo) and Ettore Bastianini (Ashton).
6. Scotto's colleagues in the Opera Orchestra of New York's *I Lombardi* were José Carreras as Oronte and Paul Plishka as Pagano. Eve Queler conducted.
7. Domingo and Scotto have recorded *Il Tabarro, Madama Butterfly, Cavalleria Rusticana,* and *Andrea Chénier.*
8. The opera was *Il Trovatore.* Scotto sang Leonora, while Shirley Verrett sang Azucena, Luciano Pavarotti sang Manrico, and Matteo Manuguerra sang di Luna. The conductor, making his Metropolitan debut, was Gianandrea Gavazzeni.
9. Renata Scotto's first Norma was sung in Cincinnati, Ohio, in May of 1977.
10. Two of Scotto's French roles include Marguerite in Gounod's *Faust* and Berthe in Meyerbeer's *Le Prophète.*

38. BEVERLY SILLS

1. "Our Gal Sunday" was a radio serial that dealt with the ups and downs of a poor girl from an American mining town who married a rich fellow. Sills's role was that of an orphaned child.
2. Rosalinde in *Die Fledermaus,* 1955.
3. Peter B. Greenough, financier, former publisher of the *Cleveland Plain Dealer.*
4. Handel's *Giulio Cesare* at the New York City Opera, in 1966.
5. In Rossini's *The Siege of Corinth* Sills replaced Renata Scotto, who withdrew because she was pregnant.
6. *Roberto Devereux, Maria Stuarda,* and *Anna Bolena.* Sills sang Queen Elizabeth I in *Devereux,* and the title characters in the other two operas.
7. Norman Treigle.
8. She sang five roles: Pamira in *The Siege of Corinth;* Violetta in *La*

Traviata; the title role in *Lucia di Lammermoor;* the title role in *Thaïs;* and Norina in *Don Pasquale.*

9. Sills and Sutherland costarred in Johann Strauss's *Die Fledermaus* in San Diego, California, in September 1980. This was Sills's last staged operatic appearance before her official retirement in October 1980. Sutherland was heard as Rosalinde, while Sills sang the role of Adele.
10. Although Sills's debut at the Metropolitan Opera House took place in April 1975, when she sang Pamira in *The Siege of Corinth,* she sang one concert performance of Donna Anna in *Don Giovanni* with the Metropolitan Opera Company at Lewisohn Stadium in July 1966 (*before* her City Opera triumph as Cleopatra in *Giulio Cesare*).
11. Sills has always had a hard time with the critics in London.
12. Julius Rudel.

39. JOAN SUTHERLAND

1. Sutherland's London debut was as the First Lady in *The Magic Flute.*
2. Franco Zeffirelli created a new production of Donizetti's *Lucia di Lammermoor* for Sutherland in 1958 at the Royal Opera House Covent Garden.
3. The first time Rudolf Bing heard Sutherland sing, he was not sufficiently impressed to offer her a Metropolitan contract.
4. Marilyn Horne and Luciano Pavarotti. Horne was a young, unknown mezzo when Sutherland heard her and began requesting her as a colleague in operatic and concert appearances. Sutherland's helping hand culminated in Horne's 1970 Metropolitan Opera debut as Adalgisa to Sutherland's Norma in Bellini's opera. Pavarotti, also unknown, auditioned for Sutherland, who was casting her tour of Australia in 1965. Pavarotti, having proven himself to the diva, was eventually recommended by Sutherland to the Royal Opera and Decca Records. The rest of his story is well known!
5. La Stupenda.
6. Richard Bonynge.
7. Sutherland performed Desdemona in Verdi's *Otello,* Eva in *Die Meistersinger von Nürnberg,* Amelia in *Un Ballo in Maschera,* among other operas.

8. Her comedy hit was in the title role of Donizetti's *La Fille du Régiment,* in which she and Pavarotti starred in London and New York.
9. Birgit Nilsson.
10. Tullio Serafin.

40. RENATA TEBALDI

1. Riccardo Zandonai (composer of *Francesca da Rimini)* and Carmen Melis.
2. Tebaldi returned to La Scala singing the title role in Puccini's *Tosca.* Giuseppe di Stefano sang Cavaradossi that night, joined by Tito Gobbi as Scarpia.
3. The San Francisco Opera.
4. Mario del Monaco sang Radames to Tebaldi's San Francisco Aida in 1950. Five years later, del Monaco's Otello welcomed Tebaldi's Desdemona to the stage of the Metropolitan Opera.
5. Tebaldi's colleagues in that wonderful *Falstaff* included Tito Gobbi as Falstaff, Giulietta Simionato as Quickly, Anna Maria Canali as Meg Page, Anna Moffo as Nannetta, and Cornell MacNeil as Ford. Tullio Serafin conducted.
6. Tebaldi's favorite role has always been the title role in Cilea's *Adriana Lecouvreur.*
7. The other three sopranos on that unforgettable 1966 "Bell Telephone Hour" were Birgit Nilsson, Joan Sutherland, and Leontyne Price.
8. Eva in *Die Meistersinger von Nürnberg,* Elisabeth in *Tannhäuser,* and Elsa in *Lohengrin.* (Although there are no surviving recordings of her Eva, records of her Elsa and Elisabeth have been available for many years.)
9. Franco Corelli.
10. Tebaldi sang the title role in Ponchielli's *La Gioconda,* an opera that she had first sung at the Metropolitan in 1966. The opera was performed at the Teatro San Carlo in Naples.

41. DEBUTS AT THE MET

1. Tebaldi's Met debut was as Desdemona in Verdi's *Otello* in 1955. Her costars were Mario del Monaco and Leonard Warren, with whom she sang on many occasions in the years to come.

2. Price's Met debut, as Leonora in Verdi's *Il Trovatore* in 1961, capped a career that had taken her to the opera houses of San Francisco, Chicago, and Vienna.
3. Del Monaco's Met debut was a one-night stand as des Grieux in Puccini's *Manon Lescaut* in 1949. The following season, the Met's then new general manager, Rudolf Bing, engaged the tenor for many more roles, and del Monaco sang regularly at the Met until he left in a huff in 1961, claiming that Franco Corelli had been given the new production of *Turandot* that Bing had promised to del Monaco.
4. Bumbry's Met debut, as Eboli in Verdi's *Don Carlo* in 1965, was the first of many occasions on which the St. Louis-born mezzo would sing the Verdi mezzo roles of Eboli, Amneris, and Azucena until, in the 1970s, she became a soprano.
5. Gobbi's debut on January 13, 1956, was a great success with the public. The role was Baron Scarpia, Puccini's most vicious villain (in *Tosca,* of course). Unfortunately for the New York public, Gobbi and the Met's Bing never really felt comfortable with one another, and the baritone's Metropolitan engagements were sporadic. Also, although public and press were ecstatic about Gobbi's performance, the baritone relates in his memoirs that Bing was furious that Gobbi changed a bit of the Met's staging. Today, incidentally, Gobbi is the stage director of the Met's current *Tosca.*
6. Marian Anderson made her Met debut as Ulrica in Verdi's *Un Ballo in Maschera* on January 7, 1955.
7. Merrill's debut in 1945, as Giorgio Germont in Verdi's *La Traviata,* found the inexperienced and–to judge from his memoirs–nervous baritone paired with Licia Albanese. Throughout Merrill's thirty-year Met career, he frequently forgot some of Germont's words!
8. Caballé's Met debut, a one-night stand at the old Met during its final season in 1965, was in the role of Marguerite in Gounod's *Faust.* She was not in spectacular voice that night, and the occasion is best remembered by many for the debut of another artist (see Question 22) and for the conductor's (Georges Prêtre) being jostled by a latecomer in the first row!
9. Siepi's first night at the Met was as King Philip II in Verdi's *Don Carlo* in 1950. Several other artists made debuts that night, as did General Manager Rudolf Bing. Siepi was a replacement for the Bulgarian bass Boris Christoff, who had visa problems.
10. Although a star in Europe since the 1940s, Giulietta Simionato made her Metropolitan debut in 1959, singing Azucena in Verdi's *Il Trovatore* on opening night, sharing the stage with Antonietta Stella, Carlo Bergonzi, and Leonard Warren.

11. Flagstad's debut, as Sieglinde in Wagner's *Die Walküre* on a broadcast matinee in 1935, was an unheralded triumph. Toscanini, long feuding with the Met, listened to her voice and telephoned the Met, demanding to be told everything there was to know about Flagstad!
12. Ponselle's Met debut in 1918 was opposite Enrico Caruso in the Met premiere of Verdi's *La Forza del Destino,* singing the role of Leonora di Vargas. Ponselle, a lifelong victim of before-the-performance nervousness, swore to friends that she nearly fainted when the curtain rose on the first act.
13. Birgit Nilsson's Metropolitan debut, as Wagner's Isolde in 1959, was reviewed on the front page of *The New York Times.* What else is there to say?
14. MacNeil flew to New York from an engagement in Milan to substitute for an ailing Robert Merrill, making his debut on the broadcast of Verdi's *Rigoletto,* singing the title role on less than a day's notice, with no rehearsal, in March 1959. MacNeil has been a fixture at the Metropolitan ever since!
15. Joan Sutherland made her Met debut in the title role of Donizetti's *Lucia di Lammermoor* at a special performance on a Sunday in November of 1961. Three years earlier, Bing had declined to offer Sutherland a contract when she, still relatively unknown, had auditioned for him.
16. Callas's Met debut, in the title role of Bellini's *Norma* in 1956, was, curiously, anticlimactic. By all accounts, including her own, she was not in best form that night. Moreover, the public was wary of her due to a hostile article that appeared in *Time* magazine the week of her debut. The audience reaction was cordial, but Callas's subsequent difficulties with Bing and the men in her life conspired to make her visits to New York all too few.
17. Franco Corelli made his Metropolitan debut as Manrico, sharing the evening with Leontyne Price in that unforgettable 1961 *Il Trovatore.* Corelli and Price sang memorable performances of Verdi's *La Forza del Destino* and *Ernani* together at the Metropolitan.
18. Marcella Sembrich, a singer of an older, legendary era, made her Met debut on the third night of the very first Met season, 1883–84, in the title role of Donizetti's *Lucia di Lammermoor.* The incredibly versatile Polish soprano sang at the Met through the first decade of the twentieth century.
19. Sills made her Met debut as Pamira in Rossini's *The Siege of Corinth* in 1975, only five years before her retirement. Technically, Sills's Met debut occurred nine years earlier, when the soprano sang the role of Donna Anna in *Don Giovanni* with the Met in a summer concert at Manhattan's Lewisohn Stadium. The diva insists in her memoirs that

a debut at the Met means singing within the four walls of the opera house. Sills's first appearance *inside* the Met attracted international attention, and she received an ovation of several minutes' duration when she stepped onto the stage for the first time. Her debut was an emotional occasion for the girl from Brooklyn and thousands of her fans.

20. Verrett's Met debut, singing the title role in Bizet's *Carmen,* took place in 1968. Reports of a fracas with her tenor, Jon Vickers, at the dress rehearsal had the fans on edge, but the performance went smoothly, and Verrett and Vickers remain good friends.
21. Domingo's 1968 Met debut was as Maurizio to the Adriana Lecouvreur of Renata Tebaldi. Domingo was signed to sing that role a week later, but Franco Corelli's sudden indisposition led to Domingo's first Met appearance being made on roughly an hour's notice. Several months later, Domingo replaced Corelli in the title role of a new production of *Il Trovatore,* when Corelli returned to Italy to be near his critically ill father. Several years later, Corelli returned Domingo's "favor" by replacing him, on equally short notice, in two Met performances of Verdi's *Ernani.*
22. Milnes's Met debut, as Valentin in Gounod's *Faust* in 1965, was shared with that of Caballé. Milnes, by no means well known even though he though he had been singing at the New York City Opera, stopped the show with "Avant de quitter ces lieux" and his powerful rendering of Valentin's death scene.
23. Renata Scotto made her first Met appearance in the title role of Puccini's *Madama Butterfly* in 1965. Although she triumphed with the audience and the press, Scotto never saw eye to eye with either Bing or his successor, Schuyler Chapin. Only after James Levine took artistic control of the Met did she become a reigning soprano there.
24. Mirella Freni made her Met debut only one night before Scotto, as Mimi in a 1965 *La Bohème.* Like Scotto, Freni captivated the public, but after her first few seasons, she sang very rarely with the Met. Although invited back many times, she has not sung there at all since 1970. (She did, however, sing at the Met with the visiting Paris Opéra in 1976 and is scheduled to return to the Met in 1983 as Elisabeth in *Don Carlo.*)
25. Pavarotti made his Met debut as Rodolfo in Puccini's *La Bohème* during a flu epidemic in 1968. He himself canceled several appearances that year due to the flu, and he sang at the Met only sporadically until his great triumph with Joan Sutherland in *La Fille du Régiment* in 1972.

42. FAMOUS FIRSTS

1. Giuseppina Strepponi, who would eventually become Verdi's wife, sang Abigaille at the world premiere of *Nabucco* at La Scala in 1842.
2. Ericlea Darclee created the title role in *Tosca* at the Rome Opera in 1900.
3. Francesco Tamagno sang *Otello*'s world premiere at La Scala in 1887.
4. The first Ariadne was sung by Maria Jeritza in Dresden in 1913.
5. Anne Trulove was first sung by Elisabeth Schwarzkopf when *The Rake's Progress* had its world premiere in Venice in 1951.
6. Elisabeth Schumann created Sophie when *Der Rosenkavalier* was given its first performance in Dresden in 1910.
7. Enrico Caruso was the world's first Dick Johnson when *La Fanciulla del West* had its world premiere at the Metropolitan Opera in 1910.
8. Leontyne Price sang Cleopatra when the work was premiered on the first opening night at the new Metropolitan Opera in 1966.
9. Francesco Tamagno created the role of Canio when *I Pagliacci* was first performed in Milan in 1892.
10. The great French baritone Victor Maurel sang Falstaff when Verdi's final opera had its inaugural performance at La Scala in 1893.
11. Mary Garden sang Mélisande when *Pelléas et Mélisande* was first performed at the Paris Opéra.
12. Gemma Bellincioni created the role of Santuzza when Mascagni's first and most successful opera premiered in 1890 at the Rome Opera.
13. Peter Pears sang the title role when *Peter Grimes* had its world premiere at London's Covent Garden in 1945.
14. Gianna Pederzini sang the Old Prioress when *Les Dialogues des Carmélites* had its first production (in Italian, surprisingly) at La Scala in 1955.
15. Claudio Muzio, deeply attached to the Jesuit priest Refice, who had composed *Cecilia,* sang in the opera's first performance in Rome in 1934.
16. Cio-Cio-San, or Madama Butterfly, was first sung by Rosina Storchio when Puccini's opera had its disastrous premiere at La Scala in 1904.
17. La Scala wasn't favored with another Puccini premiere after *Madama Butterfly* until the posthumous first performance of the composer's final opera, *Turandot,* in 1926. Rosa Raisa sang the title role.
18. Giulia Grisi was the first Norma. Bellini's opera was given its world premiere in 1831 at La Scala.

19. Beverly Sills created the role of Juana La Loca at the San Diego Opera in 1979.
20. The world premiere of the completed three-act version of Berg's *Lulu,* performed at the Paris Opéra in 1980, was graced by Teresa Stratas in the title role.

43. THE YOUNGER GENERATION

1. Katia Ricciarelli
2. Agnes Baltsa
3. Hildegard Behrens
4. Neil Shicoff
5. José Carreras
6. James Morris
7. Gilda Cruz-Romo
8. Leona Mitchell
9. Pablo Elvira
10. Tatiana Troyanos
11. Frederica von Stade
12. Richard Stilwell

44. OPERA STARS ON BROADWAY

1. Weede appeared in three Broadway musicals: *The Most Happy Fella, Milk and Honey,* and *Cry for Us All.*
2. Siepi starred in two ill-fated shows: *Bravo, Giovanni* and *Carmelina.*
3. Rounseville appeared in *Candide* and later in *Man of La Mancha.*
4. Stevens played Anna in *The King and I* at the Music Theatre of Lincoln Center.
5. Tozzi portrayed Emile in the 1967 Music Theatre of Lincoln Center's revival of *South Pacific.* More recently, he starred in the revival of *The Most Happy Fella* at the Michigan Opera Theatre, a production that was brought to Broadway and broadcast on PBS.
6. Steber sang in City Center revivals of *The Sound of Music* and *Where's Charley?*
7. Warfield's Broadway appearances include *Porgy and Bess* and *Show Boat.*
8. Irra Petina appeared with Robert Rounseville in *Candide.* She also appeared in *Song of Norway, Magdalena,* and *Anya.*

9. Chapman, a leading bass at the City Opera, has starred in the Broadway productions of *Shenandoah* and *Greenwillow.*
10. Benzell was Robert Weede's costar in *Milk and Honey.*
11. Traubel starred in Rodgers and Hammerstein's *Pipe Dream.*
12. Pinza's other Broadway show was *Fanny.*
13. Price met her one-time husband, William Warfield, when she sang Bess to his Porgy on Broadway in 1954.
14. Peerce sang Tevye in *Fiddler on the Roof.*
15. Wilson, a former Met Lucia and Norina, has appeared in several Broadway shows, including *The Yearling, Fiddler on the Roof, I Remember Mama,* and *Annie.*

45. TINY FACTS ABOUT GREAT SINGERS

1. Callas and Sills each appeared as contestants on the Major Bowes program, the forerunner of the "Ted Mack Amateur Hour."
2. Tucker had a silk-lining business in Manhattan.
3. Cossotto is the wife of bass Ivo Vinco.
4. *Subway to the Met.*
5. Cappuccilli appeared in one Met *La Traviata* in 1960, replacing Leonard Warren, who had died a few weeks earlier.
6. Flagstad ran into trouble because of her husband's association with the hated pro-Nazi government in Norway. Flagstad spent the war years at home by her husband's side, and while she never sang for the Nazis, rumors to the contrary caused her much difficulty.
7. Carreras's debut came in 1972 when he sang Pinkerton in *Madama Butterfly* with the New York City Opera.
8. Christoff, by virtue of his Bulgarian passport, was not granted a visa to enter the United States, then in the throes of anticommunist hysteria.
9. Milnes sang the Marlboro jingle: "You get a lot to like with a Marlboro."
10. Sara Tucker is Peerce's sister.
11. Domingo's first *Otello* was sung at the Hamburg Opera in September 1975. His colleagues included Katia Ricciarelli and Sherrill Milnes. James Levine conducted.
12. Samuel Barber is Homer's nephew.
13. Nilsson feuded with Herbert von Karajan, who tried to have her

removed from the cast of his proposed Metropolitan Opera *Ring* cycle.
14. Pons was once married to the late André Kostelanetz.
15. Moore's protégée was Dorothy Kirsten.

46. FAREWELLS AT THE MET

1. Alcestis, 1952.
2. Madeleine in *Andrea Chénier,* 1966.
3. Eleazar in *La Juive,* 1920.
4. Don Carlo in *La Forza del Destino.* (Warren died during the performance on March 4, 1960. His last complete role at the Met, sung three days earlier, was the title role in *Simon Boccanegra.*)
5. Tosca, 1965.
6. Official farewell: Tosca, 1975. (Her last appearance, however, was as Mimì in *La Bohème* in 1977.)
7. Canio in *I Pagliacci,* 1974.
8. Lucia di Lammermoor, 1960.
9. Desdemona in Verdi's *Otello,* 1973.
10. Carmen, 1962.
11. Rosalinde in *Die Fledermaus,* 1951.
12. Hoffmann in *Les Contes d'Hoffmann,* 1965.
13. Brünnhilde in *Die Walküre,* 1975.
14. Donna Elvira in *Don Giovanni,* 1966.
15. Gounod's Faust, 1960.
16. Norina in *Don Pasquale,* 1979.
17. Baron Scarpia in *Tosca,* 1975.
18. Zaza, 1920.
19. Don Ottavio in *Don Giovanni,* 1967.
20. Minnie in *La Fanciulla del West,* 1966.

UNFORGETTABLE CHARACTERS

47. TITLE ROLES

1. Octavian, Count Rofrano
2. Manrico
3. Fiora
4. Brünnhilde
5. Minnie
6. Philip Vanderdecker
7. Sándor Barinkay
8. Hanna Glawari
9. Mařenka
10. Amina
11. Magda
12. Figaro
13. Leonora de Guzman
14. Canio, Nedda, Tonio, and Beppe
15. Dr. Falke

48. NOBLESSE OBLIGE

1. King Philip II, in Verdi's *Don Carlo,* makes trouble for his son Carlo almost as soon as the opera begins. By marrying Elisabetta de Valois, Don Carlo's own betrothed, he causes both his son and his wife great anguish. When Carlo angers the king by drawing his sword against

Philip in public, while defending the suffering Protestants of Flanders, Philip orders Carlo's arrest. The local Grand Inquisitor convinces Philip that instead of executing Carlo, the noble (and liberal) Rodrigo, Marquis of Posa, should die for his heretical views; Philip agrees to Rodrigo's murder. Ultimately, Philip, who still suspects that Carlo and Elisabetta are lovers, stalks the two to the Cloister of St. Just, where he has them arrested for treason.

2. Cleopatra, in Handel's *Giulio Cesare,* provides the love interest for the Roman invader of Egypt. Cleopatra beguiles Caesar with her beauty, charm, and coloratura, and thus Caesar remains in Egypt, fighting Cleopatra's battles against her rivals for the Egyptian throne.
3. Good Queen Bess is painted as anything but kindly in Donizetti's *Roberto Devereux* and *Maria Stuarda.* In the first work, Elizabeth allows Devereux, whom she loves, to be executed for alleged treason, although she is more annoyed at his infidelity to her than by the possibility that poor Robert would like to have her deposed. In *Maria Stuarda,* Elizabeth has her unlucky cousin, Mary of Scotland, imprisoned at Fotheringay because Elizabeth fears that Mary schemes against her. When Elizabeth is brought to meet Mary (an operatic liberty with history–the two women never met face to face), Elizabeth goads Mary so cruelly that Mary insults her back ("Vil bastarda!") and gives Liz the excuse to have Mary beheaded.
4. Charles V, in Verdi's *Ernani,* is just plain Don Carlo for the first three of *Ernani*'s four acts. In those early scenes, he pursues Elvira, who loves the dashing bandit Ernani but is betrothed to her elderly guardian Silva. Carlo abducts Elvira, and Ernani enlists Silva's aid in freeing her, pledging his own life to Silva's command. Carlo, when crowned Holy Roman Emperor, modestly bestows Elvira on the man she loves, but Silva has other ideas that spoil the wedding–but that's another story.

   In Verdi's *Don Carlo,* Charles V is supposedly dead and buried when the action begins, but his ghost, in the guise of a friar, haunts the Cloister of St. Just. The ghost, who according to some writers is not a ghost at all but merely the retired Charles, very much alive if incognito, rescues Carlo from the Inquisition at the end of the opera, leading him into the shadowy cloister.
5. Henry the Fowler is the king in Wagner's *Lohengrin,* who is led by the evil Telramund (and the latter's witchy spouse Ortrud) to think that Elsa, his ward, has murdered her brother, the heir to the throne. Actually, Ortrud has turned the lad into a swan–an industrious fowl who lands a temporary job as Lohengrin's chauffeur. Henry is an ineffectual type who seems given more to oratory than action. Henry

does, however, arrange the trial by ordeal that brings Lohengrin to Brabant to act as Elsa's defender.

6. Gustavus III is the hero of the original libretto of Verdi's *Un Ballo in Maschera.* Local censors, worried about the effect of the plot in strife-torn Italy, refused to allow an opera dealing with the assassination of a European monarch, so the original Swedish locale was changed to the rather incongruous Boston of the Puritan era. Nowadays, many opera houses set *Un Ballo in Maschera* in Sweden, where the tale of Gustavus, the liberal, charming monarch who carries on a platonic but unwise affair with Amelia, the wife of his best friend Count Anckarström, unfolds. When Anckarström realizes that his wife is the king's beloved, the once loyal courtier joins the anti-Gustavus conspiracy and assassinates the king, who pardons all his foes as he dies.
7. Dmitri is the son of Ivan the Terrible, whom regent Boris Godunov has had murdered even before Mussorgsky's *Boris Godunov* begins. The tenor lead in *Boris*, however, is the monk Grigori, who masquerades as Dmitri in order to lead a revolt against Czar Boris. Dmitri, aided by Poland, wins, and Boris dies of a guilty conscience. The Pretender's triumph is limited, however, as history records that he was executed by still another group of insurgents three days after taking the throne.
8. Jane (Giovanna) Seymour is crowned King Henry VIII's third queen offstage, during the final scene of Donizetti's *Anna Bolena.* In the action of the opera, Seymour is portrayed as a sweet girl who, against her will, is wooed by the king and who, through no design of her own, is one of the reasons for Anne Boleyn's downfall and execution.
9. Emperor Altoum is the fa‹her of Puccini's Princess Turandot. Although the old man reigns in theory, his man-hating daughter rules the roost. All Altoum does is dodder ineffectively, first pleading with Calaf to leave before he loses his head, and then, when Calaf has won the Riddle contest, Altoum reminds his welching daughter that her vow was, after all, sacred. In the end, love wins out, and Altoum lives to see Turandot and Calaf betrothed, while his subjects wish him a reign of ten thousand years.

49. THEIR MASTERS' VOICES

1. Violetta's faithful maid in Verdi's *La Traviata* is Annina.
2. Falstaff is served by those two oafs Bardolph and Pistol, both in Verdi's *Falstaff* and Nicolai's *The Merry Wives of Windsor.*

3. In the first scene of Verdi's *La Forza del Destino,* Leonora is tended to by Curra.
4. In Verdi's opera, Amneris is the not-so-satisfied owner of the slave Aida.
5. Selim owns the villainous Osmin in Mozart's *Abduction from the Seraglio.*
6. Bartolo's servant in the Rossini opera is the sneezing Berta.
7. Médée's confidante is Neris in Cherubini's opera.
8. In Donizetti's *La Fille du Régiment,* Hortentius looks after the Marquise's varied needs.
9. In Offenbach's *Les Contes d'Hoffmann,* Crespel, unhappy father of the doomed Antonia, is served by the deaf and crotchety Frantz.
10. Timur, the old king and Calaf's father in Puccini's *Turandot,* is aided by the slave Liù.
11. Verdi allowed Rigoletto to employ Giovanna as housekeeper and duenna to his daughter Gilda.
12. In *Die Fledermaus,* Rosalinde has a chambermaid named Adele, who is not above sneaking out on false pretenses or swiping one of her employer's dresses in order to attend a fancy dress ball.
13. Dorabella, in Mozart's *Così Fan Tutte,* shares the spunky maid Despina with her sister Fiordiligi.
14. Sarastro, in Mozart's *The Magic Flute,* owns the evil slave Monostatos.
15. In Giordano's *Andrea Chénier,* Madeleine is guided through the turmoil of the Reign of Terror by Bersi, her mulatto maid, who even becomes a prostitute in order to support her timid mistress.
16. In Beethoven's *Fidelio,* Rocco is aided by his turnkey Jaquino, who loves Rocco's daughter, Marzelline, and the supposed youth "Fidelio," who is actually Leonore disguised as a boy in order to attempt to free her husband, Florestan, unjustly imprisoned in the jail that Rocco tends.
17. Donizetti's Mary, Queen of Scots, is aided by her lady-in-waiting Anna Kennedy.
18. Alice Ford, in Verdi's *Falstaff,* has four young men to help around her Tudor house–Ned, Will, Tom, and Isaac–who together find it heavy going as they toss the laundry basket (into which Falstaff has been placed) into the Thames.
19. In Tchaikovsky's *Eugene Onegin,* Madame Larina, the heroine's mother, is the owner of many serfs, among them the elderly nurse Filippyevna.
20. In Puccini's *Tosca,* Baron Scarpia has two leering henchmen, Spoletta and Sciarrone, to do his dirty work for him.

21. In Puccini's *La Fanciulla del West,* Minnie has an Indian couple, the unmarried Billy Jackrabbit and Wowkle as house servants. Nick tends the bar at Minnie's saloon, the Polka.
22. Elisabetta, in Verdi's *Don Carlo,* has the young page Tebaldo and the Countess of Aremberg, her lady-in-waiting. Unfortunately, Elisabetta's cruel husband, King Philip II of Spain, dismisses the countess, who allowed Elisabetta to have a private meeting with her stepson, Carlo.
23. Desdemona, in the *Otello* of both Verdi and Rossini, has Emilia, Iago's wife, as her maid of all work.
24. Juliette, in Gounod's *Roméo et Juliette,* is attended by her nurse, Gertrude.

50. SERVANTS, SLAVES, AND COMPANIONS

1. Annina is Violetta's maid in Verdi's *La Traviata.* She doesn't have too much to do beyond faithfully serving Violetta until the heroine's death, but her one action that has bearing on the plot is to take Violetta's reply to Flora's invitation, presumably to deliver it to Violetta's friend.
2. Mariandl is not really a servant at all, but merely the disguise put on by Octavian, in Richard Strauss's *Der Rosenkavalier,* first to avoid embarrassing the Marschallin when her cousin, Baron Ochs, comes to call, and later–as part of the plot to embarrass Ochs–Octavian (as "Mariandl") pretends to want a rendezvous with Ochs in a rustic inn.
3. Robin is the page in Verdi's *Falstaff* who delivers Sir John's love notes to Mistress Alice and Mistress Meg, when Falstaff's own servants, Bardolph and Pistol, refuse to do so.
4. Aida, in Verdi's opera, offends her mistress, the princess Amneris, by falling in love with Radames, whom Amneris loves. Since Radames loves Aida instead of Amneris, that character's jealousy leads to Radames's death, Aida's suicide, and Amneris's own bitter unhappiness.
5. Brangäne is Isolde's servant in Wagner's *Tristan und Isolde.* Although she means well, her substitution of a love potion for the death draft Isolde has commanded her to prepare for Tristan and herself leads to the ultimate destruction of the lovers.

6. Adele is Rosalinde's chambermaid in Johann Strauss's *Die Fledermaus.* More interested in good times than in washing the windows, Adele sneaks off to the same ball that her mistress and master attend, and she, wearing one of Rosalinde's own gowns, captures the fancy of Eisenstein, Warden Franke, and Prince Orlofsky.
7. Suzuki is Cio-Cio-San's faithful companion in Puccini's *Madama Butterfly.* Cynical and wiser than her mistress, Suzuki foresees disaster but is powerless to prevent it from occurring.
8. Bersi is Madeleine's servant in Giordano's *Andrea Chénier.* Although the upheaval of the French Revolution leads Bersi into a life of prostitution, she is loyal to her noble mistress and uses her earnings to support Madeleine. She also sets up the fatal assignation for Chénier and Madeleine.
9. Carlo Gérard is a colleague of Bersi's in the Coigny household in *Andrea Chénier.* First, he leads the house servants in a job action that disrupts a soiree, resulting in his discharge. Later, Gérard becomes a leader of the Revolution, abusing his power to try to press his attentions on Madeleine, whom he has always loved. Too late, he repents and attempts, unsuccessfully, to free Chénier, whom Gérard's false testimony has sent to the guillotine.
10. Curra in *La Forza del Destino* is Leonora's maid, and her only function is to help the hesitating girl to pack for her planned elopement with Alvaro.
11. Despina serves the sisters Fiordiligi and Dorabella in Mozart's *Così Fan Tutte.* The scheming Don Alfonso enlists Despina's aid in introducing the girls' disguised sweethearts into the household. Despina later impersonates both a doctor and a notary.
12. Frantz is Councilor Crespel's deaf servant in Act III of Offenbach's *Les Contes d'Hoffmann.* Not understanding Crespel's order to let no one in the house, Frantz promptly admits Hoffmann, who is in love with Crespel's daughter, Antonia.
13. David is Hans Sachs's apprentice in Wagner's *Die Meistersinger von Nürnberg.* Besides providing a love interest for Eva's companion Magdalene, thereby becoming the fifth voice in the great quintet, David's jealous attack on Beckmesser, whom he wrongly believes is serenading Magdalene, precipitates the brawl that concludes the second act of this great comedy.
14. Monostatos is Sarastro's slave in Mozart's *The Magic Flute.* His lust for Pamina earns him a thrashing, and his aiding the evil Queen of the Night in her attempt to kidnap her own daughter (Pamina) leads to his destruction, along with the queen and her three ladies-in-waiting.
15. Antonio is the gardener employed by Count Almaviva in Mozart's *Le*

Nozze di Figaro. His drunken interruption all but foils the plans of Figaro, Susanna, and the Countess Almaviva.

51. HOLY MEN AND WOMEN

1. Zaccaria is the high priest of the Hebrews held captive by Nabucco and Abigaille in Verdi's *Nabucco.* Abigaille is a slave secretly adopted by Nabucco. Zaccaria holds Fenena–Nabucco's second and natural daughter–hostage, hoping to have the Hebrews freed, but Fenena falls in love with the Hebrew Ismaele, and embraces Judaism. Nabucco frees the Hebrews and then converts also.
2. Varlaam is one of the pair of mendicant monks who arrive with the runaway Grigori at the inn at the Lithuanian border in Mussorgsky's *Boris Godunov.* Varlaam is the more jocular of the two and sings the familiar drinking song in that scene. When soldiers arrive searching for Grigori, the latter reads the warrant (the soldiers are illiterate) and changes the description to fit Varlaam. Varlaam, realizing that there is trouble in store for him, painfully attempts to read the document himself ("When it comes to hanging, I can read!") and realizes that the wanted man is his new traveling companion. Grigori escapes, and Varlaam and his partner Missail turn up again during the opera's Kromy Forest scene.
3. In Saint-Saëns's *Samson et Dalila,* the High Priest of Dagon orders the very willing Dalila to seduce Samson and learn the secret of his strength. She does so, and, in the final scene, the priest leads the worship that culminates in the miraculous destruction of the temple.
4. In Verdi's *Aida,* Ramfis is the High Priest of Phtha. His influence is great indeed: he consecrates Radames as commander of the Egyptian army; warns the king of Egypt to hold Aida and Amonasro as hostages when, as per Radames's request, the other Ethiopian captives are freed; sentences Radames to death following Radames's inadvertent treason; and defies Amneris's frantic plea that Radames be spared.
5. In Poulenc's *Dialogues des Carmélites,* de Croissy is the prioress who accepts Blanche as a novice in the Carmelite order. Her terrifying death scene is a dramatic high point of the opera, as this disciplined, strong woman curses God on her deathbed, lacking the strength to meet her end with the dignity that has otherwise characterized her life.
6. Cardinal Brogni is the villain in Halévy's *La Juive.* This elderly anti-

Semite persecutes Eleazar and his presumed daughter to death, only to learn that Rachel is actually his own, illegitimate daughter, whom Eleazar had adopted.

7. In *Nabucco* the High Priest of Baal conspires with Abigaille to wrest power from Abigaille's adoptive father (Nabucco), who has been made insane by a thunderbolt as punishment for announcing that he, Nabucco, is God. Nabucco, however, is returned to sanity when he decides to convert to the Hebrew faith, and although the libretto doesn't specifically describe the priest's eventual fate, one assumes that he will not have an easy time after the final curtain descends.
8. The Bonze is Butterfly's fanatical Buddhist uncle who, in the first act of Puccini's *Madama Butterfly,* breaks up her wedding reception to curse her for leaving her ancestral faith to become a Christian.
9. In Massenet's *Thaïs,* Athanaël is the masochistic, repressed monk who attempts to save the soul of the courtesan Thaïs, only to fall in love with her former image. Thaïs dies of exhaustion, and Athanaël must live with his sense of guilt.
10. In *Boris Godunov,* Rangoni is the Jesuit priest who urges the Polish princess Marina to seduce the Pretender Dmitri, paving the way for the ascension of Roman Catholicism in Russia. This does not work out too well.
11. In Gounod's *Roméo et Juliette,* as in Shakespeare, Frère Laurent is Roméo's friend who performs the marriage of the title characters, and later gives Juliette the potion that induces her presumed death. As in Shakespeare, Roméo learns only the bad news, not the truth, and thanks to the friar's well-intentioned meddling, both young lovers commit suicide.
12. In Meyerbeer's *Le Prophète,* John is the Dutch innkeeper whom those treacherous Anabaptist intriguers pass off as a holy prophet and then crown king. John becomes their corrupt tool, but months later, after his beloved Berthe kills herself as a result of John's cruelties, he succumbs to his own tortured conscience and incinerates himself, his mother (Fidès, the mezzo lead), and his enemies, all of whom are gathered in John's castle.

52. HI, MOM! HI, DAD!

1. Oroveso is the father of Norma in Bellini's opera. Although he condemns the errant priestess to death for her liaison with the Roman

Pollione, Norma prevails upon her father to spare her two children from the Druids' collective wrath.

2. Peter and Gertrude are the parents of Hansel and Gretel in Humperdinck's opera. The stern Gertrude sends them off to the woods to pick strawberries after Hansel spills a pitcher of milk. Peter, the kindly broommaker, warns Gertrude that the woods are haunted by a witch. The two set out to hunt for Hansel and Gretel and find them, none the worse for wear, at the opera's conclusion.
3. Archibaldo is the old blind king who strangles Fiora, his daughter-in-law and the title character, in Montemezzi's *L'Amore dei Tre Re.* Archibaldo kills Fiora because he suspects (correctly) that she is betraying her husband, Manfredo. To trap Fiora's lover, Archibaldo paints Fiora's dead lips with a poison. Sure enough, Avito sneaks into the chapel to kiss Fiora once more, and dies. Unfortunately for Archibaldo, his own son also kisses Fiora good-bye, leaving the old man childless.
4. La Cieca is the old, blind mother of La Gioconda in Ponchielli's opera. Cieca falls into the clutches of the evil spy Barnaba. Gioconda, who in no way returns Barnaba's love for her, agrees to "surrender herself," as they used to say in program synopses of the opera, to Barnaba in return for Cieca's freedom. Gioconda stabs herself as the villain approaches her. As she dies, Barnaba shouts that he had drowned Cieca anyway!
5. Mamma Lucia is Turiddu's mother in Mascagni's *Cavalleria Rusticana.* Her chief dramatic function is to listen unhappily as Santuzza tells her that Turiddu has betrayed her and gone back to Lola. Lucia runs the village tavern, thus providing the wine with which Turiddu toasts Lola. If Turiddu had not had so much to drink, he might have won the knife fight with Alfio, Lola's husband. As it is, Mamma Lucia is left by fate (and the librettist) to weep over Turiddu's death and to "be a mother to Santuzza."
6. In Mozart's *Le Nozze di Figaro* Marcellina spends the first two acts trying to trap Figaro into marrying her, and not Susanna. In Act III, however, it is revealed that Marcellina is Figaro's long-lost mother. From that point on, she becomes a staunch ally of Figaro and Susanna in their battle to keep Count Almaviva from exercising his *droit du seigneur.*
7. Antonio, also from *Le Nozze di Figaro,* is the count's gardener and father of Barbarina, the pretty lass who captures Cherubino's heart after his flirtations with Susanna and the countess. Antonio's big moment comes in the finale to the second act, when he spoils the fiction that Figaro and Susanna have concocted by bursting into the

room complaining that somebody (actually, Cherubino) has fallen into the garden, ruining some plants.

8. Rocco is Marzelline's father in Beethoven's *Fidelio.* As he is the jailer in the prison where Leonore's husband is being held, it is to Rocco's house that Leonore comes disguised as the youth Fidelio. Rocco's daughter promply falls in love with Fidelio, and Rocco encourages Leonore to pay court to Marzelline. He also allows Fidelio to help him dig the grave intended for Florestan, thus enabling Leonore to rescue Florestan.
9. Strominger is Wally's strange old father in Catalani's *La Wally.* When Wally refuses to marry Gellner as her father wishes, Strominger disowns her, forcing her to live in the Alps, and cueing the soprano for Wally's famous aria "Ebben, ne andrò lontano."
10. Erda, the earth goddess, appears in two of the *Ring* operas, *Das Rheingold* and *Siegfried.* She bears Wotan's nine Valkyry daughters and the three Norns who weave the fates in *Die Götterdämmerung,* thereby providing the cycle with its heroine, Brünnhilde, and the narrators who begin *Götterdämmerung* with a summary of the first three music dramas.
11. In Charpentier's *Louise,* only Louise and her artist-lover Julien are given names. La Mère and Le Père, thus, are Louise's folks. The mother is quite a nasty lady who disapproves of Louise's affair with Julien. Louise's father loves her and is more gentle than his wife. However, it is her father's stifling possessiveness that finally drives Louise away from home, back into Montmartre, one assumes, forever.
12. Simon Boccanegra, in Verdi's opera of that name, has a daughter named Maria who is raised by others under the name Amelia Grimaldi. Simon, the Doge of Genoa, is asked by his henchman Paolo for permission to marry Amelia. When Boccanegra discovers the girl's identity, he refuses to allow the marriage, and in retaliation, the treacherous Paolo poisons poor Simon.
13. The marquise is Marie's mother in Donizetti's comedy *La Fille du Régiment.* Although at first she pretends that she is only Marie's aunt, the marquise takes the bumptuous girl away from the soldiers who have raised her and tries to make Marie into a debutante. Ultimately, all ends happily, with the marquise acknowledging Marie and allowing the Daughter of the Regiment to marry her soldier love, Tonio.
14. Mamm'Agata is the conniving, loud mother of a young *prima donna* in another Donizetti *opera buffa, Le Convenienze ed Inconvenienze Teatrali.* Mamm'Agata creates havoc at an operatic rehearsal, insulting the other singers and showing the wretched conductor how opera

should be sung. Since this work is a satirical farce, it is perhaps not surprising that Mamm'Agata is sung by a baritone.

15. Azucena, in Verdi's *Il Trovatore,* is believed by all to be Manrico's mother. Actually, as she announces to the shocked Count di Luna, she is only Manrico's foster mother. Her real son died because the absent-minded gypsy tossed him onto the fire where her own mother had been burned as a witch. Azucena had kidnapped the count's brother to avenge her mother's death at the hands of the count's father. Her mission is accomplished when Manrico, whom she had raised as her own boy, is beheaded on di Luna's orders.

53. WHAT'S MY LINE?

1. Adriana Lecouvreur, the title character in Cilea's opera, is a leading member of the Comédie Française.
2. Nedda, in Leoncavallo's *I Pagliacci,* is a member of a troupe of players led by her husband.
3. La Gioconda, the title character in Ponchielli's opera, is a street singer.
4. Peter, the father of Hansel and Gretel in Humperdinck's opera, is a broommaker. We never learn whether or not Rosina Daintymouth, the witch who captures the children, is one of Peter's best clients.
5. Papageno, in Mozart's *The Magic Flute,* is a birdcatcher.
6. Canio is head of the company and its principal clown. Beppe and Tonio, other members of *I Pagliacci*'s cast, are also clowns. (Verdi's Rigoletto is a court jester and is an acceptable answer, too.)
7. Dr. Malatesta, in Donizetti's *Don Pasquale,* is a medical doctor, although his specialty seems to be *raising* the blood pressure of his patients.
8. Eleazar, in Halévy's *La Juive,* and David, in Mascagni's *L'Amico Fritz,* are rabbis. Interestingly, during the last years of Mussolini's reign in Italy, when Hitler pressured the Italians to persecute their Jewish citizens, Rabbi David had his profession changed to physician when this opera was presented in Italy.
9. Marcello, in Puccini's *La Bohème,* and Mario Cavaradossi, in Puccini's *Tosca,* are painters. Marcello is a bohemian unknown who must scrounge for commissions. Mario, whose fate is less pleasant than Marcello's, is, it appears, a wealthy young man who paints mostly for pleasure. Still, someone must have commissioned him to paint in the church of Sant'Andrea della Valle.

10. Figaro, in Mozart's opera, is the valet of the irascible Count Almaviva.
11. The unforgettably christened Marianne Leitmetzerin is Sophie's duenna in Richard Strauss's *Der Rosenkavalier.*
12. Minnie, in Puccini's *La Fanciulla del West,* not only owns the Polka saloon, but serves drinks, sells cigars, and acts as general "den mother" to the miners who patronize her establishment.
13. Five soldiers might include Wozzeck and Andres in Berg's opera, the strange Old Soldier in Catalani's *La Wally,* Sergeant Belcore in Donizetti's *L'Elisir d'Amore,* and Don José in *Carmen.* If you insist on including officers, there are Verdi's Radames from *Aida,* and Otello in operas by Verdi and Rossini. Cassio in the two *Otellos,* and both Alvaro and Don Carlo in Verdi's *La Forza del Destino* earn officer's commissions under assumed names.
14. Count Carnero in Johann Strauss's *Gypsy Baron* and Sergeant Belcore in *L'Elisir d'Amore* are recruiters. Each, in fact, convinces the tenor lead in his opera, Barinkay and Nemorino, respectively, to join up.
15. Ellen Orford, in Britten's *Peter Grimes,* is a schoolmistress.

54. DISGUISES

1. Ernani in Verdi's opera.
2. Count Almaviva in Rossini's *Il Barbiere di Siviglia.*
3. Cherubino in *Le Nozze di Figaro.*
4. Martha in Flotow's opera.
5. Donna Anna, Donna Elvira, and Don Ottavio in Mozart's *Don Giovanni.*
6. Eisenstein in Johann Strauss's *Die Fledermaus.*
7. Ferrando and Guglielmo in Mozart's *Così Fan Tutte.*
8. Mefistofele follows Faust in Boito's opera.
9. Magda in Puccini's *La Rondine.*
10. Alberich in Wagner's *Das Rheingold.*

55. ALIASES

1. Lindoro, in Rossini's *Il Barbiere di Siviglia,* is actually Count Almaviva, who has decided to woo Rosina wearing the guise of a poor student.
2. Don Carlo di Vargas, in Verdi's *La Forza del Destino,* claims to be a

student called Pereda as he searches for his sister Leonora, whom he has sworn to kill.

3. In Verdi's *Simon Boccanegra,* Simon's enemy Jacopo Fiesco uses the name Andrea in order to escape detection in the city from which he had been banished.
4. Amelia Grimaldi, also in *Simon Boccanegra,* is actually Maria Boccanegra, the child that Boccanegra had with Maria Fiesco. In a typically incredible operatic coincidence, Fiesco, a member of the Grimaldi family, adopts Maria without being aware of the child's true identity, and he passes her off as a Grimaldi (the actual daughter of that family had died as a small child) in order to protect the family fortune.
5. In Ponchielli's *La Gioconda,* Enzo Grimaldo, an Italian prince banished from Venice by Alvise Badoero, pretends to be Dalmatian sailor Enzo Giordan in order to find his beloved Laura Adorno, whom Alvise has married.
6. In Wagner's *Siegfried,* Wotan, the leader of the Norse gods, wanders through the forests disguised in human form, hoping to learn the whereabouts of his mortal grandson, Siegfried.
7. In *La Forza del Destino,* Don Alvaro flees from the vengeful Carlo and takes holy vows as Padre Raffaele. He finds refuge in the same cloister in which his beloved Leonora has hidden from the outside world.
8. Enrico is the name taken by Faust in Boito's *Mefistofele* after the Devil has transformed him into a handsome youth. It is as Enrico that Margherita knows Faust.
9. In Johann Strauss's *Die Fledermaus,* Eisenstein, due to begin a brief jail term, goes to Orlofsky's party instead and, at his friend Dr. Falke's suggestion, uses the name Marquis Renard instead of his own.
10. In Wagner's *Tristan und Isolde,* the heroine, in Isolde's Narrative, tells how Tristan, calling himself Tantris, wooed her for King Marke.
11. In Richard Strauss's *Der Rosenkavalier,* Octavian, the Marschallin's youthful lover, disguises himself as a housemaid called Mariandl, first to save the Marschallin from embarrassment, but later uses the same identity to foil Baron Ochs's designs on Sophie von Faninal.
12. In another Richard Strauss opera, *Arabella,* the heroine's impoverished family can't afford to bring up two girls in society and therefore force Arabella's younger sister, Zdenka, to masquerade as the boy Zdenko.
13. In Verdi's *Falstaff,* Ford disguises himself as Fontana, mythical suitor to Ford's own wife Alice, as part of an elaborate plot to punish the fat knight.
14. In Giordano's *Andrea Chénier,* Madeleine bribes a Parisian jailer to

allow her to assume the identity of a condemned woman, Idia Legray, so that Madeleine can die with Chénier.

15. In *Die Fledermaus,* Rosalinde's maid Adele attends Orlofsky's party where, in a gown borrowed without her mistress's consent, Adele passes herself off as an actress, Mlle. Olga.
16. In Verdi's *Rigoletto,* the Duke of Mantua woos Rigoletto's daughter, Gilda, posing as the poor student Gualtier Maldé.

56. WHO WEARS THE PANTS?

1. Cherubino, in Mozart's *Le Nozze di Figaro.*
2. Smeton, in Donizetti's *Anna Bolena.*
3. Fyodor, in Mussorgsky's *Boris Godunov.*
4. Oscar, in Verdi's *Un Ballo in Maschera.*
5. The Composer, in Richard Strauss's *Ariadne auf Naxos.*
6. Stephano, in Gounod's *Roméo et Juliette.*
7. Octavian, in Richard Strauss's *Der Rosenkavalier.*
8. Dmitri, in Giordano's *Fedora.*
9. Siebel, in Gounod's *Faust.*
10. Romeo, in Bellini's *I Capuletti ed i Montecchi.*
11. Nicklausse, in Offenbach's *Les Contes d'Hoffmann.* (He and Giulietta sing the Barcarolle.)
12. Prince Orlofsky in Johann Strauss's *Die Fledermaus.*

57. HOME WRECKERS

1. Luigi, the stevedore in Puccini's *Il Tabarro,* is the lover of Georgetta, the wife of Michele, Luigi's boss. Misinterpreting Michele's lighting of his pipe as the signal from Georgetta that all is ready for the lovers, Luigi is confronted by the jealous Michele, who strangles Luigi and then forces his erring wife to kiss the dead man's lips.
2. Werther, the title character of Massenet's opera, loves Charlotte, who

although returning Werther's sentiments, wishes to be loyal to her husband Albert. He suspects the truth, and when asked by Werther to lend him his dueling pistols, does so gladly. Werther shoots himself, but Charlotte finds the dying man and assures him of her love for him as he expires.

3. Turiddu, in Mascagni's *Cavalleria Rusticana,* abandons his lover Santuzza to pay court to Lola, his former sweetheart now married to Alfio. Santuzza spills the beans to Alfio, who kills Turiddu in a duel.
4. Enzo, in Ponchielli's *La Gioconda,* loves Laura Adorno, wife of the beastly Alvise Badoero. Aided by the distraught Gioconda, who loves Enzo but who has sworn to help Laura (who has saved Gioconda's mother from burning as a witch), Laura and Enzo escape the wrath of Alvise (who had "killed" Laura) and sail off into the sunset, leaving poor Gioconda to kill herself.
5. Riccardo (a.k.a. Gustavus III) is the tenor hero of Verdi's *Un Ballo in Maschera.* Riccardo loves Amelia, the wife of his loyal secretary Renato (a.k.a. Count Anckarström). When Renato discovers the affair, which incidentally has been confined to the platonic level, he joins the conspiracy to assassinate Riccardo. Renato shoots him, but he is pardoned by the dying Riccardo.
6. Roberto Devereux, the title character in Donizetti's opera, is loved by Queen Elizabeth I. Unfortunately, he loves Sara, Duchess of Nottingham. The queen orders Roberto's execution for treason, and the jealous Duke of Nottingham places his wife under arrest so that she is unable to give the queen Roberto's ring, which under a promise from Elizabeth would have made her pardon Roberto. Thus Roberto is beheaded, Sara is humiliated, and the Virgin Queen is quite distressed with the Duke of Nottingham as the final curtain falls.
7. Alfred is the strolling Italian tenor in Johann Strauss's *Die Fledermaus.* Alfred's frenzied flirtation with Rosalinde, wife of Eisenstein, costs him a night in jail, but all is put right at the end of the operetta, and the confusion is attributed to a general overdose of champagne.
8. Percy, in Donizetti's *Anna Bolena,* has the misfortune to be Anna's lover, much to the anger of King Henry VIII. Actually, Percy and Anna haven't really been lovers, but Henry has them executed anyway.
9. The countess, in Berg's *Lulu,* is the lesbian lover of the heroine. She helps Lulu to escape from prison, where Lulu has been confined after murdering her husband, Dr. Schön. The two women escape to London, where Lulu becomes a streetwalker. Her final client is Jack the Ripper, who stabs both Lulu and the countess to death.

10. The Drum Major in Berg's *Wozzeck* seduces Marie, the common-law wife of the title character. Wozzeck suspects Marie's infidelity and stabs her to death before he drowns himself.

58. GOOD DREAMS . . . BAD DREAMS

1. Pollione, in Bellini's *Norma,* dreams that Norma has pursued him and Adalgisa to Rome to punish Pollione for turning his attentions from Norma to Adalgisa. Norma is, of course, infuriated when she actually learns of Pollione's duplicity, but after hours of worrying about the situation, she spares Adalgisa's life, admits that she has broken her own vows of chastity, and, with the newly contrite Pollione, goes to her death.
2. In Richard Strauss's *Die Frau ohne Schatten,* the empress sees her husband turned to stone. By learning compassion for others, the empress's newly defined humanity suffices to allow the emperor to turn to flesh and blood once more.
3. Clytemnestra, in Richard Strauss's *Elektra,* is haunted by dreams in which she is murdered by her son Orestes as punishment for her own murder of Orestes's father, Agamemnon.
4. Elsa, in Wagner's *Lohengrin,* sees the arrival of the Swan Knight in a dream. Lohengrin does indeed sail up the river to fight for Elsa in a trial by combat. Although he wins, the evil Ortrud eventually undermines Elsa's faith in Lohengrin, leading to his departure from Brabant and Elsa's own death.
5. In Wagner's *Die Walküre,* Sieglinde dreams of her twin brother (and lover) Siegmund's death at the hands of Hunding, her husband. In spite of Brünnhilde's valiant efforts on Siegmund's behalf, Hunding indeed kills Siegmund.
6. Lady Macbeth, in Verdi's opera, sleepwalks as she relives in her dreams the murder of Duncan.
7. In Verdi's *Otello,* as in Shakespeare's tragedy, one of the fictions that Iago manufactures in his effort to destroy Otello's and Desdemona's happiness is the dream that Iago claims Cassio had, during which he murmured words of love to Desdemona. Otello, of course, swallows Iago's bait, and tragedy results.
8. In Mussorgsky's *Boris Godunov,* Czar Boris suffers a fatal heart attack when the old monk Pimen recounts the story of a blind man who

regained his sight after dreaming of the murdered Czarevitch Dmitri.

9. In Bellini's *La Sonnambula,* the sleepwalking heroine Amina dreams that her jealous suitor Elvino is restored to her. Elvino, overcome by shame as he watches Amina walk in her sleep, sinks to his knees in front of her. Thus, Amina awakens to find that her dream has come true.
10. In Gilbert and Sullivan's *Iolanthe,* the Lord Chancellor's bad dream, described in the song "When You're Lying Awake," is a very funny and very realistic description of a foolish but unnerving dream.
11. In Rossini's Cinderella opera *La Cenerentola,* Don Magnifico (the male equivalent of the wicked stepmother) is mystified by his dream of being turned into a donkey. His subsequent foolish behavior shows that the dream, at least metaphorically, has come true.

59. LOCO EN EL COCO

1. Elvira, in Bellini's *I Puritani,* sinks into delirium when Arturo, her intended, deserts her at the altar in order to save Henrietta, Queen of England, from execution. As soon as Arturo returns, Elvira recovers her faculties.
2. Ophélie is, of course, Hamlet's cast-off sweetheart in Ambroise Thomas's *Hamlet.* As in Shakespeare, the cumulative effect of Hamlet's strange behavior, which includes the murder of Ophélie's father, Polonius, is too much for the poor girl.
3. *Lucia di Lammermoor* has perhaps the most famous mad scene in all of opera. Donizetti's heroine goes mad when, after being tricked into marrying a political ally of her brother's, her true love Edgardo–whom she believed to be false–arrives to break up the wedding party. Lucia stabs her bridegroom to death.
4. Nabucco, in Verdi's opera, is struck by lightning sent by Jehovah when the Babylonian king announces to the assembled soloists and chorus that he is no longer merely the king, but God himself. There is no aria for Nabucco here, just the lead in the ensemble that ends the act. Nabucco regains his intellect after praying to God for forgiveness.
5. Marguerite, in Gounod's *Faust,* loses her mind after Faust abandons her when she is pregnant with his child. Marguerite kills her baby and is condemned to death, although her prayers for deliverance from

Méphistophélès and Faust lead to her salvation. Instead of a formal aria, Gounod lets her recall her love for Faust musically.

6. Peter Grimes, in Britten's opera, is pretty upset throughout the three acts of the opera. Grimes finally snaps completely when his new apprentice accidentally falls to his death.
7. Azucena, in Verdi's *Il Trovatore,* is demented throughout, but especially in the second act, when she is riveted by the memory of her mother's being burned at the stake. In her terror, she had thrown her own baby into the flames and has never been the same again.
8. Imogene, in Bellini's *Il Pirata,* goes berserk when her husband executes her pirate lover. Her *scena di pazzia* ends the opera somewhat abruptly. Bellini wasn't interested in the final scene of the libretto in which various plot angles are straightened out.
9. Boris Godunov, in Mussorgsky's masterpiece, suffers from the guilt he feels for the murder of the Czarevitch Dmitri. The Clock Scene in Act II finds Boris gibbering on the floor, terrified by visions of the slaughtered child's ghost.
10. Juana La Loca, in Gian Carlo Menotti's opera, is the much put-upon daughter of Ferdinand and Isabella of Spain. Betrayed by husband, father, and son, Juana spends her last forty years walled up in a dark corner of the palace. Small wonder she goes crazy for a mad scene that lasts for almost the entire third act of the opera.

60. *SUICIDIO*

1. In Catalani's *La Wally,* Wally's unexpected reconciliation with Hagenbach, whom she herself had wanted to kill earlier on, is ruined when the poor tenor is killed in an avalanche. Wally jumps into an icy chasm without so much as a backward glance.
2. In Wagner's *The Flying Dutchman,* the title character, condemned to sail the seas eternally unless he finds a wife who will be true unto death, erroneously believes that Senta has betrayed him. That Senta has not done so is established by her leap into the sea, an act of love that results in the Dutchman's own death and the pair's mystical reuniting in the Great Beyond.
3. Leonora, in Verdi's *Il Trovatore,* drinks poison from her ring in order to die faithful to Manrico. The spiteful Count di Luna, discovering

that he had been duped, orders Manrico to the block–only to be happily told by Azucena that Manrico had been di Luna's own, long-lost brother.

4. Rodolfo, in Verdi's *Luisa Miller,* is this tragically gullible fellow. As he falls dying, he manages to stab Wurm, the spoilsport who contrived all of Luisa's and Rodolfo's suffering.
5. Peter Grimes, the title character in Britten's opera, takes Captain Balstrode's stern but well-intentioned advice and sinks his boat away from shore, with himself as its passenger.
6. Aida, in Verdi's opera, plants herself inside Radames's soon-to-be-sealed crypt, so that she may die with the man she loved.
7. This is the penultimate scene of Alban Berg's *Wozzeck.* When Wozzeck walks into the water, he leaves the body of Marie to be discovered by a band of children, including their own son.
8. In the original version of Verdi's *La Forza del Destino,* performed in St. Petersburg, Don Alvaro jumps to his death after Carlo kills his sister, Alvaro's beloved Leonora. No one in this version gets to sing that beautiful trio "Non imprecare" which Verdi later used to end the opera.
9. Liù in *Turandot* dies for love, and Puccini expired shortly after composing her death scene.
10. Papageno, in Mozart's *The Magic Flute,* decides not to hang himself after all when the Three Genii remind him that his magic glockenspiel can help him find Papagena.

61. MURDERS MOST FOUL

1. In Cilea's *Adriana Lecouvreur,* the Princess de Bouillon dips a bouquet of violets into a poison and sends them to Adriana, implying that the posies come from Maurizio, Count of Saxony. Adriana sniffs the bouquet, and dies in Maurizio's arms shortly thereafter.
2. In Montemezzi's *L'Amore dei Tre Re,* old King Archibaldo manages, despite his age and the fact that he is blind, to strangle Fiora. Although his plan to entrap her lover by smearing the dead girl's lips with poison succeeds, Archibaldo did not reckon with the possibility that his own son would also offer Fiora a final kiss, and in doing so, would die too.

3. Santuzza, in Mascagni's *Cavalleria Rusticana,* blurts out the news that her lover Turiddu is once again seeing Lola to that lady's tough-minded husband, teamster Alfio. Alfio shortly thereafter provokes Turiddu into a duel with knives, and Alfio wins.
4. Aegisth, in Richard Strauss's *Elektra,* finds his stepdaughter (the title character) welcoming him home with uncharacteristic joy. The king enters his palace and is surprised by Orestes (Elektra's brother and son of Agamemnon, the slain king) waiting for him with an axe.
5. Samson, of biblical fame, is the tenor protagonist of Saint-Saëns's *Samson et Dalila.* Dalila ties up Samson and shears off his hair, which, as most will recall, is the source of Samson's tremendous strength. Blinded, Samson is led into the temple of Baal, where the Philistines make sport of him. Samson prays to God for a return of his prowess, then proceeds to push down the columns that support the structure, thus killing his enemies and himself at the same time.
6. Renato, in Verdi's *Un Ballo in Maschera,* believes that his wife, Amelia, and his best friend Count Riccardo are lovers. He therefore joins a conspiracy to assassinate the count at a masked ball. Renato takes part in a lottery and wins the privilege of stabbing poor Riccardo, who, with his last few breaths, assures Renato that Amelia's honor had not been sullied, then orders the police to free Renato, forgiving him as he dies.
7. Lucrezia Borgia, in Donizetti's opera of that name, poisons the wine offered the guests at a dinner party she gives in Ferrara, hoping to destroy Orsini, who has insulted her. Her own recently discovered illegitimate son is Orsini's best friend and shares the wine with him. Poor Lucrezia, she has little choice but to sing her *cabaletta* and go mad.
8. Giants Fasolt and Fafner have built Valhalla for the gods in Wagner's *Das Rheingold.* Although at first Wotan had offered them his sister-in-law Freia, the Goddess of Youth, he attempts to buy them off with the gold he has just stolen from Alberich the dwarf (who in turn had pinched it from the Rhinemaidens). They quarrel over ownership of the ring, and Fafner hits Fasolt over the head.
9. Baron Scarpia, in Puccini's *Tosca,* has dined well and expects his dinner to be topped off by the sweet kisses of Floria Tosca, who has promised herself to the baron in return for the life of her lover, Mario Cavaradossi. Instead, she stabs Scarpia with his own bread knife.
10. Lucia di Lammermoor, the heroine of Donizetti's opera, has been forced into marriage to Arturo Bucklaw. She'd much rather wed her brother's archenemy, Edgardo. So, as the newlyweds slip away to the

bridal chamber, Lucia stabs her husband to death during the intermission before the Mad Scene.

62. PRISONERS OF FATE

1. Piquillo, in Offenbach's comic opera *La Périchole,* is sent to the Dungeon for Recalcitrant Husbands when he refuses to acquiesce to his wife's being the mistress of the Viceroy of Peru. The wife in question, Périchole, has, of course, no intention of being unfaithful, but angrily insists on Piquillo's arrest when he insults her during her presentation at court. Since *La Périchole* is a comedy, all ends happily for the couple, for Périchole–after briefly being locked up herself–escapes with Piquillo, eventually winning the viceroy's forgiveness and a title in the bargain.
2. Margherita, in Boito's *Mefistofele,* like her counterpart Marguerite in Gounod's *Faust,* is sent to prison under sentence of death for having killed the baby she has borne Faust. Faust and the Devil endeavor to manage her escape, but Margherita prays to God for strength and for pardon, and dies in a state of grace.
3. In Puccini's opera, Manon and her impoverished lover des Grieux are surprised by Manon's wealthy old protector, Geronte de Ravoir. When the old man storms off in a fury, Manon wastes precious time gathering up her jewelry. Geronte returns with the police, to whom he has denounced the girl as a prostitute. The felony is compounded when Manon is caught hiding the jewels. Manon is deported to Louisiana where, tended by the faithful des Grieux, she dies of an unexplained malaise.
4. In Verdi's *Rigoletto,* Monterone is dragged off to the dungeon because he has dared to publicly berate the Duke of Mantua for seducing Monterone's daughter. Although we never learn Monterone's exact fate, the curse he hurls at Rigoletto is fulfilled by Gilda's murder at the hands of the assassin Sparafucile, whom the jester has engaged to do in the duke.
5. Elena, the firebrand heroine of Verdi's *I Vespri Siciliani,* is sent to "death row" after the discovery of her part in a plot against Monforte, the French governor of Sicily. Monforte's son Arrigo is Elena's lover, and she is eventually pardoned and allowed to marry Arrigo. Unfortu-

nately, the Sicilian rebel Procida ruins the wedding party by rushing in with a horde of angry Sicilians, who murder all the French soldiers, including the groom's father.

6. In Verdi's *Don Carlo,* the title character is sent to prison after he draws his sword against his father, King Philip II of Spain, in an attempt to win leniency for Protestant Flanders. A change of heart on Philip's part (after a depressing conversation with the Grand Inquisitor) sets Carlo free, but the king attempts to arrest his son the following evening, believing that Carlo and Philip's wife, Elisabetta de Valois, are lovers. The end of *Don Carlo* is quite confusing, as the prince is saved from the king's soldiers by the intervention of a rather scary friar who appears to be the ghost of Charles V, Carlo's doting old grandfather. Charles V leads the lad into the cloister of St. Just, from which he evidently never emerges.
7. In Puccini's *Tosca,* all we know about Angelotti is that he has been sent to prison by the Royalists because he was a Republican consul. The play by Sardou on which the opera is based fills in the details by having Angelotti be the former lover of the notorious Lady Hamilton. Lady Hamilton, a friend of the Roman Queen Caroline, fears that Angelotti might embarrass her by revealing her naughty past. She has the works of Voltaire planted in Angelotti's home and thereby seals the poor fellow's doom. In play and opera, Angelotti escapes from jail (the Castel Sant'Angelo) and is hidden by painter Cavaradossi in the well in Cavaradossi's villa. Cavaradossi refuses, even under torture, to reveal his friend's hiding place, but Tosca, who can't stand hearing her lover's cries of pain, gives Baron Scarpia the information. Angelotti kills himself with poison as the policemen reach him.
8. Massenet's *Manon* differs from Puccini's opera by having the heroine arrested after a card game at the Parisian Hôtel de Transylvanie. Guillot, the old man whose attentions Manon has been spurning continuously for four long acts, accuses Manon's lover des Grieux of cheating at cards and tells the arresting officers that Manon is des Grieux's accomplice. The young man's powerful father prevents des Grieux's arrest, but Manon is dragged off. In the French opera, Manon's release from custody is arranged before deportation to America, but the poor girl has suffered so greatly in prison that she dies in des Grieux's arms moments after being freed.
9. Eisenstein, in Johann Strauss's *Die Fledermaus,* has been sentenced to five days in jail for assaulting a tax collector. His incompetent lawyer, Dr. Blinde, has so badly bungled the appeal that three additional days are added to his sentence. Eisenstein arrives in prison hours after his

sentence had begun, having first gone off to Prince Orlofsky's ball. All the complications are set right at the end of the opera, and Eisenstein serves his sentence a happy man, knowing that his wife Rosalinde wasn't really unfaithful to him after all . . . probably.

10. The Old Prisoner in *La Périchole* helps Périchole and Piquillo escape from the viceroy's dungeon. As the plot is resolved, the viceroy recognizes the old man as a dear friend and asks why he had been shut away in the first place. No one can recall the crime, and therefore, unfortunately, there can be no pardon. The Old Prisoner is led away, brandishing his penknife with which–he assures the sympathetic onlookers–he can burrow his way out to freedom in a mere twelve years.

63. CAPITAL PUNISHMENT

1. The prince of Persia, in Puccini's *Turandot,* is beheaded because he has failed to answer the princess's three riddles.
2. Mario Cavaradossi, in Puccini's *Tosca,* is shot by Baron Scarpia's soldiers, although Tosca herself believes it to be a mock execution. The shooting was ordered because Mario had aided the escaped political prisoner Angelotti and, moreover, had insulted Scarpia after having been tortured.
3. Paolo Albiani dies, in Verdi's *Simon Boccanegra,* for having abducted Doge Simon's daughter. Before his arrest, however, Paolo has poisoned Simon's carafe of water.
4. Maria Stuarda, in Donizetti's opera of that name, dies mourned by all her retainers. The Queen of Scots had committed treason, in the eyes of Queen Elizabeth I, by calling her a "vil bastarda."
5. Manrico, in Verdi's *Trovatore,* is dragged away to the axeman calling out "Madre, o madre, addio" to Azucena, who–he doesn't realize–is *not* his mother.
6. Madeleine, in Giordano's *Andrea Chénier,* has bribed a jailer to let her die in place of a condemned woman, Idia Legray, in order to perish with her beloved poet, Chénier, who has been condemned to death for treasonous activities by the minions of the Reign of Terror.
7. The entire convent of Carmelite nuns in Poulenc's *Dialogues des Carmélites* (except for the incognito Mother Marie of the Incarnation)

go bravely to their deaths, having defied the French revolutionary government by keeping to their religious vows.

8. Don José, in Bizet's *Carmen,* is undoubtedly executed for murdering his gypsy sweetheart. His last words are: "You may arrest me, I killed her. Oh, my beloved Carmen." Mérimée's novel is narrated by José, who awaits execution.
9. Roberto Devereux, in Donizetti's opera of that name, is killed because Sara, the Duchess of Nottingham, is held captive by her vengeful husband, who wants Devereux dead as revenge for Roberto's affair with the duchess. If Sara could have reached Queen Elizabeth in time with the ring the queen had given Devereux, the execution would have been stopped.
10. Jokanaan, or John the Baptist in Richard Strauss's *Salome,* is beheaded at the request of Salome after Herod has promised his stepdaughter anything she wants, if she would dance for him. After Salome receives Jokanaan's severed head and makes love to it for twenty or so minutes, the shocked Herod orders his soldiers to kill her.

64. FINAL REQUESTS

1. As she lies dying, Violetta, in Verdi's *La Traviata,* hands Alfredo a locket containing her portrait. She tells Alfredo to give the locket to the innocent young girl he will some day marry, and to tell her that an angel in heaven is praying for her happiness.
2. Johnson, in Puccini's *La Fanciulla del West,* is about to be lynched by the posse led by Sheriff Rance. Johnson accepts his fate (although he will, of course, be rescued by the title character) but asks the men to allow Minnie to believe that he is alive and free in another part of the country.
3. Mario, in Puccini's *Tosca,* asks the jailer to allow him to write a farewell to Tosca.
4. Paolo, in Verdi's *Simon Boccanegra,* has been condemned to death for treason. As he is led off, Paolo tells the haughty Fiesco that he, Paolo, had abducted Fiesco's ward, Amelia. He begs Fiesco to spare him the indignity of public execution, but Fiesco angrily refuses, leaving Paolo to his fate.
5. Werther, the title character in Massenet's opera, begs his beloved to bury him beneath the shade of his favorite tree.

6. Amelia, in Verdi's *Un Ballo in Maschera,* takes seriously her husband's threat to kill her after she has revealed herself to have been the object of Riccardo's affection. She asks to be allowed to see her son once more before being murdered. Renato not only grants this wish, but decides to spare her life and to kill Riccardo instead.
7. Boccanegra, in Verdi's *Simon Boccanegra,* having been poisoned by the condemned Paolo, names his new son-in-law, Gabriele Adorno, to be the new doge after his death. He asks Fiesco, his former enemy, to see that his wish be carried out.
8. Anna in Donizetti's *Anna Bolena,* awaiting beheading, hears the offstage celebration of the wedding of Henry VIII to Jane (Giovanna) Seymour. She claims to forgive her ex-husband and his new bride, and calls down heaven's blessing upon them. Her fiery melody, however, suggests that Bolena is not entirely sincere in her leave-taking.
9. Don Alvaro, in Verdi's *La Forza del Destino,* believes himself to be dying from a wound suffered in battle. He asks his new friend, who is actually his sworn enemy Don Carlo, to burn all his personal papers upon his death. Carlo, of course, riffles through these instead and discovers Alvaro's true identity, thereby motivating the final hour of the plot.
10. Desideria, in Menotti's *The Saint of Bleecker Street*, has been fatally stabbed by her lover, Michele, during a furious argument in which Desideria insinuates that Michele has incestuous desires for his sister Annina, a frail and devout girl whom the neighbors consider a saint. Desideria falls dying and, in her terror, asks Annina to pray for her soul.

65. OPENING LINES

1. In Puccini's *La Bohème,* Marcello addresses Rodolfo with these words, jokingly blaming the sea in his painting for the cold that pervades their attic flat.
2. In Verdi's *Rigoletto,* the Duke of Mantua opens the opera by discussing his latest sweetheart (actually, Gilda) with the courtier Borsa.
3. As the curtain rises on Verdi's *Otello,* the Cypriots discuss the storm that threatens Otello's ship with these first words.
4. In Puccini's *Turandot,* the Mandarin begins the opera by announcing Turandot's pronouncement to the assembled crowd.

5. In Verdi's *Il Trovatore,* the old soldier Ferrando bestirs his restless guardsmen with this admonition, then proceeds to launch into the exposition.
6. In Richard Strauss's *Salome,* the first character to be heard is the captain of the guard, Narraboth, commenting on the beautiful Salome to his colleagues.
7. In Verdi's *La Forza del Destino,* the Marquis of Calatrava begins the turbulent opera on a quiet, tender note, as he bids his daughter Leonora good night.
8. In Mozart's *Le Nozze di Figaro,* the opera begins with Figáro measuring his new room with a yardstick.
9. In Mozart's *The Magic Flute,* the first bit of action is Tamino's rushing on stage, screaming for help, as he is being pursued by a vicious-looking serpent.
10. In Gounod's *Faust,* the title character commences his role with this despairing summation of his life's achievements thus far.
11. In Gershwin's *Porgy and Bess,* Clara sings this familiar lullaby to her baby.
12. This line opens Menotti's *The Telephone* as Ben enters and gives Lucy a piece of abstract sculpture.
13. The "spirit" of wine, actually an offstage male chorus, opens Offenbach's melodically alcoholic *Les Contes d'Hoffmann* with this surreal statement.
14. In Massenet's *Werther,* the genial bailiff, father of the heroine Charlotte, tries to bring his children to order as he attempts to rehearse them in a Christmas carol on a summer afternoon.
15. Samuel Barber's *Antony and Cleopatra* opens with these words of exposition from the chorus of Egyptians.

66. FAMOUS FIRST WORDS

1. In Verdi's *La Forza del Destino,* Don Carlo ponders his friend Alvaro's serious war wounds before singing the aria "Urna fatale del mio destino."
2. In Verdi's *Aida,* the heroine wonders about her ill-starred love for Radames as she begins the aria "O patria mia."
3. In Mozart's *Le Nozze di Figaro,* the countess anxiously waits for Susanna in order to set in motion the intrigue planned to stop her husband's philandering, and then she thinks about the count's betrayal of their love in the aria "Dove sono."

4. In Puccini's *La Fanciulla del West,* Johnson, about to be lynched by the miners, thanks Sonora for allowing him a few last words, which he addresses to the absent Minnie, in the aria "Ch'ella mi creda."
5. Upon her entrance in Act I of Bizet's opera, Carmen greets her admirers with these words before beginning the "Habanera."
6. Lucia, in Donizetti's *Lucia di Lammermoor,* waits for her lover Edgardo and describes their love in the aria "Regnava nel silenzio," which begins shortly after the quoted phrase is uttered.
7. Leonora di Vargas, in Verdi's *La Forza del Destino,* sings these words at the beginning of the Convent Scene before singing the aria "Madre pietose vergine."
8. In Mascagni's *Cavalleria Rusticana,* Mamma Lucia asks this of Santuzza, who responds with the aria "Voi lo sapete, o mamma," letting Lucia and the audience know why she is so unhappy.
9. With these words, Canio in Leoncavallo's *I Pagliacci,* begins the most famous of all tenor scenes, leading into "Vesti la giubba."
10. In Cilea's *Adriana Lecouvreur,* the actress-heroine dismisses the praise of her backstage visitors, then sings the aria "Io son l'umile ancella."
11. In Puccini's *Madama Butterfly,* Cio-Cio-San tries to calm the agitated Suzuki, as she describes her anticipated joy at Pinkerton's return in "Un bel di vedremo."
12. Donna Elvira, in Mozart's *Don Giovanni,* contemplates Don G's bad behavior as she launches into "Mi tradì quel alma ingrata."
13. These are the words uttered by Norma in Bellini's opera as she enters and calms the rebellious Druids with her peaceful "Casta Diva."
14. Cilea's *Adriana Lecouvreur;* as Adriana receives the poisoned violets sent her by her rival, Princess de Bouillon, she leads into the aria "Poveri fiori."
15. In Verdi's *Il Trovatore,* Leonora dismisses Ruiz, who has brought her to the castle where Manrico is imprisoned. The aria that follows is "D'amor sull'ali rosee."

67. DRAMATIC ENTRANCES

1. In Puccini's *Turandot,* the title character plunges directly into her first aria–addressed to her father, the unknown prince, and the assembled throng–in which she explains that her hatred for men stems from the rape of one of her ancestors, many years earlier.
2. In Act I of Wagner's *Die Walküre,* Siegmund, exhausted from battle, staggers into Hunding's home (in the hollow of a tree) begging for

water and a place to rest, not knowing that he is about to discover his long-lost twin sister Sieglinde.

3. This succinct, ironic greeting is addressed to Faust by Méphistophélès, in Gounod's opera, whom he had just summoned.
4. In Verdi's *Aida,* Radames is first heard questioning the high priest Ramfis about preparations for the coming war between Egypt and Ethiopia, and he is especially interested in the selection of the commander of the Egyptian troops.
5. In Verdi's *La Traviata,* Violetta graciously welcomes her friend Flora Bervoix and other tardy guests with these hospitable words.
6. In Ponchielli's *La Gioconda,* the title character establishes her close relationship with her mother, La Cieca, with her very first words, as she leads the old blind woman into St. Mark's Square.
7. The lovesick Leonora in Verdi's *Il Trovatore* complains thusly to her confidante, Ines, as she makes her first appearance in the opera, waiting, as usual, for Manrico's song of love.
8. Brünnhilde's blustering, if somewhat nonsensical, war cry is addressed to her father, Wotan, as the Valkyrie rushes onstage in *Die Walküre.*
9. In Verdi's *Don Carlo,* the fearsome Grand Inquisitor, brought into Philip II's study, makes plain his own desire to confront the king with his very first line.
10. Verdi's lovelorn Aida pleads concern with politics when, on her entrance, Amneris begins to question her, suspecting (correctly, as it turns out) that Aida, like Amneris herself, is in love with Radames.
11. In Richard Strauss's *Der Rosenkavalier,* the awakening Octavian caresses the Marschallin, with whom he has spent the night, crooning these tender words to her.
12. Cleopatra, in Barber's *Antony and Cleopatra,* makes a rather petulant entrance with these words.
13. Marguerite, in Gounod's *Faust,* utters what must be the most modest phrase ever to issue from the lips of a diva.
14. This is Dalila's opening pitch to Samson in Saint-Saëns's *Samson et Dalila.*

68. LOVE DUETS

1. This is sung by Radames and Aida in Verdi's *Aida.*
2. This is sung by Faust and Marguerite in Gounod's *Faust.*

3. With these words the great duet for Manon Lescaut and des Grieux begins in Puccini's *Manon Lescaut.*
4. This is the duet for Lucia and Edgardo in Donizetti's *Lucia di Lammermoor.*
5. This is the duet for Riccardo and Amelia in Verdi's *Un Ballo in Maschera.*
6. This is the duet for Desdemona and Otello in Verdi's *Otello.*
7. This is the lovely duet sung by Octavian and Sophie in the closing moments of Richard Strauss's *Der Rosenkavalier.*
8. This is the duet for Cio-Cio-San and Pinkerton in Puccini's *Madama Butterfly.*
9. This is the duet for Alfredo and Violetta in Verdi's *La Traviata.*
10. This is the duet for Nedda and Silvio in Leoncavallo's *I Pagliacci.*
11. These sarcastic words open the duet for Adalgisa and Pollione, who soon soothes her fears, in Bellini's *Norma.*
12. These are the opening words of the final duet for Turandot and Calaf in Puccini's *Turandot.* (Puccini died before completing this scene, and the duet was finished by Franco Alfano, working from Puccini's sketches.)
13. These are the opening words of the ecstatic duet for Mimi and Rodolfo in Puccini's *La Bohème.*
14. This is the duet for Werther and Charlotte in Act I of Massenet's *Werther.*
15. With these words, Brünnhilde awakens and begins the long duet for her and Siegfried in the final scene of Wagner's *Siegfried.*
16. This is the ecstatic duet for Leonore and Florestan in Beethoven's *Fidelio.*
17. This is the little duet from Mozart's *Le Nozze di Figaro* in which Figaro cools the anger of his bride Susanna, who believes she has caught Figaro flirting.
18. This is the duet with uncomfortable consequences for Alfred and Rosalinde in Johann Strauss's *Die Fledermaus.*
19. This is the final duet for Madeleine and Chénier in Giordano's *Andrea Chénier.*
20. This is the second of the three duets for Don Carlo and Elisabetta in Verdi's *Don Carlo.*
21. With these words begins the Act I duet for Mario and Tosca in Puccini's *Tosca.*
22. This is the duet for Francesca and Paolo in Zandonai's *Francesca da Rimini.*
23. This is the duet for Gilda and the Duke of Mantua in Verdi's *Rigoletto.*
24. This is the Act III duet for Mario and Tosca in Puccini's *Tosca.*

69. *CABALETTE*

1. In Act II of Verdi's *La Traviata,* Alfredo's rhapsodic aria is followed by his crestfallen *cabaletta* "O, mio rimorso!" when he learns that Violetta has been selling her property in order to support him.
2. In Act II of Verdi's *Luisa Miller,* Rodolfo's contemplative aria, in which he muses on the happiness that he and Luisa once enjoyed, is followed by the overwrought *cabaletta* "l'ara, o l'avello apprestami," in which Rodolfo vows to punish Luisa for her apparent faithlessness.
3. In Act I of Verdi's *Il Trovatore,* Leonora follows her description of Manrico's nocturnal serenades by vehemently casting aside her attendant's skepticism about the sincerity of Manrico's love in the *cabaletta* "Di tale amor."
4. Norma's prayer in Act I of Bellini's opera is closely followed by her *cabaletta* "Ah! bello a me ritorna" in which she quietly prays for the restoration of Pollione's love.
5. In Act I of Verdi's *Macbeth,* Lady Macbeth, upon learning that King Duncan will be spending the night under her roof, ceases her musings on the nature of power and, in the *cabaletta* "Or tutti sorgete, ministri infernale," calls upon evil spirits to give her the strength to induce Macbeth to murder the king.
6. In Bellini's *La Sonnambula,* Amina's dreamy expression of her love for Elvino, who has wrongly accused her of infidelity, is followed by the joyous "Ah! non giunge uman pensiero" when Elvino has awakened her, begging her forgiveness.
7. In Act I of Verdi's *La Traviata,* Violetta's introspective aria, in which she wonders if she could seriously love Alfredo, is followed by the determinedly hedonistic "Sempre libera" in which the courtesan vows to continue living solely for pleasure.
8. In Act III of Verdi's *Il Trovatore,* Manrico's tender avowal of his love for Leonora is followed by his anguished vow to save his mother, Azucena, from the family tradition of being burned at the stake. The *cabaletta* is "Di quella pira."
9. In Act II of Bellini's *I Puritani,* Elvira's delirious lament over Arturo's continued absence is sweetened by her similarly deluded, if happier, fantasy in which she imagines that her tenor has returned to her. That *cabaletta* is "Vien, diletto, è in ciel la luna."
10. In Act I of Donizetti's *Lucia di Lammermoor,* Lucia happily describes

the wonderful aspects of her love for her family's long-time enemy, Edgardo, to her uneasy confidante, Alcia, in the *cabaletta* "Quando, rapito in estasi."

70. SELF-AWARENESS

1. Iago to Cassio in Verdi's *Otello.*
2. Adriana Lecouvreur to the Prince de Bouillon, the Abbé, and Michonnet in Cilea's opera.
3. Rodolfo to Mimì in Puccini's *La Bohème.*
4. Mefistofele to Faust in Boito's *Mefistofele.*
5. Anna Maurrant in Weill's *Street Scene.*
6. Cio-Cio-San to Sharpless in Puccini's *Madama Butterfly.*
7. Annina in Menotti's *Saint of Bleecker Street.*
8. Norina in soliloquy in Donizetti's *Don Pasquale.*
9. Figaro in soliloquy in Rossini's *Il Barbiere di Siviglia.*
10. Desdemona to Otello in Verdi's *Otello.*
11. La Gioconda to Laura in Ponchielli's opera.
12. Mimi to Rodolfo in Puccini's *La Bohème.*
13. Scarpia in soliloquy in Puccini's *Tosca.*
14. Nabucco to the Babylonians and Hebrews in Verdi's opera.
15. Pinkerton to Sharpless in Puccini's *Madama Butterfly.*
16. Minnie to Dick Johnson in Puccini's *La Fanciulla del West.*
17. Bardolph and Pistol to Falstaff in Verdi's opera.
18. Manon to herself in Massenet's opera.
19. Musetta to Marcello and all his friends in Puccini's *La Bohème.*
20. Santuzza to Mamma Lucia in Mascagni's *Cavalleria Rusticana.*

71. FAMOUS LAST WORDS

1. In Ponchielli's *La Gioconda,* the evil spy Barnaba voices his rage that the heroine, who has just stabbed herself rather than keep her promise to go to bed with him, has expired before he can inform her that he had, the day before, drowned her mother.

2. In Giordano's *Andrea Chénier,* the poet Chénier and his beloved Madeleine de Coigny exclaim this decidedly peculiar sentiment as they climb into the tumbrel that will deliver them to the guillotine.
3. In Verdi's *Rigoletto,* the title character cries out in horror as his daughter Gilda dies, killed by the assassin whom Rigoletto had engaged to murder the Duke of Mantua, thus fulfilling the curse that Monterone had placed on the jester.
4. In Massenet's *Werther,* Charlotte exclaims that all is ended as Werther dies in her arms of a self-inflicted wound. Offstage, the village children are heard celebrating Christmas in this effectively Gothic ending.
5. In Verdi's *Don Carlo,* at the moment Philip II of Spain orders his soldiers to arrest Carlo and Elisabetta, he hears the voice of his father—supposedly dead for five years—from within the cloister. Philip says these words, and Elisabetta cries out, in shock, to heaven.
6. The assembled chorus, revelers at King Gustavus III's masked ball in Verdi's *Un Ballo in Maschera,* exclaims in horror as the king dies after being shot by his "best friend," Count Anckarström.
7. This simple statement, uttered by the grieving Fernando, closes Donizetti's *La Favorita,* as the repentant Leonora dies in Fernando's arms. The phrase is memorable because, while singing it, the tenor must hit a ringing high C sharp!
8. With these taunting words, Carmen, in Bizet's opera, seals her fate. Having the ring thrown in his face snaps Don José's self-control, and he stabs the gypsy to death.
9. Violetta, in Verdi's *La Traviata,* feels better just at the moment that consumption claims her life. Convinced that she is recovering, she tries to embrace Alfredo, falling dead in the process.
10. Margherita, in Boito's *Mefistofele,* addressing Faust by the alias he had given her, refuses to let him comfort her as she lies dying in prison. Her final words crush Faust, whom the Devil roughly drags away.
11. Verdi's Simon Boccanegra dies stammering the name of both his daughter and her mother. He has, of course, been poisoned by his treacherous henchman Paolo Albiani, the abductor of Amelia Grimaldi, who is, of course, Simon's long-lost daughter Maria.
12. With these frantic words to Azucena, whom he believes is his mother, Manrico, the hero of Verdi's *Il Trovatore,* is dragged to the headsman by Count di Luna's guards, leaving Azucena to inform both the count and audience that Manrico was not really her son at all, but di Luna's missing brother Garcia.
13. At the conclusion of Wagner's *Die Walküre,* Wotan invokes the demigod of fire, leaving his daughter Brünnhilde to sleep surrounded

by magic fire until a hero brave enough to pass through said fire comes upon her.

14. With these two words, the Marschallin in Richard Strauss's *Der Rosenkavalier* agrees with von Faninal's trite comment on the ways of young folks and, in the process, reveals her heartbreak at losing Octavian to Faninal's daughter, Sophie.
15. Canio, in Leoncavallo's *I Pagliacci,* after stabbing his wife Nedda and her lover Silvio to death, rings down the curtain on both the play in which he had been appearing and the opera itself.
16. In Barber's *Vanessa,* Erika utters this line as she covers all the mirrors and locks all the gates in the home that Vanessa has given to her. Seemingly, as Vanessa had done before her, Erika will sit alone and wait for her lover to return to her. (Since her lover is Anatol, who has just married Vanessa, this seems unlikely to happen.)
17. In Gounod's *Roméo et Juliette,* the lovers beg God's forgiveness for their suicides as they expire in each other's arms.
18. Chrysothemis, in Richard Strauss's *Elektra,* frantically calls out to her brother, as she witnesses Elektra literally dance herself into heart failure in her frenzied joy over Orestes' return and his slaying of their mother Clytemnestra and her paramour Aegisth.

AND THEN WHAT HAPPENS? OPERA PLOTS AND PLOTTINGS

72. EXTRA! EXTRA! READ ALL ABOUT IT!

1. Ponchielli's *La Gioconda*
2. Wagner's *Lohengrin*
3. Puccini's *Tosca*
4. Verdi's *Luisa Miller*
5. Richard Strauss's *Salome*
6. Any of these: Boito's *Mefistofele;* Gounod's *Faust;* Verdi's *Il Trovatore*
7. Verdi's *Simon Boccanegra*
8. Verdi's *Falstaff* or Nicolai's *The Merry Wives of Windsor*
9. Wagner's *Die Walküre*
10. Saint-Saëns's *Samson et Dalila*
11. Giordano's *Andrea Chénier*
12. Verdi's *I Vespri Siciliani*
13. Verdi's or Rossini's *Otello*
14. Puccini's *Turandot*
15. Wagner's *Tannhäuser*
16. Britten's *Peter Grimes*
17. Verdi's *La Forza del Destino*
18. Verdi's *Rigoletto*

19. Verdi's *Un Ballo in Maschera*
20. Leoncavallo's *I Pagliacci*
21. Verdi's *Aida*
22. Mascagni's *Cavalleria Rusticana*
23. Wagner's *Die Götterdämmerung*
24. Wagner's *Tristan und Isolde*
25. Wagner's *Die Meistersinger von Nürnberg*
26. Mussorgsky's *Boris Godunov*
27. Catalani's *La Wally*
28. Mozart's *Don Giovanni*
29. Richard Strauss's *Elektra*
30. Donizetti's *Anna Bolena*

73. THE RAIN IN SPAIN

1. In Donizetti's *Lucia di Lammermoor,* Edgardo and Enrico meet in Wolfscrag Tower, amidst crackling thunder and lightning, to challenge one another to a duel.
2. In Massenet's *Thaïs,* the playgirl turned penitent crosses the desert accompanied by the sex-starved monk Athanaël, and the privations of the journey are too much for Thaïs to bear.
3. In Wagner's *Die Walküre,* Siegmund blunders into a fateful treehouse, seeking refuge from a storm. There he discovers his twin sister Sieglinde, unhappily married to the brutish Hunding. The twins run off together, and Siegmund fathers Sieglinde's child (who, many hours later, grows up to be Siegfried). Unfortunately for Siegmund, Hunding kills him the next day.
4. In Puccini's *La Bohème,* Rodolfo and Marcello have run out of firewood in Act I, so Rodolfo throws a play he has written into the stove, providing a few minutes' warmth.
5. In Mascagni's *Lodoletta,* the title character shivers in front of her callous lover Flammen's house, surviving only long enough to perform the opera's best-known aria, "Flammen perdonami."
6. In Kurt Weill's *Street Scene,* the overheated neighbors make so many comments about Anna Maurrant's indiscretion that her ill-tempered husband discovers the truth and murders his wife and her boyfriend, Steve Sankey.
7. In Donizetti's *La Favorita,* the unhappy Leonora, once mistress of a

king, staggers through the snow to the monastery where her beloved Fernando has, once again (!), taken holy vows. Fernando finds her dying in a drift, forgives her, and the pair renew their vows of love, but Leonora expires before Fernando is forced to contemplate leaping over the wall.

8. In Verdi's *Otello,* the first act begins with a terrible storm, and the opening moments of the opera deal with the frantic attempts to dock safely the battleship that has brought Otello home from the war.
9. In Rossini's *Il Barbiere di Siviglia,* the storm interlude in Act III gives the singers a few moments of rest while the orchestra conjures a brief summer rainstorm.
10. In Puccini's *La Fanciulla del West,* the irate Minnie tosses Dick Johnson out into the snow after she learns that he is really the bandit Ramerrez, in spite of Dick's protestations of moral, if not technical, innocence. Sheriff Rance is lurking near Minnie's cabin, and he shoots Dick. The erstwhile bandit staggers back inside Minnie's place, bleeding, and the soprano finally decides that she loves Dick in spite of his past. This one, though, has a happy ending.

74. LITTLE THINGS MEAN A LOT

1. In Rossini's *Il Barbiere di Siviglia,* when Dr. Bartolo finds only four sheets of writing paper on his desk, instead of the five he had left there, and notices that some ink has been spilled, he suspects (correctly) that Rosina has been up to some mischief during his absence.
2. In Massenet's *Manon,* the heroine, preparing to leave her impoverished lover des Grieux for the wealthy de Brétigny, is overcome with remorse and sadness as she bids farewell to the little table at which she and des Grieux had shared many meals, and she sings the aria "Adieu, notre petite table."
3. In Act I of *Street Scene* by Kurt Weill, Anna Maurrant gives her little boy, Willie, a dime to buy a Coke on this scorchingly hot night, establishing herself as a sweet and generous person.
4. In Britten's *Peter Grimes,* Ellen's discovery of the sweater she had knitted for Grimes's little apprentice convinces her that the child has come to harm.

5. In Puccini's *Tosca,* the heroine sees a dinner knife innocently adorning Scarpia's supper table, and she suddenly discovers a way out of her unpleasant bargain with him.
6. In Puccini's *Madama Butterfly,* Cio-Cio-San distracts her son by giving the boy a flag to play with while she prepares to commit suicide.
7. In Puccini's *La Bohème,* the flighty Musetta demonstrates the compassion she so seldom reveals to Marcello by telling him to pawn her earrings in order to buy some medicine for the dying Mimi.
8. In Mozart's *Le Nozze di Figaro,* the gardener Antonio punctures the fib that Susanna and the countess have concocted for the count's benefit when he rushes into the countess's apartment to complain about a plant damaged by a man who jumped out of the countess's window.
9. In Rossini's *L'Italiana in Algeri,* the heroine interrupts the bullies threatening to execute Taddeo when she invites them to join her for some coffee.
10. In Verdi's *Otello,* Iago uses the handkerchief his wife had taken from Desdemona to convince Otello that Desdemona has been unfaithful to him. Iago tells the Moor that he had seen Cassio with the handkerchief. The credulous Otello immediately decides to kill his innocent wife.
11. In Puccini's *Il Tabarro,* the unfortunate Luigi mistakes his boss's lighting his pipe for the signal he had arranged with his lover Giorgetta, the boss's wife. He boards the couple's barge–and is promptly caught and killed by Michele.
12. In Ponchielli's *La Gioconda,* La Cieca gives her rosary to Laura, who has saved her life. When Gioconda discovers that the man she loves, Enzo, has a lover, she plans to kill the other woman. When she discovers that her rival is Laura (she sees the rosary in Laura's hand), she devotes herself to making possible Laura and Enzo's escape from Venice.

75. HOT TIMES

1. John of Leyden, in Meyerbeer's *Le Prophète,* devises this drastic method of atoning for his own wicked acts, while taking his even more wicked Anabaptist enemies along with him.

2. Enzo, in Ponchielli's *La Gioconda,* eludes Alvise Badoero, his beloved Laura's spouse, by jumping into the Adriatic Sea, after having diverted his enemy's attention by setting fire to his boat. (If this strikes you as nonsensical, you should know that much in *La Gioconda* defies logic.)
3. In Act I of Verdi's *Otello,* the Cypriots dance joyously around a fire moments before Iago begins working out his evil designs by getting Cassio drunk.
4. In Bellini's *Norma,* the title character, a Druid priestess, and her Roman lover, Pollione, are burned to death for having participated in this illicit romance.
5. In Verdi's *Don Carlo,* an auto-da-fé, in which a number of Flemish Protestants are burned at the stake for heresy, serves as the entertainment at the coronation of King Philip II of Spain. Although it must bring them scant comfort, these wretched victims of intolerance are welcomed into heaven by a Celestial Voice who sings one of Verdi's most exquisite melodies.
6. In Mozart's *Don Giovanni,* the unrepentant Don is sent off to Hell while devilish flames reduce his palace to a shell. The statue of the Commendatore, appearing at Don G.'s party at his bidding, commands the Don to renounce his licentious ways. When Don Giovanni refuses, all Hell breaks loose.
7. In Humperdinck's *Hansel and Gretel,* witch Rosina Daintymouth expects to make a dainty meal of her two young prisoners. Gretel, at Hansel's urging, pushes the witch into the oven, thus releasing all the children who have been bound by her spell and providing everyone with a tasty gingerbread cookie.
8. Azucena, in Verdi's *Il Trovatore,* throws the wrong baby (her son) into the fire that had devoured her own mother. She thought it was the baby of the old Count di Luna. Her rash action has, of course, devastating, if highly melodic, consequences!
9. In Wagner's *Die Götterdämmerung,* the fire from Siegfried's funeral pyre rises up, destroys what's left of Valhalla (not to mention the Gibichungs' palace), and wipes out almost all of the *Ring*'s population. The exceptions, it appears, are the three Rhinemaidens, who, having finally gotten their accursèd lump of gold back, frolic on through the ages.
10. In Verdi's *Giovanna d'Arco,* Joan of Arc is *not* burned by the English, receiving instead a seemingly mortal wound on the battlefield from which she miraculously recovers just in time to take part in the opera's finale.

76. HOLIDAYS

1. Christmas Eve figures in Puccini's *La Bohème,* Massenet's *Werther,* and Menotti's *Amahl and the Night Visitors.* In *La Bohème,* Mimi and Rodolfo meet on Christmas Eve and then go to the Café Momus with Rodolfo's bohemian friends to celebrate the holiday and their love. *Werther,* which begins with a chorus of children rehearsing a Christmas song in July, ends with Werther's suicide on Christmas Eve. The reprise of the joyous song offstage is meant to serve as a contrast to Werther's suffering and Charlotte's grief. *Amahl and the Night Visitors* is set on the original Christmas Eve, and the miracle of the crippled boy regaining his health when he offers his crutch as a gift to the Christ Child gives the opera its happy ending.
2. Mascagni's lurid *Cavalleria Rusticana* is set on Easter Sunday. The violent love triangle leads to Turiddu's murder by Alfio moments after the Easter mass is celebrated in the village church.
3. Midsummer Night, called *Johannesnacht* in Wagner's German text, is the setting for Act II of *Die Meistersinger von Nürnberg.* It encompasses Walther and Eva's declaration of love, Beckmesser's attempt to serenade Eva, and the thrashing administered to Beckmesser by David.
4. All Hallows' Eve is the setting for the *Walpurgisnacht* ballet in Gounod's *Faust,* during which Méphistophélès attempts to distract Faust's attention from Marguerite by conjuring up such beautiful women as Helen of Troy. The trick, of course, does not work.
5. The birthday of the mythical Don Andres, Viceroy of Peru, provides the occasion for the merrymaking that opens Offenbach's *La Périchole.*
6. Passover figures in the plot of Halévy's *La Juive,* which boasts a scene during which Eleazar presides over a Passover seder.
7. Good Friday is the setting for the third act of Wagner's *Parsifal.* It is also the setting for the first scene of Menotti's *The Saint of Bleecker Street,* in which Annina's neighbors come to witness her vision of the Crucifixion and the stigmata that appears on her hands.
8. Carnival, or the pre-Lenten celebrations, is mentioned in Ponchielli's *La Gioconda,* Verdi's *La Traviata,* and Johann Strauss's *A Night in Venice.* In *La Gioconda* the festivities surrounding the regatta enable the spy Barnaba to begin his evil intrigues. In *La Traviata* the dying Violetta listens to the offstage revelry early in the fourth act and instructs her maid Annina to distribute half of their remaining few

coins to the poor. Carnival forms the basis for all the merry complications of *A Night in Venice.*

9. In Menotti's *The Saint of Bleecker Street,* Annina, the feeble, saintly heroine, who exhibits the stigmata each year on Good Friday, is forcibly dragged by the Sons of San Gennaro to head the Little Italy parade on the Feast Day.
10. In Leoncavallo's *I Pagliacci,* the townspeople celebrate this day by attending the play presented by Canio and his troupe.

77. WINE, PERSONS, AND SONG

1. In Mascagni's *Cavalleria Rusticana,* Turiddu invites his friends to drink with him at his mother's tavern after Easter services. Turiddu drinks so much, toasting the beauty of his beloved Lola, that, by the time Lola's angry husband Alfio arrives, poor Turiddu is in no condition to fight a duel with the man he wronged, which is probably why Alfio wins.
2. In Act I of Bizet's *Carmen,* the heroine bargains with Don José to entertain him at the inn of Lillas Pastia only if José will let her escape from his custody. She will dance the *seguedilla* for him and drink *manzanilla* in his company. José cannot resist and ends up with a term in the guardhouse, but he ultimately does meet Carmen at Pastia's. The rest is history.
3. Hoffmann, Offenbach's poet-protagonist in *Les Contes d'Hoffmann,* gets carried away by the fellowship at Luther's tavern and relates the story of his tragic love for the doll Olympia, the courtesan Giulietta, and the doomed girl Antonia. He gets so drunk in the process that he sleeps through the arrival of his current *amour,* the singer Stella, who cheerfully accepts the attentions of Hoffmann's archenemy, Councilor Lindorf.
4. Lucrezia Borgia, in Donizetti's opera of that name, invites the youths who have insulted her to a dinner party, where she plans to kill them with poisoned wine. Lucrezia is unpleasantly surprised when her own illegitimate son drinks and, thus, dies with his pals.
5. In Act II of Puccini's *Tosca,* Baron Scarpia invites the heroine to enjoy his Spanish wine as she ponders his offer to free her lover if she spends the night with him. If the wine gives Tosca courage, it is the courage

needed to stab Scarpia with the dinner knife that she spies near the wineglass.

6. In Act I of Wagner's *Götterdämmerung,* Siegfried is given a special brew by the villainous Hagen, which is designed to make the simple hero forget his vows of love for Brünnhilde. More specifically, Hagen plans to offer his half sister Gutrune to Siegfried, and then schemes to have Siegfried snatch the ring of the Nibelung from Brünnhilde, who regards it as her wedding ring. (If you can remember all that, you don't need this book to tell you what happens thereafter!)
7. Falstaff, in Verdi's opera, orders sherry after the merry wives have conspired to dump him into the Thames as punishment for the ribald propositions he has made to Alice and Meg. The drink soothes him, but he is soon led by his lechery into the Forest of Windsor, where the wives and their friends torment him further.
8. Alfred, in Johann Strauss's *Die Fledermaus,* urges Rosalinde to drink with him now that her husband Eisenstein has gone off to jail. Before much champagne can be imbibed, Prison Warden Frank arrives to escort Eisenstein to jail. To protect Rosalinde's reputation, gallant Alfred agrees to impersonate Eisenstein.
9. In Samuel Barber's *Vanessa,* Erika, Vanessa's niece, dines with Anatol, the son of the lover Vanessa had expected to join her. Anatol takes after his dad, and after a few too many, Erika agrees to spend the night with Anatol, whom she has known for only a few minutes. By the next act, Anatol is engaged to Vanessa, and Erika is pregnant!
10. In *La Traviata,* Violetta listens to Alfredo's toast and soon finds herself considering his declaration of love. She runs off with him.

78. CRIMES MAJOR AND MINOR

1. In Mussorgsky's *Boris Godunov,* the first crime is the murder of the Czarevitch Dmitri, arranged by Boris. The second crime, at least by the laws of the day, is the escape by Grigori from his monastery. The final crime is the robbing of the Fool by the band of children who steal his money as he bewails the fate of Russia.
2. One crime in Verdi's *Don Carlo* is the assassination of Rodrigo, arranged by King Philip II and the Grand Inquisitor, and carried out by soldiers of the Inquisition. The next crime is treason, when Don

Carlo draws his sword against his father Philip. The third crime, this one of a more domestic nature, is Eboli's theft of Elisabetta's jewel box, which contains Carlo's portrait. This is calculated to make the jealous old monarch suspicious of his unhappy young wife. Lastly, there is the crime of adultery, committed by Philip and Eboli.

3. Blackmail occurs in Meyerbeer's *Le Prophète* when the sinister Anabaptists twice threaten to kill Fidès, John of Leyden's mother, if John doesn't agree to go along with their plans and schemes. Also, there is the mass murder that John commits when he blows up his own castle, taking his enemies, as well as his mother, with him!
4. In Puccini's *Madama Butterfly,* Pinkerton commits bigamy by marrying Kate while he is married to Butterfly.
5. In Ponchielli's *La Gioconda,* Alvise Badoero is guilty of the attempted murder of his wife Laura because of her infidelity. Barnaba is the opera's chief malefactor: he is guilty of bearing false witness when he accuses La Cieca of being a witch; he's guilty of extortion when he threatens to kill Cieca if Gioconda doesn't go to bed with him; and, finally, he's guilty of Cieca's murder.
6. In Puccini's *Manon Lescaut,* his heroine is accused of attempted theft when the police apprehend her about to leave Geronte's house with all his jewelry. Geronte himself is conceivably guilty of corrupting the morals of a minor.
7. In Wagner's *Das Rheingold,* Alberich steals the gold from the Rhinemaidens; Wotan and Loge steal from Alberich the ring he has had forged from the gold; and Fafner kills his brother Fasolt when the two giants quarrel over the ring.
8. In Verdi's *Simon Boccanegra,* Paolo Albiani abducts Boccanegra's newly discovered daughter, Amelia, and, an act later, murders Simon by poisoning his pitcher of water.
9. In Berg's opera, Lulu shoots her husband, Dr. Schön, and later, with the aid of the countess, escapes from prison. Later still, she violates London's public morality by walking its streets. The final crimes, however, are committed by none other than Jack the Ripper, whom Lulu brings to her rooms. Jack kills Lulu and the countess.
10. In Britten's *Billy Budd,* Squeak steals Billy's tobacco; Claggart swears falsely that Billy is plotting a mutiny; and Billy, however unwittingly, kills Claggart when he strikes him and he cracks his head as he falls to the floor.
11. In Donizetti's *Lucia di Lammermoor,* Enrico, Lucia's brother, sins by forging the letter that convinces Lucia that Edgardo has deserted her. Although Lucia murders Arturo, her husband of less than an hour,

she would, one assumes, have been acquitted by reason of insanity had she lived to stand trial.

12. No one commits a "big" crime during Johann Strauss's *Die Fledermaus,* although Adele "borrows" a dress belonging to her employer, Rosalinde, and in Act II, Rosalinde swipes Eisenstein's watch. However, before the operetta actually begins, Eisenstein has been sentenced to a week in jail for having kicked a tax collector, a fact crucial to the development of the farcical plot.

79. HIDING PLACES

1. In Mozart's *Le Nozze di Figaro,* Cherubino and Susanna take turns hiding in a closet during Act II. Cherubino hides to escape the wrath of Count Almaviva, and Susanna takes his place in order to help her mistress, the Countess Almaviva, teach the count a lesson. Since this is a comedy, all turns out well.
2. In Act III of Puccini's *La Bohème,* Mimi hides behind a tree to eavesdrop on Rodolfo's conversation with Marcello. She learns that Rodolfo still loves her, but that she is dying of consumption.
3. In Puccini's *Tosca,* Angelotti hides in a well in Mario's garden in order to escape Baron Scarpia's policemen, who are searching for him after his escape from the Castel Sant'Angelo. Tosca, unable to endure Mario's screams of agony, tells Scarpia where Angelotti has been hidden. The unfortunate Angelotti kills himself to avoid recapture.
4. In Puccini's *La Fanciulla del West,* Minnie hides her wounded boyfriend Dick Johnson in her loft, when Sheriff Rance, who has shot and wounded Johnson, arrives to search Minnie's little cabin. In a grotesque touch, Johnson's blood drips down from the loft, and Rance forces his quarry to climb down. Minnie cheats in a poker game in which the stakes are Johnson's life and freedom. All ends well.
5. Falstaff, in Verdi's opera–as well as in Nicolai's *The Merry Wives of Windsor*–is hidden by the ladies in a laundry basket, ostensibly to save the fat knight from the wrath of Master Ford, but it is actually a means of tricking the naughty Sir John, who is tossed into the Thames as punishment for his attempts to seduce Alice and Meg.
6. In Mozart's *Don Giovanni,* the Don, meeting Leporello in a graveyard, hides behind a marker and torments his servant, pretending to be a

ghost and not realizing that his own doom is about to be sealed in a supernatural encounter with the Commendatore's statue.

7. In Act I of Puccini's *Tosca,* Angelotti hides in the chapel of his sister, the Marchesa d'Attavanti, first when he hears the sacristan's approach, and later when Tosca comes to pay her morning call on Mario.
8. In Verdi's *Otello,* the Moor hides behind a partition to eavesdrop while Iago converses with Cassio, falsely supplying evidence to Otello that Cassio is Desdemona's lover. This encounter is the final straw and Otello decides to murder his wife that very night.
9. In the last act of Bizet's *Carmen,* Don José mills around in the crowd outside the arena, where Escamillo is fighting bulls, until only Carmen (who has seen him anyway) is left outside. This is the final session for the two former lovers; José stabs Carmen when she refuses to return to him.
10. In Verdi's *La Forza del Destino,* Leonora takes refuge in a cave at the monastery of Hornachuelos, where she plans to live out her life away from the world. Her lover Alvaro coincidentally takes holy vows at the same monastery, and the truth is discovered in the opera's tragic and bloody final scene.
11. In Zandonai's *Francesca da Rimini,* Francesca's lover Paolo tries to escape through a trap door when Francesca's husband, Paolo's hunchbacked brother, surprises him. Unfortunately, his cape gets caught in the door as the irate husband enters, and both lovers are stabbed by the deformed cuckold.
12. In Massenet's *Werther,* Charlotte locks herself into her own boudoir closet to escape from Werther's protestations of love. Werther leaves, crestfallen to the point of suicide. Charlotte runs to Werther's house after her husband has lent Werther a pair of pistols. She arrives, in the opera's last scene, to find Werther dying.

80. GIFTS

1. The Mikado sends a hara-kiri dagger to Butterfly's father, we learn from Goro in the first act of Puccini's *Madama Butterfly,* with the suggestion that the dishonored man use it. The suggestion is accepted. Cio-Cio-San also finds use for the knife.
2. In the first act of Bellini's *La Sonnambula,* Elvino gives his sweetheart Amina a ring that had belonged to his departed mother.

3. Arlecchino (Beppe) brings a bottle of wine to Colombina (Nedda) in the play-within-a-play segment of Leoncavallo's *I Pagliacci.* (It would have been kinder, in view of the opera's bloody ending, had Arlecchino provided his beloved with a pair of running shoes!)
4. As the curtain descends on Richard Strauss's *Arabella,* Arabella gives her betrothed Mandryka a glass of water, which somehow signifies that their love shall endure.
5. In Massenet's opera, de Brétigny dries Manon's tears after her impoverished lover des Grieux has been abducted (for "his own good" by his father) by means of some jewelry.
6. Sachs gives Beckmesser the lyrics to Walther's Prize Song, knowing that the town clerk will make a fool of himself when he attempts to perform the song at the Mastersingers' contest in Wagner's *Die Meistersinger von Nürnberg.*
7. In Ponchielli's *La Gioconda,* La Cieca gives Laura her rosary after Laura saves Cieca from a mob bent on killing her.
8. In the beginning of the second act of Puccini's *La Bohème,* Rodolfo buys a pink bonnet for Mimi.
9. In Act III of Wagner's *Die Walküre,* Brünnhilde gives Sieglinde the broken pieces of Siegmund's sword. (Years later, of course, the Walsungs' son Siegfried forges the sword back into its original state.)
10. Adriana Lecouvreur, in Cilea's opera, gives her lover Maurizio a bouquet of violets. Maurizio, trying to placate the Princess de Bouillon, gives the flowers to her later that same evening. Ultimately, this action proves to be a mistake.
11. Otello, in Verdi's opera, gives Desdemona the handkerchief that Iago later claims to have seen in Cassio's hands. Otello, believing Iago's lie, condemns his wife to death.
12. Orlofsky, in Johann Strauss's *Die Fledermaus,* gives Adele a purse filled with money to gamble with at his gala party. He is not in the least dismayed when Adele promptly loses everything.
13. Mario, in the first act of Puccini's *Tosca,* gives his friend Angelotti, who has just escaped from prison, the basket of food and wine that the sacristan has provided for Mario's own dinner.
14. Ernani, in Verdi's opera, gives the vengeful Silva his hunting horn when Silva agrees to help Ernani rescue Elvira, whom they both love, from her other would-be husband, Don Carlo. Ernani swears that his life will be forfeited when Silva sounds the horn.
15. At the end of the Venice segment of Offenbach's *Les Contes d'Hoffmann,* Dapertutto offers Hoffmann the sword with which he kills Schlémil in a duel.

81. MEMBERS OF THE WEDDING

1. In Mozart's *Le Nozze di Figaro,* Susanna agrees to meet Count Almaviva in the palace garden on the evening of her marriage to Figaro. Of course, Susanna does not intend to keep the tryst. The countess will impersonate Susanna, who, dressed as the countess, will test Figaro's loyalty. In the end, the countess catches Almaviva, but all ends with forgiveness and merriment.
2. In Wagner's *Die Götterdämmerung,* Siegfried, disguised as Gunther, kidnaps Brünnhilde, to whom he has pledged eternal faithfulness. Siegfried, however, has been given a potion that makes him forget all about Brünnhilde. Thus, Brünnhilde is given to the *real* Gunther, while Siegfried marries Gunther's rather wimpy sister, Gutrune. All of these events occur in fulfillment of the curse of the ring, but before the drama ends, Brünnhilde realizes that Siegfried, slain by her half-brother-in-law Hagen, was a victim of Hagen's treachery. Her love for Siegfried restored, Brünnhilde rides into his flaming pyre to join him in death.
3. In Mozart's *Don Giovanni,* the wedding of Zerlina and Masetto is interrupted when Don Giovanni arrives on the scene and attempts to seduce the not totally unwilling Zerlina. Don Giovanni pursues Zerlina intermittently throughout the opera, but he never succeeds in getting her away from Masetto's vengeful eye. Once Don Giovanni has been dragged off to Hell, Zerlina and Masetto are free to begin their married life.
4. In Wagner's *Lohengrin,* Elsa derails her wedding night with the Swan Knight when, upset by Ortrud's insinuations, she breaks her vow and asks Lohengrin his name and where he comes from. For reasons that defy logic, Lohengrin is thus compelled to leave Elsa, although before he goes he thwarts Ortrud's evil magic by turning his swan back into Elsa's missing brother, the rightful Duke of Brabant.
5. In Verdi's *I Vespri Siciliani,* the wedding of Arrigo to Elena ends in bloodshed when the Sicilian rebels, led by the fiery Procida, suddenly set upon and kill Arrigo's father, the French governor Monforte, and all the assembled French soldiers.
6. In Donizetti's *L'Elisir d'Amore,* the flirtatious Adina postpones her wedding ceremony because her lovesick suitor Nemorino isn't around for her to make miserable. Also, deep down, Adina must know that she really loves Nemorino and not the foppish Sergeant Belcore, whom she had impulsively promised to marry.

7. In Gounod's *Roméo et Juliette,* as in Shakespeare's play, the secret marriage of Roméo to Juliette is followed almost immediately by Roméo's slaying of Juliette's kinsman Tybalt and his subsequent banishment from Verona, which leads to the lovers' suicides.
8. In Donizetti's *La Fille du Régiment,* the *vivandière* Marie is rescued from her forced marriage to the little Duke of Krackentorp by the arrival of her beloved Tonio and the regiment he now commands. When Marie's past as Daughter of the Regiment is revealed, the duke is dragged away by his haughty mother while Marie's own, newly revealed mother, the Marquise de Berkenfeld, belatedly blesses the union of Marie and Tonio.
9. In Verdi's *Aida,* Amneris emerges from the temple, where she has been praying on the eve of her wedding to Radames, only to find her fiancé romancing Aida and revealing the hidden place of the Egyptian army. She orders Radames's arrest and later relents, but she is unable to save Radames from the death sentence handed down by the priests.
10. In Donizetti's *Don Pasquale,* Pasquale is astounded and dismayed when his supposed bride, Sonfronia (who is actually Ernesto's fiancée Norina in disguise), changes from shrinking violet to Venus's-flytrap as soon as their wedding (a put-up job arranged by Dr. Malatesta in order to teach Pasquale a lesson) is over. She bullies Don Pasquale to the limits of his sanity, but all is resolved at the final curtain.
11. In Bellini's *I Puritani,* Elvira quickly goes mad when she learns that her bridegroom, Arturo, has run away with Henrietta of England, widow of Charles I. Of course, Arturo's reasons are honorable–he saves Henrietta from certain execution by the Puritan Roundheads–and he and Elvira are reunited after two acts of *bel canto* madness from the bride.
12. In Verdi's *Don Carlo,* the rapturous love between Carlo and Elisabetta de Valois is short-circuited after approximately ten minutes of bliss, when the princess learns that, as part of a peace agreement between France and Spain, she must marry Carlo's formidable father, King Philip II. This one ends badly for all concerned.

82. STOP ALL THAT SINGING AND LET US DANCE!

1. In Cilea's *Adriana Lecouvreur,* the ballet "Judgment of Paris" begins as Adriana and her hostess, the Princess de Bouillon, are about to

scratch each other's eyes out. The princess gets the golden apple, but Adriana gets those poisoned violets.

2. In Meyerbeer's *Le Prophète,* the dancing *patineurs* entertain the Anabaptist rebels.
3. This, of course, is the Triumphal Scene ballet in Verdi's *Aida.*
4. In Verdi's *Don Carlo,* the ballet "The Pearl," commissioned by King Philip II as an entertainment for his wife, Elisabetta de Valois, is performed in a scene from Act III that is almost always omitted.
5. In Ponchielli's *La Gioconda,* Alvise's announcement that he has killed his faithless wife Laura breaks up his party at the conclusion of the "Dance of the Hours."
6. In Gounod's *Faust,* the *Walpurgisnacht* ballet finds the Devil trying to distract Faust from Marguerite's plight by introducing Faust to such fabled beauties as Helen of Troy.
7. The final scene of Saint-Saëns's *Samson et Dalila* begins with a wild *bacchanale,* a balletic and sexy version of a pagan rite. Unfortunately, Samson, having been blinded by the Philistines, is unable to enjoy it.
8. The waltz that interrupts Act II of Johann Strauss's *Die Fledermaus* may frustrate Eisenstein, but it seems to delight the audience nonetheless.
9. In the Paris version of Wagner's *Tannhäuser,* the opera's opening scene is the Venusberg ballet, after which Tannhäuser begs leave to depart from Venus's lair.
10. This, of course, is Richard Strauss's "Dance of the Seven Veils" from *Salome.* After dancing for Herod, her stepfather, Salome demands (and gets) Jokanaan's (John the Baptist) head on a platter.

83. GETTING THERE IS HALF THE FUN

1. In Puccini's *Il Tabarro,* Michele, Giorgetta, and Luigi live and work on their barge, which sails up and down the Seine.
2. Vanderdecker, Wagner's Flying Dutchman, sails a ship with blood-red sails.
3. Lohengrin, in Wagner's opera, arrives in Brabant on a boat drawn by a swan. (Incidentally, when he leaves, the swan has become Elsa's brother Gottfried once more, and the boat is propelled by a dove.)

4. In Wagner's *Die Walküre,* Fricka arrives (to nag her husband Wotan) in a cart drawn by a ram.
5. Rosina Daintymouth, the witch in Humperdinck's *Hansel and Gretel,* rides a broomstick with comic gusto.
6. Porgy, in Gershwin's *Porgy and Bess,* rides on a cart drawn by a goat.
7. In Britten's opera *The Turn of the Screw,* the governess travels by train to the country estate of her mysterious employer.
8. In the Swedish opera *Aniara* by Karl-Birger Blomdähl, all the action takes place in a spaceship millions of miles from Earth.
9. In Menotti's *Help! Help! the Gobolinks!,* the tone-deaf creatures from outer space invade a schoolbus.
10. In another Menotti opera, *The Saint of Bleecker Street,* the fugitive Michele rides the subways and arranges to meet his ailing sister Annina in an IRT station.
11. Peter Grimes, in Britten's opera, has various misadventures on his fishing boat.
12. Pinkerton, in Puccini's *Madama Butterfly,* shuttles between the United States and Japan on board the *U.S.S. Abraham Lincoln.*
13. Tannhäuser walks from Thuringia to Rome and back, doing penance for his wicked lifestyle in Wagner's opera.
14. The villains who create the city of Mahagonny, in Kurt Weill's opera *The Rise and Fall of the City of Mahagonny,* decide to create that city after the truck in which they are fleeing the police breaks down.
15. In Barber's *Vanessa,* Anatol travels by horse-drawn sleigh to dine with Vanessa.

84. FARAWAY PLACES

1. Delibes's *Lakmé* takes place in India.
2. Janáček's *Jenůfa* and Smetana's *The Bartered Bride* are set in Bohemia.
3. Hell is the setting for Offenbach's *Orpheus in the Underworld,* as well as for Gluck's serious treatment of the Orpheus legend, *Orfeo ed Euridice.*
4. Venice is the setting for Ponchielli's *La Gioconda,* Act I of Donizetti's *Lucrezia Borgia,* Act II of Offenbach's *Les Contes d'Hoffmann,* and a Johann Strauss opera that uses Venice as part of its title, *A Night in Venice.*

5. Offenbach's *La Périchole* is set in Lima, Peru.
6. Palestine is the setting for Verdi's *I Lombardi.*
7. Gaul is the setting for Bellini's *Norma.*
8. Gaspare Spontini's *Fernando Cortez,* Roger Sessions's *Montezuma,* and *The Royal Hunt of the Sun,* a contemporary opera by Iaín Hamilton, are set in Mexico.
9. An inn on the Lithuanian border serves as the one more or less comic interlude of Mussorgsky's *Boris Godunov.*
10. Offenbach's *Les Contes d'Hoffmann,* Gounod's *Faust,* and Massenet's *Werther* take place in Frankfurt.
11. Bellini's *I Puritani* is set in a Scotland that never really existed.
12. Manhattan is the setting for Weill's *Street Scene* and Menotti's *The Saint of Bleecker Street.*

85. CRUEL AND UNUSUAL

1. Manfredo, in Montemezzi's *L'Amore dei Tre Re,* dies after kissing the lips of his dead wife. His father, King Archibaldo, has poisoned the lips of his unfaithful daughter-in-law Fiora–whom the king had previously strangled–hoping to catch her lover Avito in the act of bidding Fiora farewell. That happens too, but at the unexpected cost of Manfredo's life as well.
2. Rachel, in Halévy's *La Juive,* is thrown into a vat of boiling oil with her supposed father, Eleazar, as these Jewish martyrs have defied the edicts of the local cardinal. As Rachel is being deep-fried, Eleazar allows himself the last laugh by shouting to his archenemy, the cardinal, that Rachel is actually the churchman's own illegitimate child.
3. Cecilia, an early Christian martyr in Refice's opera of that name, is skewered by a brigade of Roman soldiers after having frustrated her husband for three acts by refusing to consummate their marriage. Although stabbed from every direction, Cecilia lives long enough to warble out her final visions of salvation.
4. The Queen of the Night (along with Monostatos and the three ladies-in-waiting) is swallowed up into the earth shortly before Mozart's *The Magic Flute* reaches its conclusion. The loathsome quintet had been planning the destruction of Sarastro's righteous community and,

therefore, get exactly what they deserve, although one is never quite certain how and why the earth swallows them at just the right moment.

5. La Cieca is La Gioconda's luckless mother in Ponchielli's opera. Held hostage by the fiendish spy Barnaba, La Cieca's release is promised to Gioconda if she will make love to Barnaba. Gioconda kills herself instead, but Barnaba gloatingly shouts to the suicide that he had already drowned Cieca in the canal.
6. Hagenbach, the tenor lead in Catalani's *La Wally,* survives being tossed over a cliff by Gelner, who does so to avenge the insult Wally had suffered from Giuseppe. The remorseful Wally nurses him back to health, only to lose him to an avalanche, after which, incidentally, Wally jumps off a cliff.
7. Lisa, in Tchaikovsky's *Pique Dame,* chooses a rather picturesque method of doing herself in, namely, jumping into the River Neva when she realizes that her lover, Herman, has lost his mind in his obsession with winning at cards.
8. Antonia, the saddest of Hoffmann's three loves in Offenbach's *Les Contes d'Hoffmann,* suffers from a strange disease that makes her singing potentially lethal to her. The diabolical Dr. Miracle conjures up the voice of Antonia's mother, who had died of the same disease. The mother urges Antonia to sing, and the girl does so until she collapses and dies in her father's arms after completing a gorgeous if strenuous trio.
9. In Giordano's *Fedora,* the title character is responsible for the arrest and eventual death of the brother of her sometime enemy, otherwise lover, Loris. Loris has killed Fedora's evil fiancé Vladimir, son of the head of the Russian secret police. Fedora writes to Moscow, implicating Loris (who is in Paris with her) and his brother. The brother is drowned when a flood engulfs his dungeon cell, and his poor old mother expires upon receiving the grim news. These events lead to Fedora's eventual confession and suicide, which is accomplished with a bottle of poison concealed in Fedora's jeweled crucifix.
10. Lakmé, in Delibes's opera, realizing that her love affair with the Englishman Gerard is doomed, poisons herself by a most exotic means–sniffing the perfume of a poisonous flowering plant.
11. Glauce is Jason's young second wife in Cherubini's *Médée.* Médée's hatred for Glauce is so strong that she sends the girl a wedding dress treated with a poisonous chemical that causes the dress to catch fire, thus immolating the bride. Then Médée proceeds to prepare a special dinner for Jason, but that's another story!

12. John of Leyden, the false prophet and tool of the Anabaptists in Meyerbeer's *Le Prophète,* is joined in death by his mother, Fidès, when John, disgusted with his own corrupt behavior, and aware of a plot against him, seals the fate of his enemies and himself by igniting all the ammunition in his palace.

A POTPOURRI

86. OPENING NIGHTS

1. Marguerite was sung by Christine Nilsson (no relation to Birgit).
2. Italian.
3. Puccini's *Tosca,* with Dorothy Kirsten in the title role.
4. Enrico Caruso as the Duke of Mantua in Verdi's *Rigoletto,* 1903; Cesare Siepi as King Philip II in *Don Carlo,* 1950; Maria Callas in Bellini's *Norma,* 1956; George London as Amonasro in Verdi's *Aida,* 1951; Lucine Amara as the Celestial Voice in Verdi's *Don Carlo,* 1950.
5. *Antony and Cleopatra;* music by Samuel Barber; libretto adapted from Shakespeare by Franco Zeffirelli, who also designed and staged the production. Alvin Ailey choreographed the opera, his first assignment for the Met. Justino Diaz and Leontyne Price sang the title roles. Jess Thomas sang Caesar Octavius, Rosalind Elias sang Charmian, Ezio Flagello was the Enobarbus, and Andrea Velis sang Mardian the Eunich. Thomas Schippers was the conductor. In case you've forgotten, the date was September 16, 1966.
6. Puccini's *Madama Butterfly* starring Maria Callas.
7. Renata Tebaldi and Maria Callas conducted, at least through their

partisans, *the* operatic feud of the 1950s and 1960s. Callas attended the opening-night performance of Cilea's *Adriana Lecouvreur* on September 16, 1968. Tebaldi sang the title role, flanked by Franco Corelli as Maurizio, Irene Dalis as the princess, and Anselmo Colzani as Michonnet, with Fausto Cleva conducting. After the final act, Bing brought Callas backstage to see Tebaldi. In a scene captured by photographers, the two women fell into each other's arms, weeping with emotion.

8. December 7 – Pearl Harbor Day.
9. One year, Caruso allowed Geraldine Farrar to make her debut on opening night. Farrar sang the soprano lead in Gounod's *Roméo et Juliette.*
10. There was a special concert on December 7, 1946, conducted by Arturo Toscanini. The program included the Verdi *Te Deum,* the prologue to Boito's *Mefistofele,* the prayer from Rossini's *Mosè,* and the third act of Puccini's *Manon Lescaut.* Three of the singers that night were Mafalda Favero, Tancredi Pasero, and Renata Tebaldi, making her La Scala debut on that occasion.

87. OPERA HOUSES AROUND THE WORLD

1. Mozart's *Don Giovanni* had its first performance at the Prague Opera.
2. Mary Garden managed the Chicago Opera for one tempestuous season in the 1920s during which period the company lost nearly $1 million.
3. As the Paris Opéra-Comique, the Salle Favart was the scene, on March 3, 1875, of the first performance of Bizet's *Carmen.*
4. *Oberto,* Verdi's first opera, was also his first to be given at La Scala.
5. *La Bohème* was first produced at the Teatro Reggio in Turin. The rebuilt theater opened in 1973 with a not terribly successful production of Verdi's *I Vespri Siciliani,* staged by Maria Callas and Giuseppe di Stefano.
6. The Metropolitan Opera opened with a performance of Gounod's *Faust,* sung in Italian. The seven seasons that followed featured operas sung only in German, regardless of their countries of origin.
7. *La Forza del Destino.*
8. The Chicago Lyric Opera was organized in 1954 by Carol Fox, its director, conductor Nicola Rescigno, and the late Lawrence Kelly.

9. Tebaldi made her American debut in the autumn of 1950 in the title role of *Aida.* The debut took place at the San Francisco Opera, and her Radames that night was Mario del Monaco.
10. Sutherland made her Royal Opera House debut as the First Lady in Mozart's *The Magic Flute.* Her modest success soon led to her appearance as the servant Clotilde in Bellini's *Norma,* but she could hardly have been noticed in Bellini's opera since the Norma on that occasion was Maria Callas.
11. The Monte Carlo Opera House was home to the first performance of Puccini's *La Rondine.*
12. Both La Scala and the Vienna State Opera were practically leveled by Allied bombing. La Scala was the first to reopen, with a gala concert led by Arturo Toscanini in 1946. Vienna had to wait nine more years, until 1955, for the Staatsoper to reopen with a performance of Beethoven's *Fidelio.*
13. The Stockholm Opera has created a production of Verdi's *Un Ballo in Maschera* with a Swedish setting that is sung in Swedish to a libretto that more accurately depicts the events surrounding the assassination of King Gustavus III.
14. Parma is feared by singers around the world for the hostility heaped on offending artists by the local patrons, especially the fanatics who sit in the theater's highest gallery.
15. Gatti-Casazza managed La Scala before he headed the Metropolitan Opera.
16. The Baths of Carracalla in Rome is celebrated for the spectacular stagings of *Aida* that lure thousands of tourists each summer.
17. Puccini's *Madama Butterfly* and *Turandot* were given their premieres at La Scala. The *Butterfly* premiere, in 1904, was conducted by Toscanini with Rosina Storchio as the heroine. The performance was a fiasco, with rude behavior from the audience (an intrigue led by Puccini's enemies was rumored to have been responsible) interrupting the opera on several occasions. Puccini immediately withdrew the opera and revised it. *Turandot* was produced at La Scala in 1926, two years after the death of the composer. *Turandot* was led by Toscanini, who terminated the performance with the last music Puccini completed, the point of Liù's death in Act III. The Turandot was Rosa Raisa, and the opera was triumphantly received.
18. *La Traviata*'s unsuccessful first night took place at the Teatro La Fenice in Venice.
19. Liebermann turned the Hamburg Opera into a major operatic center before leaving that post for the Paris Opéra.
20. The Edinburgh Festival, in Scotland, had invited the La Scala com-

pany to perform Bellini's *La Sonnambula* in a production starring Maria Callas. Callas refused to take part in an extra performance that was added in response to the great demand for tickets. Her understudy, Renata Scotto, then in her early twenties and virtually unknown in or out of Italy, sang the role of Amina to great acclaim.

88. FROM PAGE TO STAGE

1. *Ivanhoe,* by Sir Walter Scott, was the inspiration for Sir Arthur Sullivan's lone serious opera, also named *Ivanhoe.*
2. Henry James's novel *The Wings of the Dove* was adapted for the lyric stage by Douglas Moore and was produced at the New York City Opera in 1961.
3. Dickens's novel was renamed *Miss Havisham's Fire* when American composer Dominick Argento composed an opera based upon it, produced at the New York City Opera in 1979.
4. Cervantes's *Don Quixote* was adapted as an opera by Jules Massenet, who, of course, gave the title character a French name, Don Quichotte. Mention might also be made of Albert Marre and Mitch Leigh's 1965 musical play *Man of La Mancha,* which straddles the thin line between "musical" and "grand opera."
5. Dostoevsky's *The Gambler* was used as a subject by Prokofiev, whose opera bears the same title as the novel.
6. This is a dead giveaway, as far as title is concerned. Walter Scott's somewhat lurid romance was turned by Donizetti into his most popular opera, *Lucia di Lammermoor.*
7. Tolstoy's epic was made into an opera by Prokofiev, and while most often performed by the Bolshoi in Moscow, the lyric *War and Peace* has been televised in the United States. It has been done in Italian at La Scala, in a production that starred Franco Corelli.
8. The Abbé Prevost's novel about an eighteenth-century nymphet inspired Massenet's *Manon,* Puccini's *Manon Lescaut,* and, before either of those two works, a now-forgotten *Manon Lescaut* by Daniel Auber.

89. PLAY VERSUS OPERA

1. Berlioz's *Béatrice et Bénédict* is based on Shakespeare's play *Much Ado About Nothing.*

2. Johann Strauss's *Die Fledermaus* is based on the comedy by Meilhac and Halévy.
3. Verdi's *Luisa Miller* is based on Schiller's tragedy.
4. Verdi's *Rigoletto* is based on this tragedy by Victor Hugo.
5. Mascagni's *Lodoletta* is based on Ouida's novel.
6. The *La Bohèmes* of both Puccini and Leoncavallo are based on this autobiographical novel by Henri Murger.
7. Verdi's *La Traviata* is based on the novel and play by Alexandre Dumas, *fils.*
8. Britten's *Peter Grimes* is based on the poem by George Crabbe.
9. Donizetti based *L'Elisir d'Amore* on this comedy adapted by Eugène Scribe from a work by Silvio Malaperta.
10. Ponchielli based *La Gioconda* on Victor Hugo's play, which also was the basis for Mercadante's recently revived *Il Giuramento.*
11. Thomas's *Mignon* is based on Goethe's play.
12. Berg's *Lulu* is based on Wedekind's play.
13. The third act of Offenbach's *Les Contes d'Hoffmann* is based on this tale by E. T. A. Hoffmann.

90. LIBRETTISTS

1. Antonio Ghislanzoni
2. Giuseppe Giacosa and Luigi Illica
3. Ruggiero Leoncavallo
4. Tobia Gorrio (pseudonym for Arrigo Boito)
5. Temistocle Solera
6. Luigi Illica
7. Eugène Scribe and Charles Duveyrier
8. Lorenzo da Ponte
9. Richard Wagner
10. Henri Meilhac and Ludovic Halévy
11. Giuseppe Adami and Renato Simoni
12. Francesco Maria Piave

91. RECORD COLLECTORS I

1. The nine Metropolitan Opera productions issued by Columbia Records were: *La Bohème,* Giuseppe Antonicelli conducting with Bidú

Sayão, Richard Tucker, and Mimi Benzell; *Hansel and Gretel* (in English), Max Rudolf conducting with Risë Stevens, Nadine Conner, and Thelma Votipka; *Faust,* Fausto Cleva conducting with Eleanor Steber, Eugene Conley, and Cesare Siepi; *Madama Butterfly,* Max Rudolf conducting with Eleanor Steber, Richard Tucker, and Giuseppe Valdengo; *Cavalleria Rusticana,* Fausto Cleva conducting with Richard Tucker and Margaret Harshaw; *I Pagliacci,* Fausto Cleva conducting with Richard Tucker and Lucine Amara; *Die Fledermaus* (in English), Eugene Ormandy conducting with Ljuba Welitsch, Lily Pons, John Brownlee, and Richard Tucker; *Così Fan Tutte* (in English), Fritz Stiedry conducting with Eleanor Steber, Richard Tucker, and Roberta Peters; *The Rake's Progress* (in English), Igor Stravinsky conducting with Hilde Gueden, Eugene Conley, Blanche Thebom, Mack Harrell, and Martha Lipton.

2. The EMI/Angel *Tosca* is led by Victor de Sabata.
3. Wotan is sung by George London in *Das Rheingold,* and by Hans Hotter in *Die Walküre* and *Siegfried.* (In *Siegfried,* of course, Wotan calls himself the Wanderer.)
4. Price's first *Il Trovatore,* for RCA, was conducted by Arturo Basile. Her colleagues included Richard Tucker (Manrico), Rosalind Elias (Azucena), and Leonard Warren (di Luna). Price's second *Il Trovatore,* also for RCA, was conducted by Zubin Mehta, and the cast included Placido Domingo (Manrico), Fiorenza Cossotto (Azucena), and Sherrill Milnes (di Luna). Price's third recording of this role for EMI/Angel was conducted by Herbert von Karajan, and the other artists included Franco Bonisolli (Manrico), Elena Obraztsova (Azucena), and Piero Cappuccilli (di Luna).
5. Among the operas recorded by the New York City Opera are *Giulio Cesare, Lizzie Borden, The Crucible, Carrie Nation, The Ballad of Baby Doe,* and *Silverlake.*
6. In this *I Pagliacci,* Luciano Pavarotti is heard as Canio, and his father is heard as a villager.
7. Caruso's first recordings were made by EMI.
8. Toscanini's 1954 broadcast of Verdi's *Un Ballo in Maschera* was supposed to have had tenor Jussi Bjoerling in the role of Riccardo. Owing to Bjoerling's absence from rehearsals, the tenor was replaced by a Toscanini favorite, Jan Peerce. Peerce was miffed because he wasn't the maestro's original choice for the performance and nearly refused to sing, throwing the entire project in doubt.
9. Olivero recorded *Turandot* in 1937 for Parlophone Records (currently on Everest/Cetra) and *Fedora* in 1970 for London Records. In *Turan-*

dot the soprano sang Liù, while Gina Cigna and Francesco Merli were heard as Turandot and Calaf, respectively. In *Fedora* Olivero sings the title role, while Mario del Monaco sings Loris, and Tito Gobbi sings di Siriex.

10. *Aida.*
11. Kiri Te Kanawa may be heard as the stable boy Cirillo on the London *Fedora* set mentioned in Question 9; she also sings the Countess Ceprano in the London *Rigoletto* with Sherrill Milnes, Luciano Pavarotti, and Joan Sutherland.
12. Carreras's first opera recording was Rossini's *La Pietra del Paragone,* issued on the Vanguard label.
13. Grace Bumbry sings Leonora and Nicolai Gedda sings Alvaro on this recording of Verdi's *La Forza del Destino,* which is known in Germany as *Die Macht des Schicksals.*
14. In each set of this album was a piece of the old Met's gold curtain, which was unceremoniously chopped up when the company moved to Lincoln Center in 1966.
15. Caterina Mancini sang Abigaille opposite the Nabucco of Paolo Silveri in Cetra's early recording of *Nabucco.*
16. The opera Bjoerling canceled was *Un Ballo in Maschera* for London/Decca. Rumor has it that the Decca vaults contain the first two scenes of this ill-fated recording. The opera was finished with Carlo Bergonzi taking over the role of Riccardo.
17. Six operas recorded by Milanov include *Cavalleria Rusticana* (Santuzza), *Tosca* (title role), *Il Trovatore* (Leonora), *Aida* (title role), *La Gioconda* (title role), *La Forza del Destino* (Leonora).
18. Ten "Callas" operas available on pirated records include *Il Pirata, I Vespri Siciliani, Macbeth, Nabucco, La Vestale, Poliuto, Anna Bolena, Alceste, Iphigénie en Tauride,* and *Armida.*
19. Maria Callas.
20. Tebaldi and Corelli made *no* complete recordings together. They did record a disc of duets from *Aida, Manon Lescaut, Adriana,* and *Francesca da Rimini.*
21. Boris Christoff, in each of his two EMI/Angel recordings of Mussorgsky's *Boris Godunov,* undertook not only the title role but those of the monks Pimen and Varlaam.
22. Tebaldi, Nilsson, and Bjoerling appear in the RCA *Turandot* and in the gala sequence of the London/Decca *Die Fledermaus.*
23. Flagstad, worried about her high C, allowed soprano Elisabeth Schwarzkopf to sing those notes, which were then spliced into Flagstad's part.

24. Santuzza was sung by Lina Bruna-Rasa, Turiddu by Beniamino Gigli, and Mamma Lucia by the very young (in 1940) Giulietta Simionato.

92. RUDOLF BING

1. He had been the director of the Glyndebourne Festival in England.
2. Bing replaced former tenor star Edward Johnson, who had run the Met between 1935 and 1950.
3. In the opening night *Don Carlo,* soprano Delia Rigal (Elisabetta), mezzo Fedora Barbieri (Eboli), bass Cesare Siepi (Philip), and soprano Lucine Amara (Celestial Voice) made their Met debuts. Rigal lasted a decade at the Met (though she turned up to replace Amara in the *La Forza del Destino* trio at the closing gala at the old Met); Barbieri visited the company sporadically for the next quarter century; Siepi remained *primo basso* until 1973; and Amara went on to sing many leading roles.
4. Zinka Milanov had been let go for no apparent reason by the Johnson administration. Bing reengaged her, and Milanov went on to sing with the Met until 1966, triumphing in such roles as Aida, both Verdi Leonoras, Santuzza, Tosca, Desdemona, Norma, and Madeleine.
5. The *Die Fledermaus* adapters were Garson Kanin (dialogue) and Howard Dietz (lyrics).
6. Igor Stravinsky's *The Rake's Progress.*
7. Bing fired Callas because she refused to sign her Met contract for the 1958–59 season without an alteration of roles. She didn't want to sing both Violetta and Verdi's Lady Macbeth within a few days of each other. Bing ordered Callas to cable acceptance by a certain hour. When Callas failed to do so, Bing fired her in a move many consider to have been his single worst mistake as manager of the Met.
8. Karl Liebl, Albert Da Costa, and Ramon Vinay were Nilsson's three Tristans in one night, in December 1959.
9. Lauritz Melchior, the eminent Wagnerian tenor.
10. Bing invited Walter Slezak, son of *heldentenor* Leo Slezak, to appear in the role of Szupán in Johann Strauss's *The Gypsy Baron.* Walter Slezak made his entrance carrying a diapered piglet. He is remembered for his

Hollywood villains, Broadway comic turns, and many eloquent appearances as an Opera Quiz contestant.

11. Lunt staged *Così Fan Tutte* (in English) in 1952, and *La Traviata* in 1966.
12. Death threats and other mischievous notes directed against soprano Leonie Rysanek were received hours before a broadcast performance of *Otello* in 1964. Bing felt that members of the Standing Room Regulars were responsible and he banished all the standees that afternoon. He relented in time for the evening performance, and Rysanek returned unscathed to perform for years to come.
13. Leopold Stokowski earned Bing's wrath during the closing gala when, in an unscheduled speech, Stokowski asked the audience to save the old Met from being torn down to make room for an office building. Bing, of course, had agreed to the old theater's destruction in order to finance the company through lease of the property.
14. Because of cold war politics, Boris Christoff was prevented from singing on Bing's first opening night. Although the Bulgarian bass eventually sang in the United States, he never came to terms with the Met. Soprano Sena Jurinac, a darling of the Viennese public, was often invited but never sang at the Met. Beverly Sills, who became a friend of Bing's, was never offered a contract that suited her. Her Met debut was made in 1975, during the Schuyler G. Chapin regime.
15. Flagstad's final Met role was Alceste in the Gluck opera.
16. Ljuba Welitsch.
17. Birgit Nilsson, whose tax troubles led to her self-exile from the States from 1975 to 1979, once claimed Bing as a dependent "because he needed her."
18. Roberta Peters, who had never sung a professional opera performance (although she was scheduled to debut later that year), made her debut as Zerlina, replacing the ailing Nadine Conner.
19. The final opera sung at Bing's Met was *Don Carlo* in the same Margaret Webster production that had opened Bing's tenure in 1950. Three artists who sang at that first night were in the cast of this broadcast matinee: Lucine Amara (Celestial Voice), Cesare Siepi (Philip), and Robert Merrill (Rodrigo), which took place on April 22, 1972. That evening, Bing was honored at a Gala Concert featuring most members of the company.
20. After leaving the Met, Rudolf Bing taught a course in opera at New York's Brooklyn College for several years and then became a member of the board of directors at Columbia Artists. He has written two volumes of memoirs: *5000 Nights at the Opera* and *A Knight at the Opera.*

93. FAMOUS OPERATIC CONDUCTORS

1. Cleofonte Campanini
2. Arturo Toscanini
3. Franco Faccio
4. Tullio Serafin
5. Thomas Schippers
6. Hans von Bülow
7. Sarah Caldwell
8. Nicola Rescigno
9. Pietro Mascagni
10. Herbert von Karajan
11. Gustav Mahler
12. Sir Georg Solti
13. Mstislav Rostropovich (married to Galina Vishnevskaya)
14. Guido Cantelli
15. Bruno Walter
16. Karl Böhm
17. Richard Bonynge (married to Joan Sutherland)
18. Wilfred Pelletier
19. Pierre Boulez
20. James Levine
21. Victor de Sabata
22. Clemens Krauss
23. Sir Thomas Beecham
24. Wilhelm Furtwängler
25. Julius Rudel
26. Rafael Kubelik
27. Carlos Kleiber
28. Leonard Bernstein (Cherubini's *Médée,* in 1955, with Maria Callas)

94. SATURDAY AFTERNOONS AT THE MET

1. Kirsten Flagstad made her debut singing Sieglinde in *Die Walküre* in 1935. In 1940 an emergency resulted in Astrid Varnay's debut singing that role and being heard coast-to-coast.
2. The only Met broadcast with Callas was a December 1956 performance of *Lucia di Lammermoor,* with Callas in the title role.
3. Tenor Giovanni Martinelli collapsed from food poisoning as he attempted to sing "Celeste Aida" one afternoon in the 1940s.
4. Baritone Cornell MacNeil rushed from Italy to the Met overnight in order to make his debut, replacing Robert Merrill in the broadcast performance of *Rigoletto* that took place early in 1959.
5. Sutherland's broadcast debut occurred less than a month after her Met debut. In both performances, she sang the title role in *Lucia di Lammermoor*. Richard Tucker was her tenor partner.

6. *Hansel and Gretel* was the recipient of the first complete broadcast from the Met on Christmas Day 1931.
7. The Met broadcasts are sponsored by Texaco.
8. Geraldine Farrar joined Cross at the microphone back in the good old days.
9. The first opera broadcast from Lincoln Center was Barber's *Antony and Cleopatra,* at its world premiere, opening night of the new Met, September 16, 1966.
10. Peerce's twenty-fifth anniversary was in 1966, and he was honored during the broadcast of *Don Giovanni* in which he sang Don Ottavio. Milanov was feted during a 1963 broadcast of *Andrea Chénier* in which she sang Madeleine. Tucker celebrated his twenty-fifth anniversary at the Met in 1970 in a broadcast *La Bohème* as Rodolfo.

95. OPERA ON THE SILVER SCREEN

1. *Carmen* (Geraldine Farrar); *La Bohème* (Lillian Gish as Mimi); *Rosenkavalier* (Maria Jeritza as the Marschallin).
2. Aida: Renata Tebaldi; Radames: Giuseppe Campora; Amneris: Ebe Stignani; Amonasro: Gino Bechi; conductor: Giuseppe Morelli.
3. In the film *Salome,* the Princess of Judea was a good girl and a convert to the preaching of John the Baptist. She performed the dance of the seven veils in order to win John's release from Herod!
4. Sylvia Sydney played Butterfly; Cary Grant was Pinkerton.
5. Eileen Farrell was the "voice" of Miss Lawrence.
6. Dorothy Kirsten and Lucine Amara sang with Lanza in *The Great Caruso.*
7. Franco Corelli was heard in a 1958 film of *Tosca,* in which the title role was sung by Maria Caniglia but acted by Franca Duval. Corelli appeared on the screen.
8. Callas made a film of *Medea* in 1970.
9. Stevens's best-known film is *Going My Way,* in which she costarred with Bing Crosby.
10. In the Salzburg Festival *Der Rosenkavalier* film, the conductor was Herbert von Karajan. Elisabeth Schwarzkopf, Sena Jurinac, and Otto Edelmann were seen as the Marshcallin, Octavian, and Baron Ochs.

11. The soprano starlet, Wilhelminia Wiggins Fernandez, was featured in the film *Diva.* In the movie, Fernandez sings "Ebben, ne andrò lontana" from Catalani's *La Wally.* Her April 1982 City Opera debut was as Musetta in Puccini's *La Bohème.*

96. RECORD COLLECTORS II

1. Maria Huder.
2. Among Cossotto's supporting roles recorded early in her career were Suzuki in *Madama Butterfly* for London/Decca, Bersi in *Andrea Chénier* for London/Decca, Teresa in *La Sonnambula* for EMI, and the Madrigal Singer in *Manon Lescaut* for EMI/Angel.
3. Serafin agreed to conduct *La Traviata* at La Scala for an EMI recording. Callas was the announced Violetta, but owing to a five-year wait clause in her previous recording contract with Cetra (with whom she had done a *La Traviata* less than five years earlier), she was unable to record the work with Serafin, Giuseppe di Stefano, and Tito Gobbi. Callas was replaced on the EMI set by Antonietta Stella, and she regarded Serafin's continued participation in the project as a personal affront. Although the diva and the aged maestro eventually resumed their friendship, Callas refused to work with Serafin for more than a year after the *Traviata* affair.
4. Gobbi recorded *Il Tabarro* with soprano Margaret Mas and tenor Giacinto Prandelli. The conductor of this still available EMI performance was Vincenzo Bellezza.
5. Carreras's first *Tosca,* released in 1977, boasts Montserrat Caballé in the title role and Ingvar Wixell as Scarpia. Sir Colin Davis conducts the performance, which has been released on the Philips label. Carreras's second *Tosca,* released in 1980, features Katia Ricciarelli as Tosca and Ruggero Raimondi as Scarpia. Herbert von Karajan conducts the set, available on the Deutsche Grammophon label.
6. The three operas the Met recorded for RCA are: Samuel Barber's *Vanessa,* with the "original cast": Eleanor Steber, Rosalind Elias, Giorgio Tozzi, Nicolai Gedda, and Regina Resnik, conducted by Dimitri Mitropoulos; Rossini's *Il Barbiere di Siviglia* with Roberta Peters, Robert Merrill, Cesare Valletti, Giorgio Tozzi, and Fernando Corena, conducted by Erich Leinsdorf; and Verdi's *Macbeth,* with

Leonard Warren, Leonie Rysanek, Carlo Bergonzi, and Jerome Hines, conducted by Erich Leinsdorf.

7. The first seven Verdi operas are: *Rigoletto* with Dietrich Fischer-Dieskau, Carlo Bergonzi, and Renata Scotto, led by Rafael Kubelik; *La Traviata* with Renata Scotto, Gianni Raimondi, and Ettore Bastianini, conducted by Antonino Votto; *Don Carlo* with Antonietta Stella, Flaviano Labo, Boris Christoff, Fiorenza Cossotto, and Ettore Bastianini, led by Gianandrea Gavazzeni; *Simon Boccanegra* with Piero Cappuccilli, Mirella Freni, Nicolai Ghiaurov, and José Carreras, conducted by Claudio Abaddo; *Il Trovatore* with Antonietta Stella, Carlo Bergonzi, Ettore Bastianini and Fiorenza Cossotto, led by Tullio Serafin; *Macbeth* with Shirley Verrett, Piero Cappuccilli, Placido Domingo, and Nicolai Ghiaurov, conducted by Claudio Abaddo; *Un Ballo in Maschera* with Antonietta Stella, Fiorenza Cossotto, Ettore Bastianini, and Gianni Poggi, conducted by Antonino Votto.
8. Corena's non-*buffo* roles include Schaunard in *La Bohème,* Geronte in *Manon Lescaut,* and the King of Egypt in *Aida.*
9. The 1970 Bolshoi *Eugene Onegin* released in the West by EMI poses difficulties in that its soprano and conductor, Galina Vishnevskaya and Mstislav Rostropovich, have since defected to the West and have therefore been stripped of their Soviet citizenship.
10. Callas's only non-Italian opera set is *Carmen,* sung in French, with Nicolai Gedda, Robert Massard, and conducted by Georges Prêtre.
11. Spanish tenor José Soler sang Chénier opposite Tebaldi's Madeleine on her first *Andrea Chénier* set, released by Cetra.
12. Warren and Varnay recorded the Recognition Scene from *Simon Boccanegra,* an opera they sang at the Met in 1949.
13. Nelli, of course, was a favorite of Arturo Toscanini's. She broadcast and recorded the *Requiem, Otello, Falstaff, Aida,* and *Un Ballo in Maschera* with him.
14. On the London *Ring,* Hans Hotter is Nilsson's Wotan, and Wolfgang Windgassen is her Siegfried. On the Philips *Ring,* the soprano is flanked by Theo Adam as Wotan and, once again, Windgassen as Siegfried.
15. Crespin has recorded Metella in *La Vie Parisienne,* and the title roles in *La Périchole* and *La Grande Duchesse de Gérolstein.*
16. Alberto Erede conducted all of Tebaldi's first series of opera recordings.
17. Simionato's early Countess de Coigny was sung in the company of Beniamino Gigli (Chénier), Maria Caniglia (Madeleine), and Gino Bechi (Gerard). Oliviero di Fabritiis conducted.

18. Pavarotti's debut recording was Bellini's *Beatrice di Tenda* in which he received third billing after Joan Sutherland and Josephine Veasey.
19. Eugenio Fernandi sang Calaf to Callas's Turandot.
20. Price replaced the ailing Leonie Rysanek in the *Aida* set, now available on London/Decca.

97. OLD VIENNA

1. Lehár's *The Merry Widow* is set in Paris.
2. Saffi, although raised by gypsies, is really an Austro-Hungarian princess.
3. Emmerich Kálman.
4. China is Lehár's Land of Smiles.
5. Valencienne is the love object of Camille de Rosillon.
6. Valencienne is married to Baron Mirko Zeta.
7. Walter Slezak (Leo's son) sang Kalman Szupán, the pig farmer, in the Met's charming but unsuccessful *The Gypsy Baron.*
8. The Vienna Volksoper is the chief theater for operettas in the world today.
9. Hanna's celebrated number is the "Vilia-Lied."
10. a. Orlofsky is the bored Russian prince who hosts the ball in Act II of Johann Strauss's *Die Fledermaus.*
    b. Mi is the prince's lovesick younger sister in Lehár's *The Land of Smiles.*
    c. Giuditta is the siren heroine of Lehár's operetta of that name.
    d. Barinkay is the tenor hero of Johann Strauss's *The Gypsy Baron.*
    e. These three girls are dancers of whom Danilo is enamored in Lehár's *The Merry Widow.*
    f. Frosch is the comic jailer in Johann Strauss's *Die Fledermaus,* a speaking part.
    g. Wittenburg is Maritza's love interest in Emmerich Kálman's *Countess Maritza.*
    h. Sonja is the love interest for the title character in Franz Lehár's *The Czarevitch.*
    i. Gabrielle is the leading lady in Johann Strauss's *Wiener Blut.*
    j. Bella Giretti is the opera singer whom Paganini admires in Lehár's *Paganini.*

11. Danilo is a habitué of Maxim's.
12. *Wiener Blut* is a pastiche of Strauss's music.
13. Robert Stolz.
14. The six "Champagne Operettas" were: *Die Fledermaus, The Merry Widow, The Gypsy Baron, A Night in Venice, Wiener Blut,* and *The Land of Smiles.* All were vehicles for Elisabeth Schwarzkopf and Nicolai Gedda.
15. Playwright Garson Kanin and lyricist Howard Dietz created the new English libretto for the Metropolitan's *Die Fledermaus.*
16. Lisa decides to return home after her husband, the prince, informs her that although he loves only her (in "Dein ist mein ganzes Herz"), he is forced by Chinese law to marry three other wives.
17. The show was *Champagne Sec;* the star was Kitty Carlisle.
18. Chevalier played Danilo in the 1930s version of *The Merry Widow* made by M-G-M.
19. The "Du and Du" waltz is from *Die Fledermaus.*
20. The Covent Garden *Die Fledermaus* was conducted by Zubin Mehta. Kiri Te Kanawa was Rosalinde, and Herman Prey was Eisenstein. The operetta was sung in German, but most of the spoken dialogue was in English. This novel idea worked very well.
21. Three Broadway shows that are often performed at the Volksoper are *My Fair Lady, Kiss Me Kate,* and *Show Boat.*
22. *The Land of Smiles* was composed for Richard Tauber.
23. Tebaldi sang "Vilia"; Nilsson sang "I Could Have Danced All Night"; Bjoerling sang "Dein ist mein ganzes Herz"; Price sang "Summertime"; Welitsch warbled "Wien, Wien, nur du allein"; and Simionato teamed up with Bastianini for a hilarious rendition of "Anything You Can Do" from *Annie, Get Your Gun.*
24. Ljuba Welitsch sang both Salome and Rosalinde at the Metropolitan.

98. THEY HAD SOME SONGS TO SING, O

1. The work which required a curtain-raiser was Offenbach's *La Périchole,* and the G & S work that filled the bill was *Trial by Jury.*
2. D'Oyly Carte was the theatrical producer who brought G & S together and organized the company that performed their operas continuously until 1982 when financial pressures forced it out of business.

3. a. *H.M.S. Pinafore*
   b. *Ruddigore*
   c. *The Yeomen of the Guard*
   d. *The Gondoliers*
   e. *The Sorcerer*
   f. *The Yeomen of the Guard*
   g. *H.M.S. Pinafore*
   h. *Trial by Jury*
   i. *Iolanthe*
   j. *Princess Ida*
   k. *Ruddigore*
   l. *The Mikado*
   m. *Iolanthe*
   n. *H.M.S. Pinafore*
   o. *The Pirates of Penzance*
4. Mrs. Cripps.
5. Captain Shaw was the chief of London's fire department at the time *Iolanthe* was written. He was a handsome, popular figure. The reference to him is made in the Queen of the Fairies' song, "Oh foolish fay," in which she warns her fairies–who may not marry mortals under pain of death–that Captain Shaw will not put out the fires in their hearts should they fall in love.
6. Richard D'Oyly Carte built the Savoy Theatre.
7. Gilbert loved to satirize *Il Trovatore,* in which gypsy Azucena mixes up two children, as do Buttercup in *H.M.S. Pinafore* and Inez in *The Gondoliers.*
8. Sullivan's other works include the opera *Ivanhoe, Onward Christian Soldiers,* and *The Lost Chord.*
9. Victoria was insulted by Gilbert's sly use, in *The Pirates of Penzance,* of the command "Surrender in Queen Victoria's name," to which the pirates reply, "With all our faults we love our Queen." Edward VII knighted Gilbert.
10. *The Pirates of Penzance* had its official premiere in the United States but the night before that performance took place, a touring company of *H.M.S. Pinafore* hastily ran through *Pirates* in England to protect its British copyright.
11. *The Yeomen of the Guard* opens not with a chorus, but with Phoebe's doleful spinning song, "When maiden loves."
12. *Princess Ida*
13. The last two G & S operas are *Utopia Limited* and *The Grand Duke.*
14. John Reed.
15. a. The chorus of Yum-Yum's friends in *The Mikado.*
    b. Josephine in *H.M.S. Pinafore.*
    c. Sir Joseph, Captain Corcoran, and Josephine in *H.M.S. Pinafore.*
    d. The Lord Chancellor in *Iolanthe.*
    e. Grosvenor in *Patience.*
    f. Ruth in *The Pirates of Penzance.*
    g. The Defendant in *Trial by Jury.*

h. The Grand Inquisitor in *The Gondoliers.*
i. Robin and Rose in *Ruddigore.*
j. Patience in *Patience.*

16. Martyn Green played in the Hollywood attempt at *The Mikado* as Koko.

99. WOMEN'S WORLD

1. Countess Clara Maffei.
2. Thea Musgrave.
3. Geraldine Souvaine.
4. Judith Somogi.
5. Cosima Wagner. She was the illegitimate daughter of Franz Liszt.
6. The Opera Company of Boston.
7. Carol Fox, head of the Chicago Lyric from 1954 through 1981, was the force behind Callas's American debut in 1955.
8. Eve Queler, founder of the Opera Orchestra of New York.
9. Margherita Wallman.
10. Mrs. August Belmont, known on the stage as Eleanor Robson.
11. Winifred Wagner was the wife of Wagner's son Siegfried. She was stripped of control over the Bayreuth Festival because of her ardent support of Hitler. Frau Wagner was born in Great Britain.
12. Claudia Cassidy of the Chicago *Tribune.*
13. Pauline de Ahna, wife of Richard Strauss. The opera is *Intermezzo.*
14. Giuseppina Strepponi.

100. OFF THE BEATEN PATH

1. The best-known opera to come out of Poland is Stanislav Moniuszko's *Halka.*
2. Four contemporary Wagnerians who hail from Finland would include soprano Anita Valkki, tenors Ticho Parly and Pekko Nuotio, and bass Martti Talvela.

3. Milanov was born Zinka Kunc (prounced *kuntz*).
4. Soprano Gabriella Tucci, tenor Nicolai Gedda, and bass Jerome Hines sang the final trio from Gounod's *Faust.*
5. *One Night of Love* was a vehicle for Grace Moore.
6. Renata Scotto's feud with Pavarotti exploded into the public eye during an April 1980 documentary film that combined behind-the-scenes moments with the San Francisco Opera's revival of Ponchielli's *La Gioconda,* which was shown on PBS television in the United States.
7. Soprano Helen Traubel was the star of Rodgers and Hammerstein's least successful musical, *Pipe Dream,* which opened on Broadway in October 1955.
8. Ponchielli's *La Gioconda,* the second opera to be performed at the first Metropolitan Opera House, was a seven-year-old newcomer to America when the Met opened in 1883. By September 1966, however, *La Gioconda,* which was heard on the Met's second night at Lincoln Center, was familiar enough to be considered the first "bread and butter" opera to be presented by the Met in its new theater.
9. Miss Martin performed an excruciatingly funny version of "Un bel di." (The performance survives on the DRG label and is highly recommended.)
10. Pinza's TV show about a music-loving widower with a houseful of children was called *Bonino.*
11. Callas's nemesis was Edward Bagarozy, who claimed to have been engaged by Callas in 1947 to act as her manager.
12. Nellie Melba, Marjorie Lawrence, and Joan Sutherland.
13. Massenet's *Werther,* which failed to interest Paris impresarios, had its first performance in Vienna in a German translation.
14. Elisabeth Schwarzkopf, beginning her career as a chorister in Berlin, is heard on that famous recording conducted by Sir Thomas Beecham.
15. Arrigo Boito, the composer of *Mefistofele* and *Nerone,* provided Verdi with the libretti for the revision of *Simon Boccanegra* and the composer's two final masterpieces, *Otello* and *Falstaff.* Under the alias Tobia Gorrio, Boito created the luridly endearing text for Ponchielli's *La Gioconda.* Gian Carlo Menotti, composer of *Amahl and the Night Visitors* and *The Consul,* provided his long-time friend Samuel Barber with the libretto for *Vanessa.*
16. The following gentlemen (plus Puccini) all had a hand in the *Manon Lescaut* libretto: Luigi Illica, Giuseppe Giacosa, Giulio Ricordi, Ruggiero Leoncavallo, Domenico Oliva, and Marco Praga.
17. Rosa Ponselle.

18. Poulenc's *Dialogues des Carmélites* was adapted from a film of the same name.
19. Francesco Cilea, of *Adriana Lecouvreur* fame, wheedled Olivero into agreeing to sing Cilea's best-known work after a decade's absence from performing. Unfortunately, the composer died shortly before Olivero reactivated her career.
20. She married Umberto Giordano, composer of *Andrea Chénier* and *Fedora.*
21. Fittingly, the opera performed at the Vienna State Opera hours before its near destruction was Wagner's *Die Götterdämmerung.*
22. Robinson was the author of *Caruso: His Life in Pictures* and *Celebration,* a pictorial history of the Metropolitan Opera.
23. Flotow's *Martha* is best remembered for the tenor aria immortalized by Caruso in its Italian version, "M'apparí." The soprano aria based on the folk ballad "The Last Rose of Summer" was for many years a favorite encore item on soprano recital programs.
24. The Jockey Club ruled the opera, as well as the race track, in Paris. It was this club that stipulated that all operas performed at the Paris Opéra have a ballet.
25. Ticker, Perlmutter, and Angelovich are better known under their stage names: Richard Tucker, Jan Peerce, and Gianna d'Angelo.
26. Kirsten was the protégée of another blond American beauty–Grace Moore.
27. Siepi appeared in *Bravo, Giovanni* in 1962, and *Carmelina* in 1979. In both ill-fated musicals, Siepi played a restaurant owner.
28. Nellie Melba and Luisa Tetrazzini had culinary treats named for them. For Melba, there was the peach, raspberry, and ice cream dessert, Peaches Melba. For the portly Tetrazzini, a casserole of *pollo* and *pasta,* Chicken Tetrazzini, was created.
29. Ezio Pinza was arrested and imprisoned for several weeks after another Met bass told the police that Pinza was a fascist spy. Pinza was completely exonerated.
30. Bass-baritone George London was the first American to sing at the Bolshoi. His debut role was the title character in Mussorgsky's *Boris Godunov.*
31. Nikolai Rimsky-Korsakov and Dimitri Shostakovitch each reorchestrated *Boris Godunov.* The Rimsky-Korsakov version is frequently performed to this day.
32. Baritone John Shirley-Quirk, of the Royal Opera, Covent Garden, was the ubiquitous character who pursued the opera's protagonist through plague-ridden Venice in seven guises.

101. DON'T BELIEVE EVERYTHING YOU READ I

1. False. *Carmen* was Bizet's last opera. The composer died three months after the first performance.
2. True.
3. True.
4. True.
5. False. Azucena informs the count that her *supposed* son Manrico was the count's long-lost younger brother.
6. False. Callas's first American success was due to the recordings of *I Puritani, Lucia di Lammermoor,* and *Tosca* that she had made in Europe. Callas starred in a nonoperatic version of *Medea* in 1970.
7. True. (The "Honor Monologue" was taken from *Henry IV*.)
8. False. Butterfly's father has been dead for years before the action of Puccini's opera begins. It is her uncle who is a Buddhist Bonze, and who curses her.
9. False. Montserrat Caballé was very impressed by Carreras when he sang the role of Flavio to her Norma in Bellini's opera at the Teatro Liceo in Barcelona in 1970.
10. False. Leoni, composer of *L'Oracolo,* never turned his affections to Manon. Daniel Auber was the third (actually first, in terms of the date of composition) to compose a *Manon Lescaut* opera.
11. True.
12. False. Pinza and Merman never worked together. Pinza's Broadway costar in *South Pacific* was Mary Martin.
13. True.
14. False. For Walter, substitute Arturo Toscanini for the correct answer.
15. True.
16. False. Siegfried marries Gutrune while in an altered state of consciousness. Sieglinde, who dies in between *Die Walküre* and *Siegfried,* is the hero's mother.
17. False. Gigli died at home, in bed, on November 30, 1957. Leonard Warren died onstage during a Met *La Forza del Destino* on March 4, 1960.
18. False. In the Rossini opera, there is no wicked stepmother at all, only a foolish, but not terribly wicked, stepfather, known as Don Magnifico. Griselda is the name of the heroine of Verdi's *I Lombardi.*
19. True.
20. True.

21. False. The Molière play in question is *Le Bourgeois Gentilhomme.*
22. True.
23. False. Although Sills did succeed Rudel at the New York City Opera, she has been married to Peter Greenough since 1956.
24. False. It was Toscanini.

102. OPERATIC SCAVENGER HUNT

1. Two sopranos who are victims of consumption are Mimi in *La Bohème* and Violetta in *La Traviata.*
2. The *Il Trovatore* Leonora and La Gioconda kill themselves rather than surrender to those creepy baritones, Count di Luna and Barnaba, respectively. Tosca has a much better idea; she simply murders the baritone, Scarpia!
3. Mignon, in Ambroise Thomas's opera of that name, is a "good," wholesome gypsy.
4. Italian tenor wife-killers include *I Pagliacci*'s Canio, who does in the adulterous Nedda; Otello in both Verdi's and Rossini's operas, who kills Desdemona; and in *Luisa Miller,* Rodolfo kills his betrothed, Luisa, under the mistaken impression that she has been unfaithful.
5. Amina in *La Sonnambula* and Elvira in *I Puritani* each have mad scenes (Amina's is a dreamy sleepwalking sequence) but recover their mental capacities when their men return to them.
6. Three operatic fathers who are directly responsible for the deaths of their children would include the cardinal in *La Juive,* who orders Rachel's execution not knowing that she is actually his own, illegitimate daughter; Rigoletto, who sets in motion the plot to assassinate the Duke of Mantua, which his daughter Gilda aborts by taking the Duke's place; and Archibaldo in *L'Amore dei Tre Re,* who sets a trap for his daughter-in-law's lover, and catches hiw own son, Manfredo, as well.
7. Five villains who don't get away are: Don Pizarro in *Fidelio,* who is denounced by Rocco, Florestan, and Leonora, and thus is subsequently arrested by Don Fernando; Monostatos and the Queen of the Night in *The Magic Flute,* who are crushed by the powers of Good embodied by Sarastro; the nurse in *Die Frau ohne Schatten,* who is condemned by the very god she serves, Keikobad; Telramund in

Lohengrin, who, influenced by his evil wife Ortrud, is slain by Lohengrin when he attempts to attack Lohengrin; Macbeth, another character influenced by a nasty spouse who pushes him to regicide and other murders, is killed by Macduff; in *Don Giovanni,* that original "anti-hero" is dispatched to Hell by the Commendatore's animated statue; and Normanno, who has encouraged Ashton in his plots to thwart the love of Lucia di Lammermoor and Edgardo, is publicly denounced by Raimondo after Lucia has gone mad and killed her husband. Iago's guilt is established at the end of *Otello,* but he runs out of the Moor's bedchamber, chased by the chorus. (One assumes he will be caught, however.) There are undoubtedly other possibilities, too.

8. Three operas that include scenes at masked balls are Verdi's *I Vespri Siciliani,* Ponchielli's *La Gioconda,* and Rossini's *Il Turco in Italia.*
9. Two German operas based on Shakespearean dramas are Wagner's *Das Liebesverbot,* based on *Measure for Measure,* and Nicolai's *Die Lustigen Weiber von Windsor,* based on *The Merry Wives of Windsor.* Also, Reimann's recent *Lear* has a Shakespearean basis.
10. Thomas Pasatieri's *The Seagull* is based on the play by Chekhov.
11. Turiddu, in Mascagni's *Cavalleria Rusticana,* loses his life in a fight with Alfio, shortly after leading the Easter celebrants in "Viva il vino spumeggiante"; John of Leyden leads his guests in a drinking song in the final scene of Meyerbeer's *Le Prophète,* shortly before his castle is blown up on his own orders.
12. Operatic characters who are beheaded include Manrico in Verdi's *Il Trovatore;* Donizetti's Roberto Devereux, Maria Stuarda, and Anna Bolena, in the operas of those names; Andrea Chénier and Madeleine de Coigny in Giordano's opera; and almost the entire convent of Carmelite nuns in Poulenc's *Dialogues des Carmélites.*
13. Susanna (married to Figaro) in Mozart's *Le Nozze di Figaro,* and Tatyana (to Prince Gremin) in Tchaikovsky's *Eugene Onegin.*
14. Three operatic fratricides include di Luna in *Il Trovatore,* the Hunchback in Zandonai's (and, for that matter, Rachmaninoff's) *Francesca da Rimini,* and Count Walter in Verdi's *Luisa Miller.*
15. Three evil priests include the High Priest of Baal in Verdi's *Nabucco,* Ramfis (not so much evil as reactionary and rigid, perhaps) in *Aida,* and the High Priest of Dagon in Saint-Saëns's *Samson et Dalila.*
16. Five baritone "good guys" would include Rabbi David in Mascagni's *L'Amico Fritz;* Dr. Malatesta in Donizetti's *Don Pasquale;* Gianni Schicchi in Puccini's comedy; Sharpless in Puccini's *Madama Butterfly;* Michonnet in Cilea's *Adriana Lecouvreur;* Marcello in Puccini's *La Bohème;* and, of course, Rossini's Figaro in *Il Barbiere di Siviglia.*

17. Five evil sopranos might include the scheming Abigaille in Verdi's *Nabucco;* the Queen of the Night in Mozart's *The Magic Flute;* Verdi's Lady Macbeth; Tigrana in Puccini's *Edgar;* Ortrud in Wagner's *Lohengrin* (the role has been shared by sopranos and mezzos). Médée in Cherubini's opera is a wronged wife, but her extreme vengefulness–not to mention the fact that in order to help Jason acquire the golden fleece, she murdered her father and brother–place her in the "naughty" category.
18. Two operatic wives who whack their husbands include Susanna in Mozart's *Le Nozze di Figaro,* who strikes Figaro whenever she thinks he is paying court to such ladies as Marcellina or Countess Almaviva, and Norina, who, while playacting the role of "Sofronia" in Donizetti's *Don Pasquale,* smacks her "husband," Pasquale, when he scolds her for her bitchy behavior.
19. Dr. Miracle in Offenbach's *Les Contes d'Hoffmann* kills Antonia with his bizarre spells. The doctor in *Wozzeck* is a quack, too.
20. Operas set in what is now the United States would include Verdi's *Un Ballo in Maschera* (sometimes set in Boston), *The Crucible* by Robert Ward (Salem, Massachusetts), Menotti's *Saint of Bleecker Street* (New York City), Marc Blitzstein's *Regina* (the South), Puccini's *Manon Lescaut* (Act IV takes place in Louisiana), Franco Leoni's *L'Oracolo* (San Francisco's Chinatown), Puccini's *La Fanciulla del West* (California), Kurt Weill's *The Rise and Fall of the City of Mahagonny* (the mythical Southwest), Floyd's *Susannah* (Tennessee), Levy's *Mourning Becomes Elektra* (New England), Moore's *Ballad of Baby Doe* (Colorado and Washington, D.C.).
21. Mascagni's lesser-known operas include *Nerone, Il Piccolo Marat, Le Maschere, Guglielmo Ratcliff,* and *Iris.*
22. Three operas based on plays by Scribe are Verdi's *I Vespri Siciliani* (*Les Vêpres Siciliennes*); Donizetti's *L'Elisir d'Amore* (*Le Philtre*); Verdi's *Un Ballo in Maschera* (*Le Bal Masqué*).
23. Piave wrote libretti for *La Traviata, Rigoletto,* and *Macbeth.*
24. Lotte Lehmann, Richard Mayr, Friedrich Schorr, and Elisabeth Schumann.

103. DON'T BELIEVE EVERYTHING YOU READ II

1. False. Verdi's first opera was *Oberto.*
2. False. Rosa Raisa was the first Turandot. Rosina Storchio was the first Madama Butterfly.

3. True. Beethoven composed three overtures for *Leonora,* and then he wrote a fourth, for the final revision of the work, which was renamed *Fidelio.*
4. False. Tebaldi never sang *Adriana Lecouvreur* under Toscanini's baton. In 1946, however, she did sing for the great maestro at the gala concert that celebrated the opening of the rebuilt La Scala, which had been heavily damaged during the World War II.
5. True.
6. True.
7. True.
8. True.
9. True.
10. False. Marian Anderson was the first black artist to sing at the Metropolitan on January 30, 1955, in the role of Ulrica in *Un Ballo in Maschera.* Price made her Met debut six years later, as Leonora in *Il Trovatore.*
11. False. Catalani never had anything to do with *La Bohème.* Puccini stole *La Bohème* from Ruggiero Leoncavallo, whose own *Bohème* was first produced two years after Puccini's masterpiece. Although Leoncavallo's opera is quite pleasant, it does not survive comparison with Puccini's indisputable masterpiece.
12. True.
13. False. Da Ponte was a little ahead of Verdi's time. He was the librettist for three of Mozart's greatest operas, *Don Giovanni, Le Nozze di Figaro,* and *Così Fan Tutte.* Da Ponte eventually emigrated to New York, where he taught at King's College (now Columbia University). He is buried on Staten Island.
14. True.
15. False. Meneghini was Callas's husband. The head of La Scala then was Antonio Ghiringhelli.
16. False. Puccini's favorite Tosca was Maria Jeritza.
17. False. Phyllis Curtin was the original Susannah, but Treigle was the first Blitch.
18. False. Milanov and Peerce had no feud. She was not fond of her frequent costar, tenor Kurt Baum, while Peerce didn't speak to his tenor colleague Richard Tucker, who was Peerce's brother-in-law!
19. True. In fact, Simionato recorded the role of Mamma Lucia with Mascagni himself conducting.
20. False. Donizetti reworked *La Fille du Régiment* to an Italian text, supplying sung recitatives to replace the spoken dialogue of the French version and adding an aria for Tonio. The Italian version was titled, simply, *La Figlia del Reggimento.*

21. False. Verdi composed *I Masnadieri* for Lind.
22. False. Caruso did indeed sing Johnson at *La Fanciulla del West*'s world premiere in December 1910. However, that performance took place *not* in Covent Garden, but at the Metropolitan in New York.
23. False. *Stifellio* became *Aroldo. I Lombardi* in a heavily revised, French libretto, was rechristened *Jérusalem.*
24. True.

104. OUT IN THE COLD

1. All four ladies are leading mezzo-soprano roles in operas by Verdi—*Don Carlo, Nabucco, Aida,* and *Luisa Miller.* Federica, however, is the misfit. The other three ladies are princesses; Federica is only a duchess.
2. One way of looking at this group would be to find that none of these operas, with the exception of *Turandot,* has a role for a leading tenor. However, it might also be noticed that *Das Rheingold* is the only German-language opera of the four.
3. Of the four Bellini operas given, *Norma* is exceptional because it does not have a "mad scene" for its heroine. Technically, the sleepwalking Amina in *La Sonnambula* is not insane. However, her aria "Ah non credea mirarti" is sung during an altered state of consciousness, and, therefore, qualifies as a mad scene.
4. Of the four gentlemen in question, des Grieux is the only tenor character not taken from a play by Victor Hugo. Ernani was adapted by Verdi from Hugo's *Hernani,* and Verdi's Duke of Mantua is based on King François I in Hugo's *Le Roi S'Amuse.* Ponchielli and his librettist Boito fashioned Enzo, in *La Gioconda,* from the equivalent character in Hugo's *Angelo, Tyran de Padoue.* Des Grieux, in Massenet's and Puccini's *Manon* operas, was created by Abbé Prevost in his novel *L'Histoire de Manon Lescaut.*
5. On the one hand, Dalila is the only one of these four mezzo characters who is *not* a gypsy. However, Preziosilla, a denizen of Verdi's *La Forza del Destino,* is the only Italian-speaking character among her three French colleagues.
6. All four of these characters are murdered. *Tosca*'s Scarpia, the title character in Cilea's *Adriana Lecouvreur,* and Gennaro in Donizetti's *Lucrezia Borgia,* are killed by women (Tosca, Princess de Bouillon,

and Lucrezia, respectively). Only Luisa is dispatched by a man, her tenor lover Rodolfo, in Verdi's opera.

7. Leonora di Vargas, the Spanish heroine of Verdi's *La Forza del Destino,* is the only non-French character listed, even though all are from Italian operas.
8. The Met is the only one of these four great opera houses that is not subsidized by the government of its nation.
9. All four operas are masterpieces by Verdi. As one would expect, three of them were composed to Italian texts, but *Don Carlo,* commissioned by the Paris Opéra, was first composed and produced in French. And, of these four works, *Falstaff* is the lone comedy.
10. Of these four noted sopranos, Garden, Moore, and Kirsten share a common artistic heritage, as Garden coached Moore, who coached Kirsten, leaving the talented Munsel out of the foursome. By the same token, Mary Garden is the only Scotswoman among the three American ladies listed here.
11. *Linda, Parisina,* and *Emilia* are relatively obscure operas by Donizetti. *Elisabetta,* however, is a little-known work by Rossini (who used its overture in *Il Barbiere di Siviglia).*
12. One way of looking at this one would find that all of these characters are servants, except that Mariandl, in *Der Rosenkavalier,* is a sham servant, being Octavian's disguise. It can also be said that Mariandl is the only one of the four who does *not* appear in a Mozart opera.

105. RECORD COLLECTORS III

1. *Fidelio* was the first digital process opera. The 1979 London release is conducted by Georg Solti and features Hildegard Behrens, Peter Hofmann, and Hans Sotin.
2. Cossotto sings Cherubino in the EMI *Le Nozze di Figaro* led by Carlo Maria Giulini, with such artists as Elisabeth Schwarzkopf, Anna Moffo, Rolando Panerai, and Eberhard Wächter.
3. Beverly Sills, Joan Sutherland, Patrice Munsel, Lisa della Casa, and Dorothy Kirsten.
4. Pollione was sung by the late Mario Filippeschi.

5. Elisabeth Schwarzkopf "fed" Christoff Fyodor's lines in that 1949 recording.
6. Maria Vitale is the heroine of the Cetra recording.
7. Anita Cerquetti completed a magnificent *La Gioconda* for Decca/London, led by Gianandrea Gavazzeni and flanked by Mario del Monaco, Cesare Siepi, Ettore Bastianini, and Giulietta Simionato.
8. Renata Tebaldi has recorded the three heroines of *Il Trittico:* Giorgetta, Suor Angelica, and Lauretta.
9. Teresa Stratas, acclaimed these days as Lulu.
10. Vickers sang his first recorded Florestan opposite Christa Ludwig's Leonore on the EMI/Angel set led by Otto Klemperer. Several years later, Vickers recorded the opera, again for EMI, opposite Helga Dernesch, under Herbert von Karajan's direction.
11. Martina Arroyo replaced the chronically ailing Montserrat Caballé.
12. Anna Moffo sang Musetta for EMI/Angel and Mimi for RCA.
13. Schwarzkopf sang in the chorus of Thomas Beecham's Berlin production of *The Magic Flute.*
14. a. Placido Domingo.
    b. Nicolai Gedda.
    c. José Carreras.
    d. Luciano Pavarotti.
15. The Callas recording of Puccini's *Manon Lescaut* was delayed for several years until Callas could be persuaded to approve the set for release. Giuseppe di Stefano was her des Grieux; Tullio Serafin conducted.
16. The late John Culshaw, who died at age fifty-five in 1980, produced the Decca/London *Ring.*
17. Ljuba Welitsch sings Marianne, Sophie's duenna, on the von Karajan EMI *Der Rosenkavalier.*
18. Verdi's *Alizira* and *Jérusalem* have yet to be commercially released, although pirated recordings exist.

106. ULTIMATE WAGNER

1. There are thirty-four separate parts in the *Ring,* and one choral group.
2. Characters in order of appearance:

Das Rheingold	*Die Walküre*	*Siegfried*
Woglinde	(New characters)	(New characters)
Wellgunde	Siegmund	Siegfried
Flosshilde	Sieglinde	Wanderer (actually Wotan in disguise)
Alberich	Hunding	
Fricka	Brünnhilde	Forest Bird
Wotan	Gerhilde	
Freia	Helmwige	*Die Götterdämmerung*
Fasolt	Schwertleite	(New characters)
Fafner	Ortlinde	First Norn
Donner	Waltraute	Second Norn
Loge	Siegrune	Third Norn
Froh	Rossweise	Gunther
Mime	Grimgerde	Hagen
Erda		Gutrune
		The Vassals

107. OPERA PIX

1. Baritone Franz Mazura, costumed as Alberich in *Das Rheingold.*
2. Mezzo Elena Obraztsova, costumed as Dalila in Saint-Saëns's *Samson et Dalila.*
3. Renata Scotto, shown as Norma in Bellini's opera, created a furor when she unveiled her druid priestess at the Met's 1981 opening.
4. José Carreras.
5. Lucine Amara, as Aida, has been singing leads at the Met since her 1950–51 debut season.
6. Franco Corelli, shown as Romeo in Gounod's *Roméo et Juliette.*
7. Eleanor Steber, seen here in an early studio portrait.
8. Mr. New II.
9. Renata Tebaldi was making her Metropolitan debut as Desdemona, while "old-timer" Mario del Monaco sang Otello in Verdi's opera.
10. William Walker (left) and Paolo Montarsolo in Donizetti's *Don Pasquale.*
11. Alfredo Kraus and Régine Crespin are seen as the ill-fated lovers in Massenet's romantic *Werther.*
12. Geraldine Farrar is shown as Louise to Caruso's Julien in Charpentier's *Julien,* the sequel to *Louise.*

13. Enrico Caruso as Samson in Saint-Saëns's *Samson et Dalila.*
14. Nicolai Ghiaurov, as Philip II of Spain in Verdi's *Don Carlo.*
15. Renata Tebaldi and Placido Domingo in the Connecticut Opera's *Manon Lescaut* by Puccini.
16. Eberhard Waechter, Victoria de los Angeles, and Elisabeth Schwarzkopf in a key moment in *Don Giovanni.*
17. Jussi Bjoerling and Victoria de los Angeles in Gounod's *Faust* at the Metropolitan Opera, 1953.
18. Joan Sutherland as the Merry Widow in San Francisco, 1978.
19. Aida: Leonie Rysanek; Radames: Jussi Bjoerling; Ramfis: Jerome Hines; and Amneris: Giulietta Simionato.
20. Luciano Pavarotti and Mirella Freni in a production of Puccini's *La Bohème.*
21. Giorgio Tozzi as Ramfis in *Aida.*
22. Ezio Pinza in a pre-*South Pacific* moment as Méphistophélès in Gounod's *Faust.*
23. Leonie Rysanek as Lady Macbeth in Verdi's *Macbeth.*
24. Maria Callas in Pasolini's 1970 film *Medea.*
25. Régine Crespin dies in her role of the Old Prioress in Poulenc's *Dialogues des Carmélites* at the Met in 1977.
26. Marian Anderson making her Metropolitan Opera debut in Verdi's *Un Ballo in Maschera,* January 30, 1955.
27. Leonard Warren as Baron Scarpia.
28. The delectable Lily Pons, the French singer whose American career lasted forty years.
29. Paul Robeson, who *should* have sung at the Met, in a scene from the nonoperatic film of Eugene O'Neill's *Emperor Jones.*
30. Beniamino Gigli in *Le Roi d'Ys* by Edouard Lalo. The aria, for tenor–still a frequently programmed "encore" piece–is "Vainement, mon bien aimé."
31. Richard Tucker as King Gustav in *Un Ballo in Maschera.*
32. Carlo Bergonzi as Nemorino in Donizetti's *L'Elisir d'Amore.*
33. Mario del Monaco as Canio in *I Pagliacci.*
34. Lauritz Melchior as Siegfried.
35. Jon Vickers as Aeneas in Berlioz's *Les Troyens.*
36. Giuseppe di Stefano as Don José in *Carmen.*
37. Mario del Monaco as Radames in *Aida.*
38. Enrico Caruso as Nemorino in *L'Elisir d'Amore.* Singing this opera with the Met in Brooklyn in 1920, Caruso began to bleed internally. His final performance was given on December 24, 1923, and he was dead eight months later.